GLO
THE DIVINE MOTHER
(DEVĪ MĀHĀTMYAM)

SRI GHANDI YANTRA

S. SANKARANARAYANAN

GLORY OF THE DIVINE MOTHER

by

S. SANKARANARAYANAN

Publishers
Prabha Publishers
Chennai
Distributed by
Nesma Books India
Bangalore/Chennai
E-mail: nesmabooks@yahoo.com
Typesetting & Printing
D C Press (P) Ltd.,
Kottayam, Kerala 686 001

ISBN 81-87936-00-2

Price : Rs. 300.00

FOREWORD

This exposition of *devi mahatmyam* has been undertaken primarily to share the spiritual gains derived from this sacred text with like-minded seekers.

At a very early age, my mother's father arranged for teaching me the Sanskrit language and securely laid in me the foundation for a spiritual life. After him, my uncle encouraged and initiated me into the japa of *navakṣari mantra* and the recital of *devi mahatmyam*. As a member of the family, wherein there was the daily worship of *meru* (the Yantra of Devi) and on occasions the recital of the *candi* , I was also in those days, knowingly or unknowingly, doing the worship and the *parayana* of the text with devotion of a sort. And these never went in vain. I refer to my good fortune of acquiring later on Sri Kapali Sastriar as my Guru.

I was groping in the blind alleys and fumbling in the bylanes of Spiritual Quest and he it was who brought me to the Royal Road, paving for me the way for the Hereafter. Granting me refuge as a God in human form, he it was who, besides other things, graciously revealed to me the secrets of *devi mahatmyam*. Once I asked him: While the *devi mahatmyam* speaks of only three great Shaktis, Mahakali, Mahalakshmi and Mahasaraswati, how is it that Sri Aurobindo in his epoch-making work, *The Mother,* has spoken of another great Shakti, Maheshwari? Sastriar explained to me in detail the verse "*medhasi devi viditakhila sastrasara,*" occuring in the fourth chapter of the *Devi Mahatmyam*, opening my eyes to the fact that the four great Shaktis, Maheshwari, Mahakali, Mahalakshmi and Mahasaraswati, are mentioned in the *devi mahatmyam* itself. Through his writings as well as oral teachings, he favoured me, time and again, with explanations of the principles underlying this text and other spiritual subjects. Just as a son would, without compunction, use the wealth inherited from his father, I have largely drawn upon his works and his teachings to me in the course of this exposition.

S. Shankaranarayanan

THE MOTHER OF MIGHT

I have come down into the human world
And the movement watched by an unsleeping Eye
And the dark contrariety of earth's fate
And the battle of the bright and sombre Powers.
I stand upon earth's paths of danger and grief
And help the unfortunate and save the doomed.
To the strong I bring the guerdon of their strength,
To the weak I bring the armour of my force;
To men who long I carry their coveted joy:
I am fortune justifying the great and wise
By the sanction of the plaudits of the crowd,
Then trampling them with the armed heel of Fate.
My ear is leaned to the cry of the oppressed,
I topple down the thrones of tyrant kings:
A cry comes from proscribed and hunted lives
Appealing to me against a pitiless world,
A voice of the forsaken and desolate
And the lone prisoner in his dungeon cell.
Men hail in my coming the Almighty's force
Or praise with thankful tears his saviour Grace.
I smite the Titan who bestrides the world
And slay the ogre in his blood-stained den.
I am Durga, goddess of the proud and strong,
And Lakshmi, queen of the fair and fortunate;
I wear the face of Kali when I kill,
I trample the corpses of the demon hordes.
I am charged by God to do his mighty work,
Uncaring I serve his will who sent me forth,
Reckless of peril and earthly consequence.
I reason not of virtue and of sin
But do the deed he has put into my heart.
I fear not for the angry frown of Heaven,
I flinch not from the red assault of Hell;
I crush the opposition of the gods,
Tread down a million goblin obstacles.
I guide man to the path of the Divine.

(Sri Aurobindo: Savitri)

CONTENTS

Foreword
The Mother of Might
  Introduction 1
  Preliminaries 57
  पूर्वाङ्गविधि: 71
  The Mode of Recital 75
  Kavacha, Argala, Keelaka 79
  Kavacham : text 85
  Argala Stotram : text 95
  Kilakam : text 99
  Navaksari 103
  Nyasa 107
  एकादशन्यासा : 111
  Ratri Sukta 117
  Ratri Suktam : text 123
THE THREE EPISODES
  The First Episode 127
  First Chapter 128
  The Second Episode 147
  Second Chapter 148
  Third Chapter 162
  Fourth Chapter 171
  The Third Episode 183
  Fifth Chapter 184
  Sixth Chapter 200
  Seventh Chapter 205
  Eighth Chapter 211

Ninth Chapter 223
Tenth Chapter 231
Eleventh Chapter 237
Twelfth Chapter 249
Thirteenth Chapter 257
Devi Sukta 263
Devi Suktam : text 267
The Triple Secret 271
Pradhanika Rahasya 274
Vaikrtika Rahasya 281
Murti Rahasya 290
A Prayer Craving Pardon 295
Prayoga 297
Some Questions Answered 308

GLORY OF
THE DIVINE MOTHER
(DEVIMAHATMYAM)

INTRODUCTION

GREATNESS OF THE TEXT

The edifice of our eternal Dharma is built on the solid foundations of the Veda and the Tantra. In both these ways of knowledge, sufficient importance has been given to the path that worships the Supreme as the Mother. The Veda gave to the Prime Mover the appellation Aditi, the primordial Force which extends in all and contains all, the Supreme *sakti*, the Divine Mother who gives birth to the gods and the goddesses. The Tantra proclaims: "*sakti* is the origin and source of all; she is the cause of creation; nothing is there if she be not there."

It has been said that whatever the God one worships, one worships only the *sakti*. The twice-born cannot brand themselves as *saivites* or *vaisnavites*. They are all *saktas*, worshippers of the *sakti* for they fervently worship daily *Gayatri*, the Primordial Goddess, the Mother of the Spoken Word[1].

Thus, worship of *sakti* is the life-breath of our great Dharma. Worshippers of the Divine Mother are spread everywhere in India, from Kashmir to Kanya

---

[1] सर्वे शाक्ता द्विजाः प्रोक्ता न शैवा न च वैष्णवाः ।
आदिदेवीमुपासन्ते गायत्रीं वेदमातरम् ॥

Kumari, from Bengal to Kerala. There are many sacred texts and many well-trodden paths which are capable of bringing the grace of the Mother. Even so, there is a sacred text which occupies a special place, a scripture of undying fame. Crowning all Tantric literature and traditions, it acts as a touchstone to all the doctrines established by them. It is a great *sādhana sāstra*, practical science, teaching how to approach with special privilege and win the favour of the unique manifestaion of the Mother, *durgā* whose name signifies that she is not easily approachable, *duhkhena gantum śakyā*. The text is devi mahatmya, *saptaśati*.

This scripture is in the Markandeya Purana which is in the form of a dialogue between Markandeya and Kroshtuki. The seer of this Purana is the Rishi Markandeya. He is not the author. The Seer in him has seen with the inner eye and has perceived the *darsana*, ever-existent. Like the Veda, the Devi Mahatmya is *apouruseya* not origined in man. It is the inspired word. "Just as Vedas have no beginning, so is *Saptasati* considered", says *bhuvaneśwari samhitā[1]*. Also, it is said that the basis of the text is found in the Veda. The *devī sūkta* (Rv.X.125), the seer-perception of *vāk-ambhṛni*, is said to provide the source-material for Devi Mahatmya. At the end of the Mahatmya itself, we have a significant hint *devī-śuktam param japan*, doing the japa of the great Devi Sukta.

---

[1] यथा वेदो ह्यनादिर्हि तद्वत् सप्तशती स्मृता ।

Again, this scripture is highly occult.[1] It is a secret science bestowing all Siddhis. "There is the Devi Mahatmya, the most secret, giving all the Siddhis", declares *rudrayāmala*.[2] *meru tantra* goes further: "This is highly occult. The Devi only knows the inner sense of Saptasati. Vishnu knows three-quarters, Brahma half and Vyasa a quarter portion. Rest of the people know only a myriadth of it.[3]" *dāmara tantra* extols: "Like Aswamedha amongst sacrifices, like Vishnu amongst gods, so Saptasati amongst all lauds.[4]" Verily, this scripture can claim to be the repository of Mantras and this commands a very high position amongst the Tantric texts as in each chapter are mentioned covertly many Mantras.[5] "Only those who have eyes will perceive the hidden truths: others know not."[6] *kātyāyani tantra* considers each *śloka* of the

---

1. It is significant that Sri Bhaskараraya named his exposition, commentary of this occult text also as occult, *guptavati*

2 अस्ति गुह्यतमं देव्या माहात्म्यं सर्वसिद्धिदम् ।

3 सप्तशत्यास्तु सकलं तत्त्वं वेद्यहमेव हि ।
पादोनं श्रीहरिर्वेत्ति वेदर्धं तु प्रजापतिः ।
व्यासस्तुर्यांशकं वेत्ति कोट्यंशमितरे जनाः ॥

4 यथाऽश्वमेधः क्रतुषु देवानां च यथा हरिः ।
स्तवानामपि सर्वेषां तथा सप्तशतीस्तवः ॥

5 निर्विशेषपरा मन्त्राः सविशेषपराश्च ये ।
प्रत्यध्यायं निगूढास्ते तेनेयं सर्वतः परा ॥

6 चक्षुष्मन्तोऽनुपश्यन्ति नेतरे तद्विदो जनाः ।

text as a Mantra. All the seven hundred slokas in the text do not sing the glory of the Devi. Three-fourths of the text is occupied by description of battles and narrative material. Yet if each verse is considered as a potent Mantra, it shows the great importance attached to the text in the *sādhana* and the high reverence in which it is held.

And so in this *sādhana* the recital of the text, *pārāyana*, is considered more important than any japa of a Mantra. It is true that the great *navākṣari*, the nine-lettered Mantra for worshipping Chandika, is advocated, but it is traditionally held as forming a part of the recital of the text. We said that the whole text is nothing but Mantra, *mantramaya*, and so every word of it has got the power of manifesting the presence of the Deity. The Devi herself has given the assurance that "this *mahātmyam* of mine in its entirety evokes my presence.[1]"

The whole text has to be audibly recited. It should not be silently read, nor used for Dhyana or meditation. As the recitation goes on, the word-power of the *slokas* pervades and purifies the surrounding atmosphere and prepares it for receiving the Divine Presence. The whole place where the text is recited becomes flooded with waves and waves of vibrations, immersing the Sadhaka in thrills of devotion and delight. Immediately he becomes conscious of a living Presence of the Mother. By faith and practice, he

---

[1] सर्वं ममैतन्माहात्म्यं मम सन्निधिकारकम् ।

learns to keep the Presence and a conscious concourse starts between the Deity and the devotee. And what more is needed? The Devi leads the devotee at every step through the labyrinths of life. He gets her *anugraha*. He "is seized and held in her grace so closely that time and place could not separate the human and the divine, Jiva and Deva;[1]" and he attains everything that is worth attaining in life, including the highest purpose for which the life on this earth is intended.

To quote Sri Kapali Sastriar,

"The mystical reverence in which the *devi mahatmya* is held can be best understood if we remember a tradition that comes down to us through orthodox Vaidiks who are worshippers of Chandi. The Saptasati, they hold is a great *arthaśāstra* i.e. a Shastra that teaches us the means of realising all ends in life, not *artha* in the restricted sense of wealth or economics. Thus the standard texts for the four purposes of life, *puruṣartha*, are in order. : Manu for Dharma Shastra (which is said to have been orginally 700 verses), Devi Mahatmya for Artha, Vatsyayana for *kāma* (which also is said to have been at first 700 sutras) and the Bhagavat Gita for Moksha (which is also 700). Whether there is significance in the number 700 or not is not quite material for our consideration here. But the tradition shows that the aim of Saptasati is not in a limited or one-sided direction. It includes the aims of life here and the supreme purpose as well.[2]"

1. *Further Lights : The Veda and the Tantra* by Sri Kapali Sastriar.
2. Ibid.

Now let us examine the different names through which this sacred scripture has become famous.

mahātmā means a great soul. *māhātmyam* is its quality. The great soul of the Mother, one without a second, by its own glory becomes many souls, many little mothers, *mātṛkās* and these emanations of the Mother, after finishing their appointed task converge back into the great soul of the Mother.The story of all these emanations and their deeds, the glory of the great soul of the Mother is delineated in the text which also incorporates the sublime utterance, *mahāvākya*, of the Devi embodying the Upanishadic Truth of One without a second, viz: "I alone am there in the universe. Who is the second person other than me ?!" For this reason, the text is known as Devi Mahatmyam.

This is the glory or *māhātmyam* of Chandi and so it is popularly known as *caṇḍi pāṭh* or briefly *caṇḍi*. A fierce prowess, a force which progresses breaking all obstacles, a divine goodness which cannot brook wickedness in any form, a blaze of knowledge which in its trail utterly dispels the darkness of ignorance, the valour which is ever victorious in the battle of life-these are the traits of *caṇḍi*, endearingly called *caṇḍikā*. The mother's calm insistent force is *lalitā* while her terrific impatient force is *caṇḍī*.

---

¹ एकैवाहं जगत्यत्र द्वितीया का ममापरा ।

As the text contains 700 slokas, the name *saptasati* has become famous. They say that the name Saptasati is very apt as the categorisation of 700 applies to *pārāyana*, *japa*, *homa*, *tarpana*, the sentences and the sense alike.[1]

Some opine that the name should be सप्तसती *saptasati* instead of सप्तशती *saptaśati*. The Mahatmya deals with the story of seven Satis. But there is a difference of opinion about the identification of these Satis. The seven mothers, *brāhmi*, *māheśwari*, *kaumāri*, *vaisnavi*, *vārahi*, *indrāni* and *cāmunda* are the seven Satis, aver some. Some others would have the seven incarnations of the Mother, *nandā*, *śākambhari*, *bhimā*, *raktadantikā*, *durgā*, *bhrāmari* and *śatākṣi* as the seven Satis. Anyhow, this name *Saptaśati* instead of *saptaśati* has not found much favour with the followers of the cult.

The name *devi māhātmya*, *candi pāth* or *saptaśati* not only describes the text of 700 slokas comprised of the three *caritas*, but it includes in its compass the *angas*, the limbs that go with the body of the text. Here, there are two schools—three parts or nine parts. But as Sri Bhaskararaya in his Guptavati, a commentary on Saptasati, has dealt with only three *angas*[2] and as that is the *sampradāya* that is largely in vogue

---

[1] वाक्यैरथैश्च पदैश्च सप्तशत्यात्मकं शुभम् ।

[2] कवचार्गले च कीलकमादौ मध्ये त्रयोदशाध्यायी ।
अन्ते प्राधानिकवैकृतिके मूर्तित्रयं रहस्यानाम् ॥

amongst Devi worshippers, we have also dealt only with the three *angas* in our present work.

THE STORY

Let us turn to the story. Two unlucky men meet in a forest. They are deeply disappointed, but not disillusioned. They still cling to those men and objects that have abandoned them. Each comes to know the state of the other. One has lost his kingdom; the other has been deprived of all his wealth. They both approach a Sage and enquire from him the reason for their plight. The sage dispels their doubts, teaches them the method of worshipping the Goddess in the occult way, *rahasyokta-vidhānena*. They follow his teaching meticulously, subject themselves to a great discipline and after three years of strenuous sadhana get the grace of the Devi. Suratha, the Kshatriya, gets back his lost kingdom, while Samadhi gets the supreme knowledge he aspires for. One attains happiness here, the other elsewhere. One who wants enjoyment *bhoga*, gets the enjoyment of his kingdom, while the other aspiring for liberation, *moksa*, gets the great release. We see in the story that there is nothing fundamentally wrong with the lives led by the two men. Suratha was a very good king: he was looking after his subjects as he would his own children, *prajāḥ putrānivaurasān*. Samadhi was born in a wealthy family, *utpanno dhaninām kule*, and shared his prosperity with his whole family. Yet, in spite of their goodness, they were both treated badly by their respective kinsmen. Even after receiving such treatment, their hearts clung to their old associations. They both knew that it was absurd to have such warm feelings towards those who did not respond that way. but they could not help the attachment.

A sense of introspection and self-analysis makes them approach the Sage, in quest of the truth which eludes their thinking mind. The Sage explains : "All creatures have a consciousness of their own and are instinct with their desire to preserve themselves and their knowledgs is spread over the objects of senses. Of the created beings, some are born day-blind, some night-blind, while others are, day and night, of equal vision. The knowledge of man is in no way better than that of birds and beasts which show great skill in preserving *themselves* and what is *theirs*. Here again, the sense and feeling of "mine" is spread over all creation—man and beast alike; know then, the cause of all this is Ignorance, *avidyā*, which is not the creation of any being on earth or in heaven. It is a product of the workings of *mahāmāya*, the great illusory Power of Lord Vishnu. She is the power for bondage as well as for liberation, for ignorance and for knowledge. By Her, the whole universe is set in motion revolving incessantly and containing in it all that is mobile and immobile. She, in short, is the Power of Hari, the Lord of the Universe-called *yoga nidrā*, the sleep-power of Yoga or the super-conscious poise of the Supreme Being.[1]"

---

1. *Further Lights : The Veda and the Tantra* by Sri Kapali Sastriar.

At the outset the Sage makes it quite clear that all their misery is due to *mamatā*, the sense of mine. They are filled with self-pity that their love and attachment towards their kinsmen are not responded and are misplaced. But why do they love ? It is the ego in them, the sense of I-ness and my-ness which make them cling. If the love and attachement is turned towards the Divine without expecting any return whatsoever, all misery comes to an end. By attaching oneself to the Divine, one gets the release. But this is not easy. The whole life is a battle waged between divine and anti-divine forces. In the three *caritas,* the Sage relates to them the exploits of the Supreme Sakti and her numerous emanations,the grim battles fought on various planes with the anti-divine forces. The Rishi talks of the Divine intervention at the crucial moments, the eternal vigilance and the saving Grace which shape the destiny of mankind on earth. And finally, he teaches them the method of approach, the Sadhana. Both start the same Sadhana driven by misery. Both realise the same truth, each in his own way. An exclusive this-worldliness or otherworldliness is not preached by the Saptasati. The Devi grants both *svarga* and *apavarga*. But, Bhoga, enjoyment and Moksha, release, have to be founded upon *tyāga* , renunciation of I-ness and my-ness, a complete abandonment of the ego in man, a consecrated surrender in all parts of the being to the Divine.

THE TWO PATHS

In fact, Suratha and Samadhi represent the two distinct types in humanity that ever forge their way towards the Godhead. They both resort to the Sage Medhas whose name signifies that he has the knowledge born out of unison with the Divine (from *medh* to unite). His is not mere intellect, his is a knowledge of identification with the Divine and whatever he teaches carries with it the authority of Revelation, the Divine Sanction.

Suratha is one who has a good chariot. *ratha*, chariot, represents the body while the *rathi*, charioteer, is the soul.[1] To transform the physical and establish the divine in the physical is his aim. For that purpose, birth as a Kshatriya in itself endows him with a good body, a strong physique. He is capable of protecting himself as well as extending protection to others. Being a king, he starts with all the facilities to enjoy the physical life. With all these advantages, he does the Sadhana. Bhoga, enjoyment of the physical with a spiritualised vital, is his aim and he attains it by the grace of the Devi. For, he is not merely endowed with a perfect physical body, his vital is strong. He is capable of great activity, strenuous devotion. Ultimately he becomes the master of material existence, *sāvarṇi manu,* the leader of mankind.

Samadhi, on the other hand, as his name signifies, has an one-pointed devotion in all his pursuits.

---

[1] आत्मानं रथिनं विद्धि शरीरं रथमेव तु ।

He is a Vaishya by birth. He has the advantage of worldly riches. By training, he concentrates on the gain he gets in every transaction, the ultimate profit in the commerce of men and things. When he finds that his gain is ephemeral, he rejects all the things that stand between him and the Eternal Gain and to the exclusion of everything in this worldly life, he seeks with a concentrated devotion, with an one-pointed sincerity, the supreme knowledge and attains it in the end by the grace of the Devi.

Seeing that this world of ours is full of false-hood, deceit, cunning, ignorance and misery, Samadhi becomes disgusted, rejects the world to find the Divine. With his one-pointed pursuit he gets the supreme knowledge which confers on him the great release. The King Suratha knows the shortcomings of the world and worldly life. But his is not the way of rejection, his is one of transformation. He seeks to see God in life, bring the Beyond in Here and taste *tyaga* in Bhoga.

The story of Suratha and Samadhi proves that an aspirant can reach the goal by following any one of the two famous paths in the Tantric Sadhana. Samadhi went the way of knowledge, *dakṣiṇa mārga*, while Suratha took the path of Delight, *Vama Marga*. It requires great courage and mental fortitude to seek the light in darkness, to search for the Beauty and Delight in the ugliness and misery of mortal existence. This is the aim of *vāmācāra* and in this Sadhana, things that degrade the soul of man are themselves utilised for its upliftment. It is a dangerous path and it is like walking on razor's edge, *asidhārā vrata*. One mistake, one slip on this steep course is enough for a disastrous fall. Only a *vīra,* a Kshatriya, a hero-warrior, can pursue this path. Suratha had the necessary physique, strength of mind and facilities for enjoying the material life. He could pursue the path easily. Samadhi had the knowledge to amass and accumulate worldly wealth and *dakṣina mārga* came naturally to him to use the same knowledge to amass *spiritual wealth.*

The teachings of the Tantra provide for the deficiencies found in the individual. They classify the aspirant into three groups, according to his capacity and fitness, *adhikāra*, to follow the Sadhana. These are *paśu*, the beast, *vīra*, the warrior and *divya* ,the divine types. They correspond to a predominance of physical, vital and mental and higher mental faculties in man respectively. The doctrine is that one who begins the Sadhana with predominant physical leanings, *paśu* can gradually by the very Sadhana reach the stage of the *vira* and then the *divya*. Usually, *paśu* is a stage of short duration while *vira* and *divya* exist as temperamental types or two classes of Sadhana according to the necessity of the evolving soul. The *vira* corresponds to the *vāma mārga* while *divya* denotes the *dakṣina mārga*. There has always been a dispute to ascertain which of the two paths is the greater, which is *vaidic*, according to the Vedas-orthodox and which is heterodox. It is quite true that both the methods are Tantric. It is also true that participants in *Vamacara* have brought the *acara* into disrepute.

dakṣiṇa means dexterous, right and skill which is inherent in the right hand. It is a skill born out of right knowledge in thought, word and deed. On the other hand, *vāma* means left, beauty[1] and the delight of existence. It is a delight running through the warp and woof of things, the very sap of life that sustains existence. Both these paths receive equal respect in *śri lalitā sahasranāma, soundarya lahari* and in the *devi māhātmyam*—the basic scriptures of the Devi cult. Whatever might have been the misunderstandings and mis-applications in later times, it is evident that initially these two paths were well understood and practised to perfection. A failure to understand and grasp the symbolism employed in *vāmācāra* has led to its misinterpretation. The Tantras only followed the Vedic practice in clothing their teaching in symbolism as throughout the world, down the ages, the mystic tradition has always been to protect the truth from the sight of the unworthy and the uninitiated by hiding it in symbolism. If *madhu* in the five M's is merely understood as wine, instead of as the Divine delight, the Soma in the Veda, then no doubt all drunkards can claim to be the worshippers of Devi.

---

1. It is to be noted that the left part of *siva's* body is the abode of beauty and delight, Ambika.

THE BATTLE OF LIFE

The text comprising the three *caritas* is a chronicle of the battles fought between the Devi and divine forces on one side and the Asuric, antidivine forces on the other. In the first *carita* is described the greatness of Mahakali and her encounter with the Asuras, Madhu and Kaitabha. The second *carita* deals with the manifestation of Mahalakshmi from all the gods and her grim battles with and ultimate victory over Mahishasura. The third *carita* is full of the prowess of Mahasaraswati and the patient and systematic way in which she and her emanations, *vibhutis* , vanquish the Asuras ,Shumbha and Nishumbha and their hosts. All these incidents, the text says, did not happen on the earth plane, neither are they related to our times, the cycle of Vaivasvata Manu. They took place in the cycle of Svarochisha Manu.

In this creation, apart from this world in which we live, there exist other worlds and universes, a regular gradation spreading over a rising tier of conciousness and planes. One rarely comprehends why a particular incident happens in a particular way on the earth plane. It is sometimes a resultant, some times an echo of happenings in other worlds. The significance of these stories of battles between Devas and Asuras is lost on those who hold this physical universe and material existence as the sole and fundamental reality. To them, at best, these are mythological stories intended to intimidate man into a moral or ethical behaviour. But, "the ancient mind more open than ours to the truth of things behind the physical veil, saw behind the life of man great Cosmic Powers or Beings representative of certain turns or grades of the Universal Shakti, divine, titanic, gigantic, demoniac and men who strongly represented in themselves these types of nature were themselves considered as Devas, Asuras Rakshasas, Pishachas." [1] In the Rig Veda, Indra, the master of illumined mind is always confronted with Vritra, the coverer. In fact, "the fundamental idea of the Rig Veda is a struggle between the Gods and their dark opponents, between the Masters of Light, sons of infinity and the children of division and night, a battle in which man takes part and which is reflected in all his inner life and action." [2] The same idea is carried on in the Puranas and in the epics Ramayana and Mahabharata.

Our life on earth is a battle and this battle is waged on all the fronts of terrestial existence. Every minute there is a fight, a struggle is going on in all the parts of one's being. This is a war between good and evil, light and darkness, knowledge and ignorance, truth and falsehood, delight and delusion, immortality and death. "The soul of man is a world full of beings, a kingdom in which armies clash to help or hinder a supreme conquest, a house where the Gods are our guests and which the demons strive to possess." [3] There are certain forces whose sole purpose is

---

1.Sri Aurobindo
2.Sri Aurobindo
3.Sri Aurobindo

to hinder and if possible block a man's progress towards the Godhead. There are equally powerful forces that encourage him at every step, lift him up when he stumbles, help him to reach the goal of God he has set forth for himself. "The soul is a battlefield full of helpers and hunters, friends and enemies, all this lives, teems, is personal, is conscious, is active."[1]

The anti-divine is inherent in the very process of creation. He is a concomitant of the evolving Prakriti. This fact is brought out clearly in the first *carita* . Vishnu, the all pervasive principle of preservation, lies in super-conscient sleep *yoganidrā* on Ananta, the infinity coiled up from aeons of time amidst the waters of the inconscient ocean *apraketam salilam*.[2] The creation is about to start. There is a stir, a throb, a vibration-a sound rises from the navel of the

---

1. Sri Aurobindo

2. Discussing the Vedic imagery in the Hymn of Creation (RigVeda, X, 129), Sri Aurobindo says:

"This Vedic imagery throws a clear light on the similar symbolic images of the Puranas, especially on the famous symbol of Vishnu sleeping after the *Pralaya* on the folds of the snake Ananta upon the ocean of sweet milk. It may perhaps be objected that the Puranas were written by superstitious Hindu priests or poets who believed that eclipses were caused by a dragon eating the sun and moon and could easily believe that during the period of non-creation the supreme Deity in a physical body went to sleep on a physical snake upon a material ocean of real milk and that therefore it is a vain ingenuity to seek for a spiritual meaning in these fables. My reply would be that there is in fact no need to seek for such meanings; for these very superstitious poets have put them there plainly on the very surface of the fable for everybody to see who does not

Primordeal Person. The word is born as a precursor to creation, which is described in the Puranic language as a Brahama coming out of the *nābhi-padma* of Vishnu. Immediately Madhu and Kaitabha are born out of the wax in the ear of Vishnu, *Viṣṇukarṇa-malodbhūtan*. The field of activity for the sound is the ear, *Karna* and as soon as sound is born, an obstruction comes in the ear hampering the reaching of sound, in the form of wax. The two Asuras born out of the wax proceed to Kill Brahma. The coming into being of antidivine forces is as natural as the formation of wax in the ear and they will last as long as the creation lasts. They can be vanquished, but they cannot be totally annihilated. In the twelfth chapter, closing the narrative by relating the exinction of Shumbha and Nishumbha, the sage says that the rest of them went to nether regions, *seṣhāh pātālam ayayuh*, meaning thereby that they chose to be dormant for the time being. These forces are typal beings, having no soul to evolve. They represent a fixed principle of the creation, opposing the divine intention.

---

choose to be blind. For they have given a name to Vishnu's snake, the name Ananta means the Infinite; therefore they have told us plainly enough that the image is an allegory and that Vishnu, the all-pervading Deity, sleeps in the periods of non-creation on the coils of the infinite. As for the ocean, the Vedic imagery shows us that it must be the ocean of eternal existence and this ocean of eternal existence is an ocean of absolute sweetness, in other words, of pure Bliss. For the sweet milk (itself a Vedic image) has evidently a sense not essentially different from the *madhu*, honey or sweetness, of Vamadeva's hymn." (on the Veda.)

Again, these anti-divine forces are so much like the divine.[1] They possess tremendous strength, power light, will-power and in some cases even *tapas* and knowledge. But they are all opposed to Divine Law and Truth. They usurp the functions of the divine and beguile the unwary into thinking that they are the divine. But they can be spotted out by their exaggerated ego-sense which preponderates over all their qualities and actions. All perversion and distortion in the world is the work of these forces and their hold on man and earthly existence is as powerful - if not more-as the hold of the divine forces.

Just like the divine forces, the Asuric forces can change themselves into many forms, send out emanations charged with their power. In the story, Mahishasura leaves for a while his original form of Mahisha, takes the form of a lion, then the form of a man with a sword in hand, and then the form of an elephant to fight with the Devi. Raktabija's exceptional capacity to multiply himself is astounding. Each drop of blood touching the ground, when he is struck, instantaneously produces a Raktabija and soon the whole world is filled with Raktabijas. He has to be vanquished by a skilful device.

Now, dealing with the second *carita* , the name Mahishasura signifies a Vastness (from *mahi* , vast). His stupendous proportions are described in these striking verses. "When he swaggered round with speed,

---

1. In fact, the Veda speaks of them as ancient Gods, *purvē devah* . The Asuras were orginally Gods before they chose to go and develop against the Law.

the earth crumbled into pieces under his hooves: lashed by his tail the ocean flooded everywhere; broken by his moving horns the clouds went into pieces; his heaving breath lifted up mountains in the sky and brought them down."[1] But his is not a vastness of Prishni, the Vedic dappled Cow of radiant light and all-penetrating knowledge; neither his strength is that of Indra, Vrisha, the Bull, the Male, the leader of the herd, the pourer of plenitudes. He is the Mahisha, the buffalo; he belongs to the bovine class, no doubt. But his vastness is a distortion. It is a vastness of dense *tamas*, darkness and ignorance, not of light and knowledge. Mahishasura represents a vast dense mass of stubborn stupidity puffed up with insolence and egoism.

Similarly, Shumbha and Nishumbha represent the Light (from *sumbh* to shine) just like the Devas (from *div* to shine). In fact they usurp the posts and functions of all the Gods and begin ruling the three worlds. But their light does not come out of the Sun of Truth, theirs is a reflection of their stupendous ego. They want to possess all the rare things in the world, all that is best, the gem in every field. So, when they see in Devi, a gem of a woman, they want to possess her as they are the enjoyers by right of all the precious things, *ratnabhujah*. They want to use the Divine for their own purpose.

---

[1] वेगभ्रमणविक्षुण्णा मही तस्य व्यशीर्यत ।
लाङ्गूलेनाहतश्चाब्धिः प्लावयामास सर्वतः ॥

धुतश्रृङ्गविभिन्नाश्च खण्डं खण्डं ययुर्घनाः ।
श्वासानिलास्ताः शतशो निपेतुर्नभसोऽचलाः ॥

Thus, it is clear that the anti-divine forces have some characteristics of the divine forces but entirely to a different purpose. Because they are so much like the divine forces, the struggle between them is long drawn out and bitter. The anti-divine has to be encountered under its own terms and conditions. Shumbha complains to Devi that she is fighting with him relying on other people's strength, *anyāsām balam āśritya*, meaning that she is taking help from the Matrikas. Immediately the Devi obliges him by withdrawing all the Matrikas into her own body and then asks him to face her. The anti-divine is full of snares and ruses and is strong in its own den. But, no victory is complete unless these forces are tackled under the conditions they impose. A Dhumralochana (literally smoky eye) of hazy perception can be dissolved like smoke by a *humkara*, grunt, from the Devi; but a Raktabija has to be studied in his own tactics and finally a skilful device has to be employed by making Chamunda drink the drops of blood as they fall from Raktabija's body. Chanda and Munda are killed by Kali, an emanation of the Devi while she herself has to wage a relentless war to kill Nishumbha.

A careful reading of all the three episodes would bring home to the aspirant the cardinal teaching of Saptasati. The whole life is a battle and for one who has taken to Sadhana, to a path of seeking the Divine, the opposition from the antidivine forces is all the more, as their avowed purpose is to thwart the seeker in his godward endeavour. If the seeker admits the gods into himself, is receptive to divine forces, the forces nourish and increase him while if he admits the anti-divine forces into himself, the hostile forces get aggrandised, while he perishes. In the battle of life, the sadhaka has to ally himself with the divine forces of Truth and Light and face a relentless battle with the anti-divine forces. Even a small short-coming in the sadhana, a chink in the armour is enough, to make the hostile forces hold sway.

DIVINE INTERVENTION

But there is no cause for despair. The Divine is ultimately victorious and Truth alone triumphs, *satyameva jayate* . The victory of the divine forces is a thing decreed, inevitable and irresistible. In the first *carita*, we find the sage affirming "Though she is eternal, immanent in the whole universe which is her embodiment, she takes birth again and again, incarnates herself in a special form of her choice for the successful regime of the Gods, Devas— for establishing divine principles in the world—in order that its functionings may increasingly harmonise with the eternal verities and higher laws of the creative Godhead." [1] In the second *carita* , the Gods get their task accomplished and pay homage to the Devi in gratitude. She promises her intervention when they need her protection against the anti-divine forces. In the third *carita* also, as soon as the Asuras are destroyed, the Gods sing

---

1. *Thoughts on Tantra* by Sri Kapali Sastriar

the glory of the Devi and her manifestations. The Mother is pleased and graciously gives an assurance that she would be constantly on their side to protect them from the evil and also declares that her presence would abide wherever the Devi Mahatmya is recited, *sānnidhyam tatra me sthitam.*

Thus, there is a divine vigilance over human affairs on earth. Whenever there is a crisis, when the world seems to be under complete control of the Asuric forces, when all the higher values of life are on the verge of extinction, when all is apparently lost, then the Divine descends with its Grace. The Supreme Power intervenes, destroys the anti-divine forces, puts the world back again on its feet and gives it an impetus to march ahead. In the sadhana of the individual, the Divine intervention and the saving Grace are facts of spiritual experience. The Grace "is a power superior to any rule, even to the Cosmic Law." [1] It can annual the workings of Karma and Fate and can change the destiny of the individual. A recital of Saptasati is a sure way of earning the grace of the Divine Mother. In the 12th chapter of the text, the Devi herself re-counts the effect of reciting this sacred text with devotion, gives visible signs of the working of her grace. "And when the grace and protection of the Divine Mother are with you, what is there that can touch you, or whom need you fear? A little of it even will carry you through all difficulties, obstacles and dangers; surrounded by its full presence, you can go

---

1. Sri Aurobindo

securely on your way because it is hers, careless of all menace, unaffected by any hostility however powerful, whether from this world or from worlds invisible. Its touch can turn difficulties into opportunities, failure into success and weakness into unfaltering strength. For, the grace of the Divine Mother is the sanction of the Supreme and now or tomorrow its effect is sure, a thing decreed, inevitable and irresistible."*

SPIRITUAL CONCEPT

The spiritual concept of Saptasati is in conformity with the teachings of the Veda and the Upanishads. The text speaks of the Transcendental, the Universal and the Individual nature of the Godhead, the manifest and the unmanifest and the immanent Divine in creation. Only it is here the *ādyā śakti*, the Mother of all origins, instead of Brahman. The Nirguna and Saguna, the impersonal and personal aspects, the dualities and beyond the dualities—all are dealt with. There are four *stutis* in the text, one by Brahma and the other three by all the gods made in the praise of Devi on appropriate occasions. Even a casual perusal of these *stutis* would bring home the lofty spiritual concepts embedded in these moving verses. These are not mere spiritual concepts but actual spiritual experiences of the lauders. When the Rishi addresses the Devi as one who resides as Intelligence in the heart *sarvasya buddhirūpeṇa janasya hṛdi samsthite*, he is only giving an expression to what he actually experiences.

* *The Mother:* Sri Aurobindo

The verses beginning with *yā devi sarva bhutesū* 'the goddess who in all beings' and the verses in *nārāyaṇi stuti* are unsurpassed in hymnal literature for their inspired authentic utterance of lofty spiritual concepts. They have in them the innate power of effectuating the concepts into realisations.

The Tantra discards nothing, rejects nothing: it uses everything for the Divine purpose as all this is *Sakti*. "Wherever, whatever, thing be there existent or non-existent, thou art the force, *sakti* of that all, O All-Soul!" [1]exclaims Brahma. The Many becoming One does not negate the One becoming Many. Both the realisations are commended and the scripture sees no contradiction. For destroying Mahishasura, the *sakti* in each god comes out and unites as Para Sakti, *niśśeṣa devagaṇa ṣakti-samūhamūrti*, who goes to fight the demon. The Many become One. In her battles with Shumbha, Nishumbha and their hosts, the Devi, the One manifests as the many Vibhutis. The Tantra emphasises that if One is real, the Many too are real.

THE OCCULT SIDE

The occult side of Saptasati is natuarally hidden and only those who have an eye for such things would see and not others.[2] Especially on Mantra Sadhana, the text throws a flood of light. "Mantra Sadhana proceeds

---

1 यच्च किञ्चित् कचिद्वस्तु सदसद्वाऽखिलात्मिके ।
तस्य सर्वस्य या शक्तिः सा त्वं ·········· ॥

2 चक्षुष्मन्तोऽनुपश्यन्ति नेतरे तद्विदो जनाः ।

on the basis that there are distinct Individualities, Gods, Goddeses with Forces, and beings dependent on them and emanating from them, even as they themselves are emanations and personalities of the Supreme; and this fact will be evident from a casual perusal of source-books on Tantra Shastra and some of the standard books like *Prapancasara*, whose authorship is ascribed to Shankaracharya. But nowhere is it so pronounced and clearly brought to light as in the second and third section of the threefold episode of the Devi Mahatmya." [1] A careful study of the second and third *caritas* shows that emanations are of many kinds and they can come to be in many ways. "An emanation of the Mother is something of her consciousness and power put forth from her which, so long as it is in play, is held in close connection with her and when its play is no longer required, is withdrawn back into its source, but can always be put out and brought into play once more. But also the detaining thread of connection can be severed and loosened and that which came forth as an emanation can proceed in its way as an independent divine being with its own play in the world. All the gods can put forth such emanations from their being, identified with them in essence of consciousness and power though not commensurate." [2] "He is the soul; all the gods are his limbs" [3] declares the Upanishad. The Supreme

---

1. *Further Lights: The Veda and the Tantra* by Sri Kapali Sastriar
2. Sri Aurobindo
3. स आत्मा । अङ्गान्यन्या देवताः ।

Sakti is one without a second, *ekaivaham jagatyatra dvitiya ka mamaparu* but her emanations are her members and are no less a fact. Each limb in the body has its own special function. The eye sees, the ear hears. The ear does not see, neither does the eye hear. Similarly, each god or goddess has a particular function to perform in the rising tier of consciousness outwardly represented by a heirarchy of worlds. Each has his own particular form, particular vehicle, particular colour, particular weapons and particular retinue, *vāhana, varṇa, āyudha,* and *parivāra*. In this way he can be distinguished, approached and propitiated. This is the secret of Mantra Sadhana. An emanation of a god is only a delegated power of the god and as such has the same form, weapons vehicles etc. *brahmāṇi, kaum-ari,vaisnav*, for instance, are exactly like Brahma, Kumara and Vishnu in form, dress and vehicle. *Yadvadeva hi yad rupam yatha bhūṣaṇavāhanam, tadvadeva hi tat śaktih.* Of course, the vehicle, the weapon etc. are symbolic representations of sentient beings and at times they themselves act as emanations from the god who possesses them. This is the principle behind worshipping the *sudarsana cakra* as the delegated godhead of Vishnu, the *daṇḍa* as the representative of Kumara etc. In the text, one cannot fail to notice the exploits of the Devi's vehicle, the lion. It acts as an emanation, as a guided missile of the goddess and engages quite independently with devastating effect the fighting hosts of Asuras. Again, for killing Mahishasura, each god sends forth an effulgence from himself and all these effulgences join together

to form a resplendent universal form of Para Sakti.
Not only the gods partake in this process, their weapons also, sentient beings as they are, send out their
manisfestations to serve as weapons for Para Sakti.
We shall quote a verse of this nature: "The holder of
pināka gave to her the trident drawing it out of his
trident. The dark God also gave the discus, whirling
it forth from his own discus."[1]

When the effulgences emanating from the gods
united to manifest the form of Para Sakti, they did not
unite indiscriminately. The characteristic function of
the deity is reproduced by the emanation of the deity
on the common form. A close study of the relavant
verses will amply reward the earnest seeker. We shall
give one or two illustrations. The effulgence from
Vishnu goes to make the arms of Para Sakti. Vishnu's
characteristic is preservation and protection which are
physically represented by the strength of arms. And
so arms are from the effulgence of Vishnu, *bahavo
viṣṇutejasā.* Her hips are formed by the light of the
earth, *nitambas tejasā bhuvaḥ* denoting stability and
foundation of existence. Similarly, when Brahmani
vanquishes her foes, she does not combat with ordinary weapons, but with water, sanctified by Mantra,
toyena mantrapūtena, thus revealing in her the characteristics of the original deity, Brahma. *vārāhi* at-
tacks by her snout, *tundaghātena,* and *narasimhi* tears
by her claws *nakhair vidārita.*

---

[1] शूलं शूलाद्विनिष्कृष्य ददौ तस्यै पिनाकधृक् ।
चक्रं च दत्तवान् कृष्णः समुत्पाट्य स्वचक्रतः ॥

The manifestation of the Devi to kill Mahishasura is formed by the union of effulgences of all the gods. These effulgences spring forth as a result of intense anger on the part of Siva, Vishnu and other gods. The onrush of wrath produces the emanation. So this is a partial Vibhuti coming out of the illumined vital consciousness, as far as each god is concerned though all these partial Vibhutis join to form an integral manifestation of the great goddess. Similarly, Kali the terrible-faced emanates from the Devi's face, black like ink with anger, as the text says. The exact place wherefrom she emanates is the forehead, at the point where the eyebrows of the Devi knit in anger meet. This is the centre between the eye-brows, the seat of Ajna Chakra, the seat of will and vision. Thus Kali is put forth from a highly mentalised vital consciousness, a power of effectuating will and vision. The *ganas*, the hosts of Devi, on the other hand are created from her sighs, *nisvāsa*, as she is fighting and they become hundreds and thousands, *sata sahárasah*, and they are aggrandised by her own force, *devīsaktyupabrmhitāḥ*. They are vital formations for a limited purpose and they are withdrawn as soon as their allotted work is finished. The Devi who lures Shumbha and Nishumbha by her enthralling beauty is Koushiki, an emanation from the *sarīrakośa*, bodysheath of the Devi. She has been put forth from the Mother's physical consciousness and that is why she is an acme of perfection in her limbs and entices the whole world with her exquisite charm. Then there are the Vibhutis of Vishnu, Brahma etc., which are not partial manifestations but carry in them the full characteristics of their parent godheads.

These emanations are a spiritual fact and any aspirant taking up the Mantra sadhana is able to feel the presence of these emanations at various stages of his seeking. When a seeker seeks and calls the deity, the deity responds by sending out an emanation and if a person sticks to one deity because it is congenial to him, the deity through its emanation abides in him becoming near and dear to him, *iṣṭa*.There begins a living concourse between the sadhaka and his Ishta-devata who takes the burden of leading him to the goal. Similarly, if a disciple looks to his Guru, the deity in human form, for help, an emanation of the Guru goes forth and gives the necessary help to the disciple. In the case of great spiritual personalities, the prayers for help and succour are always answered by the emanations proceeding from such a spiritual personality. A question arises whether the conscious participation of the spiritual personality is there in giving such help and when the calls for help are so numerous and constant, is it possible for anybody, however spiritually great he may be, to be physically aware of such calls. Nothing prevents a Guru or a Master from applying his consciousness to the problem of the disciple who needs help. But even if the Guru is not physically aware, as soon as a call is made by the disciple, automatically an emanation goes out of the Guru to help the disciple. This may not be known to the surface consciousness of the Guru but the help comes from his subliminal consciousness. This remarkable occult truth is illustrated in Saptasati. The gods resort to the foot of Himalayas and make their *stuti* to the Devi so that she may appear before them and do what is required to kill Shumbha and Nishumbha. As the gods are making the *stuti*, the text says, the Devi comes to bathe in the waters of the Ganges. And she questions the gods, "Whom are you praising here?" Then, an auspicious goddess comes out of her physical sheath and explains to her: "Ah, this laud is made to me by the gods who have been defeated by Shumbha and Nishumbha."

ESOTERIC SENSE

There exist many commentaries on this text. Out of them all, *guptavati*, the commentary written by Bhaskararaya, is considered to be authoritative. It enjoys as much reputation as *sowbhāgya bhāskaram*, his commentary on Lalita Sahasranama, among the worshippers of the Devi. There is also now prevalent a commentary in Bengali "Sadhana Samara" by Brahmarishi Satya Dev which deals with the esoteric sense implied in the three episodes. According to this, the whole Mahatmyam is a text on Yoga and the three Charitas represent the cutting of the three knots, Brahma, Vishnu and Rudra Granthis in the subtle body.

Vasishtha Ganapati Muni, the seer-poet, has explained, on the basis of his direct vision and realisation, the esoteric significance of the seven Mothers in his monumental hymnal poem *umāsahasram*. These seven verses occurring in the seventh stabaka of the poem are of immense help to the aspirants in understanding the cosmic purpose of these Manifestations, who are known as *matṛkā* or little Mothers.

Brahmi represents the primordeal Nada, the first throb not yet manifest in sound, which is the origin of all creation. This Nada is the Pranava or Omkara of the Upanishads pervading and permeating the mind regions, Antariksha. This Prime cause is effected in the creation as words. All the Tantras and the seerpoets acclaim her as the primordeal Nada and the evolved speech of created beings.[1]

Brahmi creates the universe with her *nāda* and it is Vaishnavi who gives it a shape. She has a mighty force and gives birth to a network of universes by giving the creation a definite shape. Waves and waves of her deep effulgence full in all parts spread and pervade and make the forms of things distinct and clear. In all the myriad forms of the universe is hidden the *kalā*, a portion, a ripple of Vaishnavi's effulgence. In short, the symmetry, beauty, the organisation and pattern of form itself is the work of Vishnu's *sakti*.[2]

---

[1] अव्यक्तशब्दकलयाऽखिलमन्तरिक्षं
     त्वं व्याप्य देवि सकलागमसम्प्रगीते ।
     नादोऽस्युपाधिवशतोऽथ वचांसि चासि
     ब्राह्मीं वदन्ति कवयोऽमुकवैभवां ताम् ॥

[2] नानाविधं भुवनजालसवित्रि रूपै-
     र्व्याप्तैककनिष्कलग भीरमहत्तरङ्गैः ।
     व्यक्तं विचित्रयसि सर्वमखर्वशक्ते
     सा वैष्णवी तव कला कथिता मुनीन्द्रैः ॥

Maheshwari holds the strings of the puppet show of the universe. Hers is the directing consciousness but in each heart she abides as a distinct consciousness so that the individual soul has an illusion that it is different and distinct from the supreme Soul and it is bound, though its nature is free. It is the case of the puppets imagining that they run the show. Maheshwari sits in each heart and makes all beings revolve as mounted on a wheel.[1]

Kaumari represents the force of aspiration of the evolving soul. She is the flame, the Agni of the Veda mounting towards the Godhead, ever young, Kumara of the Puranas. How is the flame kept burning ? By the in-take; the intake should be pure. And the intake not only means food that is taken in, but all things and perceptions that are taken into the consciousness of a person. Usually the sense perceptions are inter-twined with the senses and sense-objects. By separat-ing oneself from the doings of Prakriti, by having the sense of the witness Purusha, a person is not tainted by the intake. A constant vigilance and a sadhana of rejecting what is impure ensures *āhāra śuddhi*, the purity of the intake and that leads to the purity of the

----

[1] व्यक्तित्वमत्र हृदये हृदये दधासि
येन प्रभिन्न इव बद्ध इवान्तरात्मा ।
सेयं कला भुवननाटकसूत्रभर्त्रि
माहेश्वरीति कथिता तव चिद्विभूतिः ॥

34

being.[1] In that pure being, a constant steady remembrance becomes possible in the heart which is open and receptive (*vikasat saroje* -full blown lotus).There in the ever-wakeful heart shines the unsullied Truthflame which is the force of *guruguha* .Then *guha* , the heart-cavern itself becomes *guru*, the guide.[2]

Varahi is the all-consuming power in the universe. By her force the residents of heaven get their

---

1. The seventh chapter of the Chhandogya Upanishad closes with this paragraph:

आहारशुद्धौ सत्त्वशुद्धिः । सत्त्वशुद्धौ ध्रुवा स्मृतिः । स्मृति-
लम्भे सर्वग्रन्थीनां विप्रमोक्षः । तस्मै मृदितकषायाय तमसः
पारं दर्शयति भगवान् सनत्कुमारः । तं स्कन्द इत्याचक्षते,
तं स्कन्द इत्याचक्षते ॥

"In the purity of nourishment, *āhāra* , lies the purity of the stuff of being, Sattwa: Sattwa being pure, the immediate remembrance becomes constant and fixed: by this remembrance, there is release from all the knots. To such a one, stainless, the Blessed Sanat Kumara shows the shore beyond darkness: they call him Skanda, yea, they call him Skanda."

In a masterly exposition of this paragraph, Sri Kapali Sastriar says (*Lights on the Upanishads*: Skanda Sanatkumara) "These concluding lines give us an idea of the sadhana that helps one to realise the *bhūma* , the Vast Self which is the All and includes the All -the Immortal which seen, dispels all darkness and sorrow, sickness and death."

2. आहारशुद्धिवशतः परिशुद्धसत्त्वे
नित्यस्थिरस्मृतिधरे विकसत्सरोजे ।
प्रादुर्भवत्यमलतत्त्व विभासिका या
सा त्वं स्तुता गुरुगुहस्य सवित्रि शक्तिः ॥

sweet *havyam*, oblations and the Pitris, the fathers, get their tasteful *kavyam*, offerings. And all the beings in terrestrial existence eat the food and enjoy the physical by her grace. She provides the universe with food and the universe is her food. "The eater eating is eaten" as the Upanishad trenchantly explains the law of the universe. Varahi represents this law.[1]

'Great terror, the Vajra uplifted' *mahat bhayam*, *vajram udyatam* .In these words the Upanishad explains the eternal vigilance of the Divine against the anti-divine forces. This vigilance is the *śakti* of Indra, *indrāṇi*.To protect the world she herself directly annihilates evil and also causes their eradication through other great beings of shining strength. The play of her thunderbolt is the measure of her strength. Indrani is the manifestation of the Mother specially sent out to put down all that opposes the cosmic law and the Divine Truth.[2]

---

[1] हव्यं यया दिविषदो मधुरं लभन्ते
    कव्यं यया रुचिकरं पितरो भजन्ते ।
    अश्नाति चान्नमखिलोऽपि जनो ययैव
    सा ते वराहवदनेति कलाऽम्ब गीता ॥

[2] दुष्टान्निहंसि जगतामवनाय साक्षा-
    दन्यैश्च घातयसि तत्प्रबलैमहेन्द्रि: ।
    दम्भोलिचेष्टितपरीक्ष्यबला बलारे:
    शक्तिन्यगादि तव देवि विभूतिरेषा ॥

Cāmuṇḍā; the last of the seven Mothers, gets her name because she comes to the Devi offering Chanda and Munda whom she has killed in battle.[1] She is the great Kali who opens her wide mouth and drinks the drops of blood of Raktabija in order to prevent further Raktabijas from cropping up and finally by this process destroy Raktabija.

Chanda means fierce and he represents the fierce fire ever burning in the basic centre, *mūlādhāra*, of all beings. The Yogis talk about certain centres or plexuses in the subtle body, springs of consciousness which normally lie dormant in man. By Yoga, these centres become active; these lotuses, as they are picturesquely called, blossom and the dormant faculties and capacities become manifest as the play of consciousness is increasingly felt in these centres. *mūlādhāra* is the lower-most centre while *sahasrāra* in the head is uppermost. While Chanda represents the fierce fire in Muladhara, Munda represents the head, the moon in the Sahasrara centre which is the seat of illumined mind. Normally, the Muladhara fire burns with smoke and the Sahasrara is clouded with mental activities. Instead of being a help they act as a bar, a hindrance. In sadhana, in the initial stages, the Muladhara and Sahasrara, Chanda and Munda, take the role of the hostiles. When one takes to sadhana, all the impurities come to the surface, all the previous *vasanas* and inhibitions are brought to light. Muladhara

---

[1] यस्माच्चण्डं च मुण्डं च गृहीत्वा त्वमुपागता ।
चामुण्डेति ततो लोके ख्याता देवी भविष्यसि ॥

hinders the sadhana by throwing out the passions and activities belonging to the lower physical. Similarly, Sahasrara, the head is plagued with incessant trivial mental activities which are mistaken for a healthy state of mind. Muladhara and Sahasrara, Chanda and Munda, have to be subjugated by breaking the knots, *granthis*, so that the initial difficulties are tided over and a sure path to progress is laid out. This subjugation is done by Chamunda who is the force of concentrated awareness in the waking state, *jāgrat samādhi kalā*. An awareness, a consciousness, with the one-pointed aim towards progress, with a concentrated effort, can alone by constant rejection and detachment bring about the subjugation of these activities of the lower physical and the mind which pull one away from the path. Chamunda abolishes all thinking from the mind, makes it empty to be filled up by the divine descent which happens from the responding Sahasrara to the call of the aspiring Muladhara. Raktabija represents this incessant mental activity. The mental activities are born in succession, one from the other, just as one drop of blood produces a Raktabija and a drop of blood from that Raktabija produces another Raktabija and so on. The endless activity of the mind, one thought leading to the other, is represented by Raktabija and the Raktabija episode signifies the act of Chamunda who puts an end to all the rising thoughts in the mind by swallowing as and when they spring up. And she it is, situated in the *anāhata*, heart-centre, who brings down peace,

38

light and delight by the subordination of Muladhara and Sahasrara.[1]

FOUR POWERS

The Mother praised in the Saptasati is generally known as *durgā* or *caṇḍikā*. The seven mothers *saptamatrkas* have already been dealt with and there is also a mention of nine Durgas, *navadurgās* in the text. Many other emanations are also spoken of.

A fundamental doctrine of the Tantra Shastra is to be borne in mind. There are so many planes, gradations, tiers in Creation and presiding over these, there are many gods and goddesses. At the summit of this pyramidal heirarchy, there are certain godheads who are identified with the Supreme, the Brahman of the Vedas and Upanishads. The knowledge leading to such cardinal godheads is known as *brahmavidyā*. The Ten Mahavidyas of the Devi represent ten distinct cults and are Brahmavidyas leading to the Supreme Brahman through the ten distinct deities. Similarly the cardinal deities, the great Powers mentioned in the Saptasati are also Brahmavidyas leading the sadhaka to the Supreme. These should not be confused with *śrividyā*, neither are they the others of the ten

---

[1] सङ्कल्पपरक्तकरणपानविवृद्धशक्त्या
जाग्रत्समाधिकलयेश्वरि ते विभूत्या ।
मूलाग्निचण्डशशिमुण्डतनुत्रमेऽया
चामुण्डया तनुषु देवि न किं कृतं स्यात् ॥

Mahavidyas. They are equally powerful and equally lay a distinct path for the aspirant to reach the Supreme.

These are the three great deities Mahakali, Mahalakshmi and Mahasarasvati. A perusal of the *rahasyatraya* at the end would indicate that these deities are quite different from the generally known triad Parvati, Lakshmi and Sarasvati. These are source-deities for the Mantra, *navākṣari* and for the three *caritas* in the text. They represent, respectively, the gunas Tamas, Rajas and Sattva and have the colours dark, red and white, *ajāmekām lohita śukla kṛṣṇām*. Many contend that only these three deities, Mahakali, Mahalakshmi and Mahasarasvati are dealt with in the Devi Mahatmyam. There is a deity, Maheshwari, who is above these three deities. This is clearly explained, without room for any doubt, in the verse, मेधासि देवि विदिताखिलशास्त्रसारा occurring in the text.

The expression दुर्गाऽसि दुर्गभवसागरनौरसङ्गा indicates clearly the form of Maheshwari. She is *durgā*, difficult of access, seated above all these Powers, detached. She is the ship for crossing the difficult ocean of births and deaths.

In his work The Mother, Sri Aurobindo has explained the principle and field of operation of these four great powers of the Mother, as he has perceived them in his inner vision. In order that the perception of the great seer may also become available to traditional scholarship in the land, Sri Kapali Sastriar has rendered the relevant chapters of the book in beautiful Sanskrit verses under the title 'matrtattva prakasa' which has been acclaimed as *Matr upaniṣad* by discerning worshippers of the Mother. As an understanding of the principles and working of these Four Powers is very desirable to understand the Saptasati, we proceed to quote the relevant lines :

"Four great aspects of the Mother, four of her leading Powers and Personalities have stood in front in her guidance of this Universe and in her dealings with the terrestrial play. One is her personality of calm wideness and comprehending wisdom and tranquil benignity and inexhaustible compassion and sovereign and surpassing majesty and all-ruling greatness. Another embodies her power of splendid strength and irresistible passion, her warrior mood, her overwhelming will, her impetuous swiftness and world-shaking force. A third is vivid and sweet and wonderful with her deep secret of beauty and harmony and fine rhythm, her intricate and subtle opulence, her compelling attraction and captivating grace. The fourth is equipped with her close and profound capacity of intimate knowledge and careful flawless work and quiet and exact perfection in all things. Wisdom, Strength, Harmony, Perfection are their several attributes and it is these powers that they bring with them into the world, manifest in a human disguise in their Vibhutis and shall found in the divine degree of their ascension in those who can open their earthly nature to the direct and living influence of the Mother. To the four we give

41

the four great names, Maheshwari, Mahakali, Mahalakshmi, Mahasaraswati.

Imperial Maheshwari is seated in the wideness above the thinking mind and will and sublimates and greatens them into wisdom and largeness or floods with a splendour beyond them. For she is the mighty and wise One who opens us to the Supramental infinities and the cosmic vastness, to the grandeur of the supreme Light, to a treasurehouse of miraculous knowledge, to the measureless movement of the Mother's eternal forces. Tranquil is she and wonderful, great and calm for ever. Nothing can move her because all wisdom is in her; nothing is hidden from her that she chooses to know, she comprehends all things and all beings and their nature and what moves them and the law of the world and its times and how all was and is and must be. A strength is in her that meets everything and masters and none can prevail in the end against her vast intangible wisdom and high tranquil power. Equal, patient and unalterable in her will, she deals with men according to their nature and with things and happenings according to their Force and the truth that is in them. Partiality she has none, but she follows the decrees of the Supreme and some she raises up and some she casts down or puts away from her into the darkness. To the wise she gives a greater and more luminous wisdom; those that have vision she admits to her counsels; on the hostile she imposes the consequence of their hostility; the ignorant and foolish she leads according to their blindness. In each man she answers and handles the different elements of his nature according to their need and their urge and the return they call for, puts on them the required pressure or leaves them to their cherished liberty to prosper in the ways of the Ignorance or to perish. For she is above all, bound by nothing, attached to nothing in the universe. Yet has she more than any other the heart of the universal Mother. For her compassion is endless and inexhaustible; all are to her eyes her children and portions of the One, even the Asura and Rakshasa and Pisacha and those that are revolted and hostile. Even her rejections are only a postponement, even her punishments are a grace. But her compassion does not blind her wisdom or turn her action from the course decreed; for the Truth of things is her one concern, knowledge her centre of power and to build our soul and our nature into the divine Truth her mission and her labour.

Mahakali is of another nature. Not wideness but height, not wisdom but force and strength are her peculiar power. There is in her an overwhelming intensity, a mighty passion of force to achieve, a divine violence rushing to shatter every limit and obstacle. All her divinity leaps out in a splendour of tempestuous action; she is there for swiftness, for the immediately effective process, the rapid and direct stroke, the frontal assault that carries everything before it. Terrible is her face to the Asura, dangerous and ruthless her mood against the haters of the Divine; for she is the Warrior of the Worlds who never shrinks from the battle. Intolerant of imperfection, she deals roughly with all in man that is unwilling and she is severe to all that is obstinately ignorant and obscure; her wrath is immediate and dire against treachery and falsehood and malignity, ill-will is smitten at once by her scourge. Indifference, negligence and sloth in the divine work she cannot bear and she smites awake at once with sharp pain, if need be, the untimely slumberer and the loiterer. The impulses that are swift and straight and frank, the movements that are unreserved and absolute, the aspiration that mounts in flame are the motion of Mahakali. Her spirit is tameless, her vision and will are high and far-reaching like the flight of an eagle, her feet are rapid on the upward way and her hands are outstretched to strike and to succour. For she too is the Mother and her love is as intense as her wrath and she has a deep and passionate kindness. When she is allowed to intervene in her strength, then in one moment are broken like things without consistence the obstacles that immobilise or the enemies that assail the seeker. If her anger is dreadful to the hostile and the vehemence of her pressure painful to the weak and timid, she is loved and worshipped by the great, the strong and the noble; for they feel that her blows beat what is rebellious in their material into strength and perfect truth, hammer straight what is wry and perverse and expel what is impure or defective. But for her what is done in a day might have taken centuries; without her Ananda might be wide and grave or soft and sweet and beautiful but would lose the flaming joy of its most absolute intensities. To knowledge she gives a conquering might, brings to beauty and harmony a high and mounting movement and imparts to the slow and difficult labour after perfection an impetus that multiplies the power and shortens the long way. Nothing can satisfy her that falls short of the supreme ecstasies, the highest heights, the noblest aims, the largest vistas. Therefore with her is the victorious force of the Divine and it is by grace of her fire and passion and speed if the great achievement can be done now rather than hereafter.

Wisdom and Force are not the only manifestations of the supreme Mother ; there is a subtler mystery of her nature and without it Wisdom and Force would be incomplete things and without it perfection would not be perfect. Above them is the miracle of eternal beauty, an unseizable secret of divine harmonies, the compelling magic of an irresistible universal charm and attraction that draws and holds things and forces and beings together and obliges them to meet and unite that a hidden Ananda may play from behind the veil and make of them its rhythms and its figures. This is the power of Mahalakshmi and there is no aspect of the Divine Shakti more attractive to the heart of embodied beings. Maheshwari can appear too calm and great and distant for the littleness of earthly nature to approach or contain her; Mahakali too swift and formidable for its weakness to bear ; but all turn with joy and longing to Mahalakshmi. For she throws the spell of the intoxicating sweetness of the Divine: to be close to her is a profound happiness and to feel her within the heart is to make existence a rapture and a marvel; grace and charm and tenderness flow out from her like light from the sun and wherever she fixes her wonderful gaze or lets fall the loveliness of her smile, the soul is seized and made captive and plunged into the depths of an unfathomable bliss. Magnetic is the touch of her hands and their occult and delicate influence refines mind and life and body and where she presses her feet course miraculous streams of an entrancing Ananda.

And yet it is not easy to meet the demand of this enchanting Power or to keep her presence. Harmony and beauty of the mind and soul, harmony and beauty of the thoughts and feelings, harmony and beauty in every outward act and movement, harmony and beauty of the life and surroundings, this is the demand of Mahalakshmi. Where there is affinity to the rhythms of the secret world-bliss and response to the call of the All Beautiful and concord and unity and the glad flow of many lives turned towards the Divine, in that atmosphere she consents to abide. But all that is ugly and mean and base, all that is poor and sordid and squalid, all that is brutal and coarse repels her advent. Where love and beauty are not or are reluctant to be born, she does not come; where they are mixed and disfigured with baser things, she turns soon to depart or cares little to pour her riches. If she finds herself in men's hearts surrounded with selfishness and hatred and jealousy and malignance and envy and strife, if treachery and greed and ingratitude are mixed in the sacred chalice, if grossness of passion and unrefined desire degrade devotion, in such hearts the gracious and beautiful Goddess will not linger. A divine disgust seizes upon her and she withdraws, for she is not one who insists or strives; or veiling her face, she waits for this bitter and poisonous devil's stuff to be rejected and disappear before she will found anew her happy influence. Ascetic bareness and harshness are not pleasing to her nor the suppression of the heart's deeper emotions and the rigid repression of the soul's and the life's parts of beauty. For it is through love and beauty that she lays on men the yoke of the Divine. Life is turned in her supreme creations into a rich work of celestial art and all existence into a poem of sacred delight ; the world's riches are brought together and concerted for a supreme order and even the simplest and commonest things are made wonderful by her intuition of unity and the breath of her spirit. Admitted to the heart, she lifts wisdom to pinnacles of wonder and reveals to it the mystic secrets of the ecstasy that surpasses all knowledge, meets devotion with the passionate attraction of the Divine, teaches to strength and force the rhythm that keeps the might of their acts harmonious and in measure and casts on perfection the charm that makes it endure for ever.

Mahasaraswati is the Mother's Power of Work and her spirit of perfection and order. The youngest of the Four, she is the most skilful in executive faculty and the nearest to physical Nature. Maheshwari lays down the large lines of the world-forces, Mahakali drives their energy and impetus, Mahalakshmi discovers their rhythms and measures, but Mahasaraswati presides over their detail of organisation and execution, relation of parts and effective combination of forces and unfailing exactitude of result and fulfilment. The science and craft and technique of things are Mahasaraswati's province. Always she holds in her nature and can give to those whom she has chosen the intimate and precise knowledge, the subtlety and patience, the accuracy of intuitive mind and conscious hand and discerning eye of the perfect worker. This Power is the strong, the tireless, the careful and efficient builder, organiser, administrator, technician, artisan and classifier of the worlds. When she takes up the transformation and new-building of the nature, her action is laborious and minute and often seems to our impatience slow and interminable, but it is persistent, integral and flawless. For the will in her works is scrupulous, unsleeping, indefatigable; leaning over us she notes and touches every little detail, finds out every minute defect, gap, twist or incompleteness, considers and weighs accurately all that has been done and all that remains still to be done hereafter. Nothing is too small or apparently trivial for her attention; nothing however impalpable or disguised or latent can escape her. Moulding and remoulding, she labours each part till it has attained its true form, is put in its exact place in the whole and fulfils its precise purpose. In her constant and deligent arrangement and rearrangement of things, her eye is on all needs at once and the way to meet them and her intuition knows what is to be chosen and what rejected and successfully determines the right instrument, the right time, the right conditions and the right process. Carelessness and negligence and indolence she abhors : all scamped and hasty and shuffling work, all clumsiness and *a peu pres* and misfire, all false adaptation and misuse of instruments and faculties and leaving of things undone or half done is offensive and foreign to her temper. When her work is finished, nothing has been forgotten, no part has been misplaced or omitted or left in a faulty condition; all is solid, accurate, complete, admirable. Nothing short of a perfect perfection satisfies her and she is ready to face an eternity of toil if that is needed for the fullness of her creation. Therefore, of all the Mother's powers, she is the most long-suffering with man and his thousand imperfections. Kind, smiling, close and helpful, not easily turned away or discouraged, insistent even after repeated failure, her hand sustains our every step on condition that we are single in our will and straightforward and sincere; for a double mind she will not tolerate and her revealing irony is merciless to drama and histrionics and self-deceit and pretence. A mother to our wants, a friend in our difficulties, a persistent and tranquil counsellor and mentor, chasing away with her radiant smile, the clouds of gloom and fretfulness and depression, reminding always of the ever-present help, pointing to the eternal sunshine, she is firm, quiet and persevering in the deep and continuous urge that drives us towards the integrality of the higher nature. All the work of the other Powers leans on her for its completeness: for she assures the material foundation, elaborates the stuff of detail and erects and rivets the armour of the structure."

CONCLUSION

Thus the Devi Mahatmya is a great Sadhana Shastra. Even if it is taken as a mere story without any symbolism, one cannot miss its arresting style. It is like an interesting novel exciting the curiosity of the reader to know what is going to happen next. It is true that the text is full of descriptions of battles. But the manner of telling is not boring; on the other hand, the unexpected turns in the handling of the theme have in store for the reader many surprises. The oft-repeated phrases like *caṇḍikā, caṇḍavikramā, durgā durgārtināśinī and kāli karālavadanā* bring home the epic grandeur of the piece. In keeping with the super-human characters, the poetic embellishments employed also are unique. Phrases like the following, "He perhaps hurled the orb of the Sun itself from the sky", "Those chakras striking the Devi in succession looked like so many Suns entering successively a dark cloud and emerging out of it", cannot be classed as *atiśayokti* or exaggeration. As Sri Kapali Sastriar has remarked in a different context, in such an epic setting, the supernatural becomes the natural element and the mythological quite logical.

Most of the verses are in the *anuṣtubh* metre. But their simple grandeur and telling force can be found only in a Sadhana Shastra like this. The impact of the words and the vibrations they create in and around the reciter have to be experienced to be believed. Translation of such a work in another tongue is naturally beset with shortcomings. The Sanskrit has its own grandeur and when coupled with the grandeur of the theme, the effect is unsurpassed. Lines like

नमस्तस्यै नमस्तस्यै नमस्तस्यै नमो नमः

baffle translation into any other tongue. The line is not a mere case of alliteration, neither it is an oriental mannerism of repeating oneself to bring home a point. In the word *namah* is implied not only a salutation, but a surrender, a plasticity (*nam* -to bow) and receptivity to the Divine. Each *namah* succeeding the other forms a rising crescendo of salutation and supplication borne on the crests of the waves of adoration and surrender.

This English translation tries its best to provide at least a pale echo of the marvellous nuances and shades of sound in the original. That is why, if an apology is required, the translation in certain places seems unnatural to the idiom of the English language.

Such a text has to be carefully read and the correct meaning grasped. In this regard, Guptavati, the commentrary of Sri Bhaskararaya is of great help. Pointing out the necessity of his commenting upon the text, Bhaskararaya himself says that the commentaries of his times were useful only in dealing with the rites and practices of japa, homa, tarpana etc relating to the text and did not satisfy the learned who sought to know the inner sense of Chandi worship.[1] A major portion of his commentary is taken up by his careful classification of the text into seven hundred verses. Here he makes a bold departure fom his predecessors in the classification of the 21 verses beginning with *yā devī sarvabhūteṣu*. While others take each verse as equivalent to three verses because of the repetition of the phrase *namastasyai* thrice, Bhaskararaya has stated that each of these 21 verses has to be repeated thrice, the first line as found in the verse and the second line as *namastasyai namo namah*, making a verse of 24 letters and he holds that these verses are Mantras in Gayatri metre of the 21 aspects[2] of the Goddess mentioned in these verses. While dealing with the incarnation of the Goddess Bhramari, he identifies her with his family deity Chandrala Parameswari and dedicates his commentary to her.

His definitions are arresting. He defines *śraddhā* faith, as the certainty that the result will surely come, *phala-avaśyambhāva-niścaya* and defines *nidrā*, sleep, as a change conducive to the cessation of activity of

---

1 ताश्चण्डीजपद्बेमतर्पणमुखानुष्ठानमात्रोपयो-
ग्यर्थंज्ञानमभीप्सतां न विदुषां चित्ते चमत्कुर्वंते ।

2. No. 21 is significant. The triple aspect of the Goddess in each of the seven planes of consciousness, *anna, prana, manah, vijnana, anand, cit, sat* corresponding to the seven *vyahritis* of the Veda and the seven *lokas* of the Purana.

the external senses, *bāhyendriya vyāpāroparamānu-kulavikārah*. At times he is refreshingly original. Commenting on the verse in the twelfth chapter, *sā yācitā ca vijnānam tustā rddhim prayacchati*, he splits *sā yācitā* as *sā ayācitā* and says that Goddess gives what the devotee asks of her. But if she is not asked anything, *ayācitā* by the devotee, she gives to him the supreme knowledge *vijnānam*. To acquaint the modern reader with Bhaskararaya's deep erudition and logical reasoning, we shall give excerpts from his exposition of the word *candi*:

"Chandi denotes the deity, the sovereign queen of the supreme Brahman. We see the use of the term *canda* in words like *candabhanu, canda vada* fierce sun, fierce argument, etc., to denote a sense of extra-ordinary quality not limited by any standard or measure; and a measure is limited in three ways by time, space and object and freedom from this triple limitation is the sign of only the supreme Brahman. Though the term is derived from the root *cad* meaning anger, from statements like the following: "Whom even the Gods fear when he gets angry in battles." A woman does not like a man to be her husband whose favour is of no value and anger is of no avail and treats him as she would an impotent", we find that anger finds its fulfilment only in the creation of immense fear and only in the sense of such an anger the root *cad* is primarily used. That is why in statements like *namaste rudra manyave*, "O Rudra, salutation to thy wrath", the salutation is first to the wrath. From the utterances of

Upanishads like "Through the fear of Him the wind blows; through the fear of Him the sun rises; through the fear of Him Indra and Agni and Death hasten in their courses," the argument is fortified that the anger that instils fear into the wind and others is the sign of the supreme Brahman. That is why Uttaramimamsa in the *adhikāra, kampanāt* says that in the *śruti , mahat bhayam vajram udyatam*, the term *vajra* denotes Brahaman and not any particular weapon because of its indication to create fear. Therefore, the term *caṇḍi* is derived as the feminine gender of the verbal derivative formed from the root *cad*."

In our translation, we have considered the relative merits of various interpretations. We shall explain our approach by giving some instances in point:

In the verse *nirantarāh śaraughena* (II.60) the popular reading is *senānukāriṇah*. But in Bengal, the reading *śalyānukārināh* is prevalent. *śalya* means a porcupine. It is quite appropriate to compare those whose bodies are pierced with a volley of arrows, leaving no inch of space, with porcupines. So, the reading *śalyānukārināh* has been adopted.

In the verse *tān viṣannān surān dṛstvā candikā prāhasattvara*, 'it is usual to split the phrase *prāhasattvara* as *prāha satvarā*, 'said quickly.' Then, there is a repetition *uvaca* in the next line. To get over the difficulty, they say that the Goddess *suran praha kālīm uvāca*, told the gods and said to Kali. The verse does not tell us what she told the gods while what she said to Kali *vistīrṇam vadanam kuru* is mentioned.

But if we split the phrase as *prāhasat tvarā*, how nicely the verse makes sense! Seeing the gods dejected, Chandika laughed; quickly she said to Kali. If we recall the words *bhayam ājagmur uttamam* in the previous verse, it will be clear that splitting the phrase as above is the correct way. When the gods saw the world full of Raktabijas, they became terribly afraid. There was no cause for fear when the Goddess was with them. The Goddess laughed at their dejection and lack of confidence, but to allay their fear she immediately said to Kali.

Similarly in the verse *devyā hate tatra mahāsurendre* (XI.2), instead of translating *abja* in the phrase *vikasi vaktrabja-vikasitāsah* as lotus, it is more appropriate to give *abja* the meaning 'moon' (*vide Amarakosa*: *abjo jaaivātṛkah somah*). The moon, more than the lotus makes the quarters shine.

vidyāh samastāstava devi bhedāh striyah samastah sakalā jagatsu (XI.6) is a verse of great import. The commentators are intrigued by the word *sakala* which seems to be a repetition considering the usage of *samastah*. To overcome this difficulty, they interpret *sakala* as possessed of *kalas* and wax eloquent on the sixtyfour *kalas*, gentle arts an elegant woman should possess. The verse seems to imply that only women well-versed in 64 kalas are portions of the Devi and not the ignorant ordinary women who abound in the world. The true import is missed. *kalā* means portion and *sakalā* means 'all parts, in entirety.' The real import of the verse is that all branches of knowledge are different parts of the Devi, while all the women in the world are all the parts in entirety, the full form of the Devi. To quote Sri Aurobindo, "The sense is that wherever the feminine principle is found in the living personality, we have the entire presence of the world-supporting maternal soul of the Divinity. The Devi with all her aspects, *kalas*, is there in the woman; in the woman we have to see Durga, Annapurna, Tara, the Mahavidyas, and there it is said in the Tantra, 'Wherever one sees the feet of woman, one should give worship in one's soul even as to one's guru.' Thus, this thought of the Shakta side of Hinduism becomes an uncompromising declaration of the divinity of woman completing the Vedantic declaration of the concealed divinity in man which we are too apt to treat in practice as if it applied only in the masculine. We put away in silence, even when we do not actually deny it, the perfect equality in difference of the double manifestation."

Likewise, the verse in the kilaka, *śanaistu japyamane'smin stotre sampattir uccakaih bhavatyeva samagrā'pi* is interpreted as follows: "there will be effect if recitation is done slowly, but all the riches will result if the recitation is done loudly." According to this, the extent of riches depends upon the loudness of one's voice; ultimately vociferation pays! *Sanaih* and *uccakaih* are opposite terms and the meaning is that when this laud is recited slowly, the result, however, is lofty riches, *asmin stotre sanaistu japyamane samagra'pi sampattir uccakaireva bhavati.*

The verse *utthāya ca mahāsimham devi caṇḍam adhavata* (VII.20) presents real difficulty to all the old commentators. It is Kali who jumps at Chanda to kill him and as the lion is the mount of Goddess and not of Kali, they split *mahasimham* into *mahasim* and *ham* and say raising the great sword and *ham*, the Devi jumped at Chanda. They explain *ham* as an expression of anger; but *hum* is the normal expression. Even then, the usage will be *hamkara*, not mere *ham*. They have missed the significance of the word *Devi* in the verse. There are many verses where Devi and Kali are distinguished. e.g. *Devi simhas tathā kāli sarosaih parivāritah*. Here *Devi* is used for Kali, for, as the manifestation of the Devi, she kills Chanda and so in the act, the mount of the Devi, the great lion, *mahasimha*, becomes her mount as well. There is no need for any ingenious explanation.

The recitation of the text, we have said, is absolutely necessary to invoke the Powers of the Goddess mentioned in the text and when the recitation is done with a knowledge of the meaning of the verses, it becomes a sure vehicle of the Divine Presence.

PRELIMINARIES

There are certain preliminaries that have to be observed before one proceeds with the recital of Saptasati with its limbs. These make the recital very effective.

SNĀNA

At the outset, the aspirant has to purify himself. The external purification is accomplished by a good bath in clean water. Those who are unable to do this because of illness or other reasons are advised to drench themselves with the waves of vibration raised by the repetition of the Mantra, Vaidic or Tantric.

ĀCAMANA

One proceeds to do *ācamana*, slowly sipping the water held in the palm of his right hand reciting the *Tattva-mantras*. The *tattvas*, principles, are three in number-*ātma tattva*, *vidya tattvā*, and *śiva tattva*. They denote the self, the knowledge that makes the self realise the Godhead and God. The knowledge is given by the Mantra, rather it is the Mantra itself. When the principle of *sat cit ānanda*, Existence, Consciousness, Bliss, is involved in creation, *sat* represents the true self-existent Self, *atma*, *cit* the Consciousness which is the fruit of knowledge, *Vidyā* and *ananda* the Bliss, Siva. The *acamana* is to purify the three principles *atma*, *vidya* and *siva*, so that they may get evolved to the original principles of *sat*, *cit* and *ananda* and finally transcend

58

them. That is why the *acamana* is crowned with the fourth sip of water *sarva tattvam sodhayami*.

PRĀṆAYĀMA

pranāyāma is the regulation of breath, the ultimate aim being the extension, *āyama*, of the Pranic forces in the body. By regulating breath, the activities of the mind are regulated and after some time, the mind falls silent. Thoughts which arise from outside do not disturb the mind. Silence reigns in the mind with an expectancy, with the readiness to receive the word of the Divine. Here the Pranayama is done with the *mūlamantra, nāvakṣari*. One draws in the breath through the left nostril, repeating the Mantra once, retains the breath repeating the Mantra four times and exhales through the right nostril repeating the Mantra twice.

SANKALPA

Sankalpa is the resolution, an expression of the will of the aspirant about what he proposes to do. In the *sankalpa*, the act is clearly spelled out and the expression of the solemn resolve helps to materialise the will of the aspirant into action. The purpose of the act also is defined; generally the purpose is all-embracing; at times, the purpose is limited or special. Fulfilment of a special purpose rests on the performance of the specified acts and conditions. It is true that the aspirant puts his will behind the *sankalpa*, but it is the Divine that gives him the will and he does the act for the delight of the Divine, for His satisfaction, *parameswara prītyartham*.

"Whereas for us and for our families a constant

increase is desired in well-being, security, valour, victory, life, health and wealth, whereas the attainment of auspiciousness on all sides is sought after and whereas I having such and such a name and belonging to such and such a clan ask, by the grace of the World-Mother, for the removal of all distress and for the attainment of desired ends through the aquisition of the fourfold purposes of life, *dharma, ārtha, kama* and *mokṣa*, I now will perform the recital of the seven hundred verses of Chandi by prefacing the text with *kavaca, argala, kilaka, ekādaśa nyāsa, navakṣari japa* and *ratrisukta* and by concluding the text with *devi sukta, navākṣari japa* and the three *rahasyas*, for securing the satisfaction of the deities Mahakali, Mahalakshmi and Mahasarasvati."

This is the usual text of the resolution.

PRĀRTHANA

Then the invocation is done to Ganesha and Guru. The first God to be worshipped and the God through whom all the other gods are approached is Agni in the Veda and Ganesha in the Tantra. Both are the sons of the supreme God Maheshwara. Agni of the Veda becomes Skanda, Kumara of the Purana and the Tantra, while Ganesha of the Tantra has evolved from the Brahmanaspati of the Veda. In fact, the Mantra used in the Tantra to invoke Ganesha is the famous Rik of *śaunaka gṛtsamada* addressed to the Deity Brahmanaspati. The elephantheaded God is the superb lord of the hosts, *gaṇānām gaṇapatih*, the superb seer-poet amongst seer-poets *kavinām kavih* and the superb master of the word *brahmaṇām brahmaṇaspatih*. He is the eldest of all the shining ones, *jyestha raja*. He is superb in hearing *upamaśravastama* and so hears our invocation *ā nāh śrnvan*. He is *Brahmacari*, moves and has his activities in Brahma, the Word, and represented as a bachelor in the popular sense of the term *Brahmacāri*. But the Tantra does not make any concessions to its doctrine that one becomes a *śakta* only when endowed with *Sakti*. Ganesha is conceived not as a bachelor, but as having two consorts, *saktis, siddhi* and *buddhi*, accomplishment and effectuating intelligence. He is invoked as the Word that breaks through the barriers of ignorance and as the force of knowledge that removes all obstacles.

Next comes the obeisance to the Guru, the human representative of the Divine to the disciple. The disciple gets all that he has to get from the Godhead through his Guru who has in him the delegated power of the Godhead. Once a Guru accepts a disciple, his grace to the disciple is always there; and he himself cannot undo what he has already done. But the action of grace largely depends upon the receptivity of the disciple and the strength of his inner relationship with the Guru. As Sri Aurobindo says: "Much depends on the inner relation between *guru* and *śiṣya* (disciple). One can go to a very great spiritual man and get nothing or only a little from him: one can go to a man of less spiritual capacity and get all he has to give and more."

The inner relation is maintained by an utter surrender and supplication to the Guru. One recites the *guru pāduka mantra* and bows in great reverence to the holy sandals of his Guru, *parama guru*, the Guru of his Guru and *paramestti guru*, the Guru of his *parama guru*.

ĀSANA

"The sadhaka has to seat himself in a posture which is most convenient, physically, and helps the body to acquire the sustained poise-*āsana*. *padmāsana* is the one usually adopted as it secures a settled fixity to the erect position of the body-specially of the spine-a position which is particularly favourable to the coursings of the subtle nerve currents and the movement of the Force acting in the body during the sadhana." [1] In the first place, one should draw with water the figure of a triangle on the ground and worship the sustaining force, *ādhāra śakti*. Then, one should spread a seat over it and sit comfortably. The seat may be made of wool, skin of animals or reeds like *darbha*. *merutantra* says that the use of a tiger-skin ensures all-round accomplishment, a seat made of sheep's wool destroys diseases, a silk cloth promotes welfare and a cane mat increases prosperity.[2] Then earth is worshipped in the following terms "O Earth-goddess, people are borne by thee: thou art borne by Vishnu. Bear me as well and purify the seat." The seat is then sanctified with the sprinkling of water and salutations are offered. The names used in the salutation are significant.

---

1 M.P. Pandit - *Upasana* in *Lights on the Tantra*.

² सर्वसिद्ध्यै व्याघ्रचर्म त्वाविकं रोगनाशनम् ।
कौशेयं पौष्टिकं प्रोक्तं वेत्रजं श्रीविवर्धनम् ॥

The posture should be kept as long as possible and so the seat is identified with the seat of the primordial person, Vishnu, with *Ananta* signifying endless time. And so it is saluted as *ānāntasana*. Just as a tortoise withdraws all its limbs into its shell and remains immobile for hours, the posture should ensure the withdrawing of all outward going senses into oneself and the immobility of the body and the mind, *kūrmasāna*. The seat should be pure and should purify the sadhaka, *vimalāsana*. Just as a lotus blooms forth petal by petal, the posture should be conducive to the gradual unfoldment of the innate possibilities of the sadhaka, *padmāsana*. It should ensure the union of the sadhaka with the object of his quest in all parts of his being, *yogasana*. Then its becomes the basis for support, the sustaining force, *ādhāra sákti*. It strikes terror in the heart of the wicked and drives them away as the man-lion of yore, *duṣṭa-vidrāvana nṛsimhāsana*: and it continues throughout to be a posture of ease and comfort *madhye parama sukhāsana*. Then if the sadhaka has flowing locks of hair, he ties them into a knot symbolically representing the restraint of all his wayward tendencies and then invokes Chamunda thus: "O Chamunda of lofty upturned tresses, unshapely eyes, O thou devouring on flesh and blood. O goddess unvanquished, stand in the knot of the hair." Here it is to be noted that Chamunda is described as devouring on flesh and blood. When one sits in an *āsana*, Chamunda the deity of the *āsana* draws sustenance from the flesh and blood of the sadhaka; in other words, she is fostered by the physical base of the sadhaka. Then she shoots forth rays of light, leading the sadhaka up in the realms of light, *urdhva kesi* [1] and her eyes are not restricted to two, *virupāksi*. She endows the sadhaka with the necessary perception on various planes of his being. And in the act, she is unvanquished, *aparajita*.

When a sadhaka sits in an *asana* he normally faces east or north.

BHŪTĀPASARPAŅA

"Whatever may be the beings that abide in the place of worship, let them clear out. Let all beings that cause obstruction be destroyed by the command of Shiva. Let beings and spirits clear out of all directions; without obstruction from them, I commence the act of japa." With this prayer, the sadhaka drives away the undesirable and obstructive forces. He then takes permission from the terrible Bhairava of sharp fangs, *tīksṇa damṣṭra*, of stupendous body, *mahākāya*, and who resembles the fire at the time of the end of a Kalpa, *kalpānta dahanopama*. The ten quarters are fenced by striking the earth with the left foot, uttering the word *phat* and by snapping the fingers round the head.

BHŪTASUDDHI

To explain fully the significance of *bhūtasuddhi*, we can do no better than quote from the profound writings of Sri Kapali Sastriar on the subject:

---

1. *keśa*, hair, represents a ray of light in the Veda. Indra's horses are qualified by the word *keśi* having manes of light.

Devi Mahatmya : *samasta romakūpeṣu nijaraśmin dtvākarah* (11.24)

"Bhutasuddhi is the most important and even indispensable discipline both for the outer worship as well as for the *mantra sādhana* which leads to the inner life. The literal meaning of the term is the 'purification of the elements' but its effect is to cleanse the atmosphere in and a round the person of the worshipper and clear it of the influences of the elemental forces or beings, the lower spirits, the blind unintelligent forces to which men in their ordinary lives are subject; and the weaknesses on the mental or moral plane that pertain to the material body of man are indeed the result of the play of these forces of universal nature. The loosening and ultimate riddance of the Tamasic forces of the dense and elemental nature is indeed *sine quanon* for qualifying oneself for the *mantra sādhana* that aims high at contacting the deity in the deeper layers of one's consciousness or on the higher levels of one's being that are supra-physical. And it is also necessary and to some extent possible in the case of a beginner preparing for the external worship, *bāhya pūja*. For, without the *bhūtaśuddhi*, the *prāṇa pratiṣthā* could not be done, since the latter is meant to evoke the presence or power of the deity from the spirit of one's own being which itself is lodged in, and a portion of the supreme self, *parama atman* the indwelling godhead in all creatures. In fact, the Tantric works everywhere reiterate the value and necessity of this purification without which the *pratiṣthā*, the installing of the power and the presence either within oneself in the inner worship, or instilling the spirit and power into the image or symbol in the outer worship is not possible. The outer worship, as is done commonly by the generality of devotees, will be ineffective without the essential *pratiṣṭhā* on which everything else depends.

Its (*bhuta suddhi*) basic importance in the *mantrasādhana* cannot be too much emphasised, since in the yogic path of the Tantrik it affords the foundation on which the whole edifice of Yoga is raised, with devotion, knowledge and will as its constituent elements. But even before entering straight into the inner apartments of Yoga where the psycho-physical centres are concentrated upon and opened for progress in the sadhana and building the inner life, the Tantrik beginner devoted to his chosen deity is advised to effect the *bhūta-śuddhi* without which the presence of the deity cannot be felt and the grace of the deity, even when it comes in response to an ardent call of the *upāsaka*, worshipper, or a fervent emotional appeal to the deity could not be properly received, or even when received, be adequately held and effectively retained in the vessel, the body. Hence its importance and its value are recognised for any form of serious worship. It must be noted here that the purification of the various limbs, outer physical and the inner mind-stuff aims not only at the eradication of the narrowing and obscuring influences of the elemental forces and the universal weakness of the lower Nature, but inviting in their place the opposite good influences of the benign forces, the powers of the supraphysical worlds. That is why in the actual *bhūta śuddhi*, every part is offered to a deity, and the group of deities that are invoked to occupy their places in the body-vessel, *ādhāra*, constitutes indeed the minor gods who are the *parivāra* of the chosen chief, *pradhāna*. In some Tantric works, instead of the minor gods and the chief Deity, the tattwas or cosmic principles with the soul, and the supreme self for the Chief Deity are mentioned in the culmination of the *bhūta śuddhi*. And this is to give a pure spiritual turn with a philosophic basis to the *upāsana*.

The conception of the Tantric in regard to the body was so complete and ideal that all the *tattwas* (or the higher powers) are understood to be lodged in it and the supreme godhead abides in the centre and depths of one's being, the heart-lotus. Nor is the purification of the body and preparing it for Divine worship achieved by sheer physical purity and strength to be decided by medical opinion and judged according to hygienic standards. For the purity of the kind in the body is to be accomplished in such a manner that the god or gods could discover in it their actual temple consecrated for their advent or manifestation. And indeed the body is the field of battle between the dark and the luminous forces in the cosmos, engendering bad will and good will with their brood of feelings and ideas and their consequent subtle effect on the body, nerves and muscles, in the shape of ill-health and good-health and general disharmony running riot in the system. Thus, the *bhūta śuddhi* has a double function, the negative and the positive, the former paving the way by the clearance of the disagreeable forces for the positive side i.e. the filling of the purified parts by the presence of the Powers that are invoked to occupy their right places in the system."[1]

---

1 *Further Lights : Veda and Tantra* by Sri Kapali Sastriar.

By a powerful mental process, the coiled-up energy, *kuṇḍalini*, in the *mulādhāra* centre is lifted up centre by centre, each preceding element being dissolved into the higher succeeding element i.e. the earth-element in the *mulādhāra* is dissolved into the water-element in the *swādhiṣṭhāna* centre, the water-element there dried up by the fire-element in the *maṇipūra* centre and so on.

By reciting the Mantra *Soham* "He, I am", the Sadhaka lifts up his self from the heart, takes it along with the Kundalini force to the *sahasradala* centre in the head and unites them with the supreme Self there. Then he thinks of the body of the evil person in him and by the process of Pranayama, uttering the seed-sound *yam* he withers it up ; uttering the seedsound *ram*, he burns it; uttering the seed-sound *vam* he drenches it with nectar and uttering the seed-sound *lam* he consolidates the sinless shining body. Now, by reciting the Mantra *hamsah*, the sadhaka brings down his Self from the supreme self into his heart and the Kundalini back to *muladhara*.

PRĀṆAPRATIṢṬHĀ

The effective installation of Life-Force, *prāṇa-pratiṣṭhā*, becomes possible only when *bhūta-śuddhi* is performed. The whole recital of the text will become a lifeless ritual if the power and the presence is not installed within oneself in the inner worship or in the sacred symbol of *murti*, image, or *yantra*, diagram, in the outer worship. When by means of *bhūta-śuddhi* the body of the sadhaka is looked upon as a luminous form of light, having become quite competent for the worship of the Deity, *tejorūpam kalevaram devatopāsāna-yogyam utpannam*,[1] from such a body the power of the Pranic force and Divine is infused into the object of worship and firmly installed thus:

"My life-breaths are life-breaths here. My soul is established here. May all my sense organs, my speech, mind, skin, eyes, ears, tongue, nose and breath come here and with ease abide long."

DĪPASTHĀPANA

In keeping with the Vedic tradition that Agni, the immortal amongst the mortals, the Divine guest who has sought the house of man, is witness, *sākṣī*, to all the acts of man, generally in outer worship and rituals. a lamp, *dīpa*, is lit and the flame is carefully kept burning till the act of worship is over. The steady flame of the lamp is the outward symbol of the unflagging aspiration of the sadhaka and the *dīpa* itself is considered to be the form of the Goddess. It is common experience amongst devout worshippers that no sooner than the sacred lamp is lit, an auspicious spiritual atmosphere is created in the place of worship.

ŚAPODDHĀRA AND UTKĪLANA

The Veda speaks of the powers of darkness and ignorance who oppose the aspirant of truth and immortality and impede his spiritual progress at each step. The Vritra who covers the truth and knowledge and obstructs the free flow of light, the Panis who hide and hoard like a miser all the spiritual wealth, trading and trafficking

---

1 *Meru Tantra.*

in them and the Vala who erects barriers and encloses the truth from the perception of the aspirant, have all to be conquered. Apart from these, there are certain forces whom the Veda calls *Nidah*, "Powers of limitation, the confiners, Restrainers or Censurers, who without altogether obscuring the rays of Light of damming up the energies, yet seek by constantly affirming the deficiencies of our self-expression to limit its field and set up the progress realised as an obstacle to the progress to come."[1]

The Tantra also speaks of hostile undivine forces corresponding to the Vedic Vritra, Panis etc., who obstruct Siddhi in the Mantra Sadhana. Apart from these, corresponding to *nidah*, restrainers or censurers, there are certain seers of yore and in some cases even certain gods who have cast a spell, pronounced a curse, *śapa*, over the Mantra and that delays the Siddhi. These givers of *śapa* are not against the sadhaka attaining siddhi in the Mantra, neither are they opposed to the Divine. The spells they cast and the curses they have administered serve as check-posts on the spiritual path. The sadhaka's competency is questioned at each stage, he is discouraged to proceed further, being made aware of his deficiencies and the pass-word is given only when his credentials are proved. By the *śapoddhāra mantra*, the aspirant prays to these seers and Gods to lift up the curse and allow him to proceed on the path towards the siddhi of the Mantra.

---

1. Sri Aurobindo

Also, there are certain pivotal conditions to be fulfilled on which hinge the whole realisation of the Mantra. As long as this pivot, *kīlaka* , is not perceived, the door to progress stands slammed in the face of the sadhaka. Once the *utkīlana* is accomplished, the portals to siddhi in the Mantra swing wide open. That is the purpose of the *utkilana mantra*.

After these preliminaries, the sadhaka proceeds to the recital of the text.

पूर्वाङ्गविधिः ॥

अथ साधकः कृतस्नाननित्यविधिः आचमनं कुर्यात् ।

ॐ ऐ आत्मतत्त्वं शोधयामि नमः स्वाहा ।

ॐ ह्रीं विद्यातत्त्वं शोधयामि नमः स्वाहा ।

ॐ क्लीं शिवतत्त्वं शोधयामि नमः स्वाहा ।

ॐ ऐं ह्रीं क्लीं सर्वतत्त्वं शोधयामि नमः स्वाहा ॥

ततः प्राणायामं कुर्यात् । मूलेन वामनासया वायुमापूर्य कुम्भके चतुर्वारं मूलं पठित्वा द्विवारं मूलमुच्चरन् दक्षनासया रेचयेत् ॥

ततः सङ्कल्पं कुर्यात् । यथा - अस्माकं सर्वेषां सकुटुम्बानां क्षेमस्थैर्यवीर्यविजयायुरारोग्यैश्वर्याभिवृद्ध्यर्थं समस्तमङ्गलावाप्त्यर्थं अमुकगोत्रोत्पन्नस्य अमुकनाम्नः मम श्रीजगदम्बाप्रसादेन सर्वापत्ति-वृत्तिसर्वाभीष्टफलावाप्तिधर्मार्थकाममोक्ष चतुर्विधपुरुषार्थसिद्धिद्वारा श्रीमहाकाली महालक्ष्मीमहासरस्वतीदेवताप्रीत्यर्थं कवचार्गलकीलक-पठनैकादशन्यासपूर्वकं नवार्णमन्त्राष्टोत्तरशतजपराविनियुक्तपठनपूर्वकं देवीसूक्तपठननवार्णमन्त्राष्टोत्तरशतजपरहस्यत्रयपठनान्ते श्रीचण्डी-सप्तशत्याः पाठं करिष्ये ॥

अथ श्रीमहागणपतिं गुरुत्रयं च प्रणमेत् ।

ॐ गणानां त्वा गणपतिं हवामहे कविं कवीनामुपमश्रवस्तमम् ।

ज्येष्ठराजं ब्रह्मणां ब्रह्मणस्पत आ नः शृण्वन्नूतिभिः सीद सादनम् ॥

सिद्धिबुद्धिशक्तिसहित श्रीमहागणपतये नमः ॥

ॐ नमो गुरुभ्यो गुरुपादुकाभ्यः नमः परेभ्यः परपादुकाभ्यः ।

आचार्यसिद्धेश्वरपादुकाभ्यो नमोऽस्तु लक्ष्मीपतिपादुकाभ्यः ॥
श्री गुरुपरमगुरुपरमेष्ठीगुरुश्रीगुरुश्रीपादुकाभ्यो नमः ॥

अथ आसनविधिः ।   आसनाधो जलादिना त्रिकोण
विलिख्य ॐ ह्रीं आधारशक्तिकमलासनाय नमः   इति संपूज्य
तदुपरि आस्तरणं कृत्वा,   ॐ पृथ्वीति मन्त्रस्य मेरुपृष्ठ ऋषिः कूर्मो
देवता, सुतलं छन्दः   आसने विनियोगः ।

ॐ पृथ्वि त्वया धृता लोका देवि त्वं विष्णुना धृता ।
त्वं च धारय मां देवि पवित्रं कुरु चासनम् ॥

ॐ भूर्भुवःस्वः   इत्यासने प्रोक्ष्य प्राङ्मुख उदङ्मुखो वा
उपविश्य

ॐ अनन्तासनाय नमः ।   ॐ कूर्मासनाय नमः ।   ॐ विमला-
सनाय नमः ।   ॐ पद्मासनाय नमः ।   ॐ योगासनाय नमः ।
ॐ आधारशक्त्यै नमः ।   ॐ तुष्टिद्रावणनृसिंहासनाय नमः ।
ॐ मध्ये परमसुखासनाय नमः ।   इति नत्वा

ॐ ऊर्ध्वकेशि विरूपाक्षि मांसशोणितभक्षणे ।
तिष्ठ देवि शिखाबन्धे चामुण्डे ह्यपराजिते ॥
इति शिखां बध्नीयात् ॥
अथ भूतापसर्पणविधिः ।
ॐ अपसर्पन्तु ते भूता ये भूता भूमिसंस्थिताः ।
ये भूता विघ्नकर्तारस्ते नश्यन्तु शिवाज्ञया ॥
अपक्रामन्तु भूतानि पिशाचाः सर्वतो दिशम् ।
सर्वेषामविरोधेन जपकर्म समारभे ॥
इति भूतानुत्सार्य

तीक्ष्णदंष्ट्र महाकाय कल्पान्तदहनोपम ।
भैरवाय नमस्तुभ्यं अनुज्ञां दातुमर्हसि ॥

इति भैरवाज्ञां गृह्णीयात् ॥

अथ भूतशुद्धिः ।

सोऽहमिति मन्त्रेण हृदयात् जीवात्मानं मूलाधारस्थ-कुण्डलिन्या सह सुषुम्नामार्गेण शिरःस्थितसहस्रारकमले परमात्मनि संयोज्य प्राणायामक्रमेण सपापपुरुषं देहं यं बीजेन शोषयित्वा रं बीजेन दग्धं मत्वा यं बीजेन अमृतवृष्टिं निपात्य लं बीजेन दिव्य-शरीरमुत्पन्नमिति ध्यात्वा हंसबीजेन परमात्मनः सकाशात् जीवात्मानं हृदयमानयेत् ॥

अथ प्राणप्रतिष्ठा

हृदि हस्तं निधाय ॐ आं ह्रीं क्रों मम प्राणः इह प्राणः ॐ आं ह्रीं क्रों मम जीव इह स्थितः ॐ आं ह्रीं क्रों मम सर्वेन्द्रियाणि ॐ आं ह्रीं क्रों मम वाङ्मनस्त्वक्चक्षुःश्रोत्रजिह्वाघ्राणप्राणा इहागत्य सुखं चिरं तिष्ठन्तु स्वाहा ॥

अथ दीपस्थापनम् ।

भो दीप देवीरूपस्त्वं कर्मसाक्षी ह्यविघ्नकृत् ।
याघत् कर्मसमाप्तिः स्यात् तावत् त्वं सुस्थिरो भव ॥

अथ शापोद्धारमन्त्रः ।

ॐ ह्रीं ह्रीं श्रीं क्रां क्रीं चण्डिके देवि शापानुग्रहं कुरु कुरु स्वाहा । सप्तवारं जपेत् ॥

अथ उत्कीलनमन्त्रः ।

ॐ श्रीं क्लीं ह्रीं सप्तशति चण्डिके उत्कीलनं कुरु कुरु स्वाहा ।
एकविंशतिवारं जपेत् ॥

THE MODE OF RECITAL

The sadhaka should recite in the following order: He should first recite *kavaca, argala, kilaka,* do the *nyasas* and *japa* of the Mantra *navākṣari,* recite Ratri Sukta and then the text of three episodes containing 13 chapters. He follows up with Devi Sukta, the japa of Navakshari with the *nyāsas* and then with the three secrets, *rahasya traya.* He does again the *utkilana* Mantra and finishes by dedicating the whole act of recital to the Goddess and recites the *aparādha kṣamāpana,* prayer craving pardon for all the faults and mistakes he might have committed.

The first episode is the first chapter of the text and deals with the destruction of the Asuras, Madhu and Kaitabha. The deity is Mahakali, predominating in the *guna tamas* . The seer is Brahma, the metre is Gayatri, the force Nanda and the seed Raktadantika. The principle, *tattwa* is that of Agni, fire and the form represented is Rig Veda. The purpose is the pursuit of *dharma.*

The second episode consists of the second, third and fourth chapters and deals with the destruction of Mahishasura. The deity is Mahalakshmi, predominating in the *guna rajas* . the seer is Vishnu, the metre is Ushnik, the force Shakambhari and the seed Durga. The *tattwa* is that of *Vayu*, wind and the form represented is Yajur Veda. The purpose is the pursuit of *Artha*.

The third episode comprises the next of the chapters of the text and in it are portrayed the deeds of the Devi in vanquishing Shumbha, Nishumbha and their hosts. The deity is Mahasaraswati, predominating in the *guna satwa*. The seer is Siva, the metre is Anushtub, the force Bhima and the seed Bhramari. The *tattwa* is that of Surya, the Sun and the form represented is Sama Veda. The purpose is the pursuit of *kāma*.

There are certain rules to be followed in the recital. The recital should not be stopped in the middle of a chapter. If by mistake there happens a break in the middle, the chapter has to be read again from the beginning. The reading should be in the proper order and not haphazard. All unnecessary movements like shaking the head etc. should be avoided. The Pranic force that is to be carefully conserved and preserved leaks out of the body by these movements. The reading should never be done mentally. There should be audible recitation.[1] And it should not be done fast, in a hurry. The reading should be in a slow even manner, *śanaistu japyamāne*.

---

[1] यावन्न पूर्यतेऽध्यायः तावन्न विरमेत् पठन् ।
यदि प्रमादादध्याये विरामो भवति प्रिये ।
पुनरध्यायमारभ्य पठेत् सर्वं मुहुर्मुहुः ।
अनुक्रमात् पठेदेव शिरःकम्पादिकं त्यजेत् ।
न मानसं पठेत् स्तोत्रं वाचिकं तु प्रशस्यते ॥

It is very commendable to read all the three episodes at one sitting. If it is not possible, the middle chapter alone can be read, *ekena vā madhyamena* and not any one of the other two, *naikena itarayoh*. It is not right to read a portion of the episode and leave it half-finished: then it will be a chink in the armour, an opening for the hostile forces to attack. *Caritārdham tu na japet, japan chidram avapnuyāt.*

But yet there is a practice followed in Kerala, finishing the text of three episodes in seven days reading. And this is continued week after week. The first chapter is read on the first day, the second and third chapters on the second day, the fourth chapter on the third day, the fifth, sixth, seventh and eighth chapters on the fourth day, the ninth and tenth on the fifth day, the eleventh on the sixth day and the twelfth and thirteenth chapters on the seventh day.[1] According to this practice, an episode is not finished in a single day.

Those who cannot recite themselves can hear with devotion a recital by another and derive benefit. Special modes of recital are dealt with in the chapter on Prayoga.

---

1. This is remembered by a mnemonic *pāthoyam dvi prakārah.* The letters in this, as per the usual *katapayādi sankhyā* stand for 1, 2, 1, 4, 2, 1, 2 denoting the number of chapters to be read each day of the week.

KAVACHA, ARGALA, KEELAKA

The physical body is obscure and obstinate and prone to ailments. It is not plastic and supple like the vital or the mind. Because of its innate inertia, it is considered an impediment to spiritual progress and there are many spiritual paths that advocate a total ignoring or suppression of the physical. But that is not the way of the Tantra. The body is the basis of the sadhana, the receptacle for the play of the Divine. It has to be enlightened and made to share the experiences and progress in the mental and the vital. It has to be made strong to resist the onslaughts of the forces that stand in the way of such a change. The body has to be guarded and protected and the physical envelope surrounding it made strong so that these forces do not make inroads into it and attack the body in the form of illness. The device used by the sadhaka is the *kavaca*, a prayer acting as an armour effectuating the divine protection. The *kavaca* is used to guard and protect the body, ward off illness from it and cure it from illness when it has already besieged the body. It ensures the proper distribution and operation of forces in the very cells of the body, *piṇḍāṇḍa*, in consonance and harmony with the operation of the Divine Law in the Cosmos, *brahmāṇḍa* and sets right all discord.

The prayer for protection is made to the *pradhāna*, principal deity and the *parivāras*, the subsidiary deities, that form the retinue of the principal deity. The sadhaka spells out the parts of the body to be protected, limb by limb, part by part, and assigns them to the protection of a particular deity. Thus the entire body is left to the care and protection of the principal and subsidiary deities. Thus fortified, the sadhaka pursues his Sadhana.

Apart from other deities, the *kavaca* makes mention of the nine Durgas who compose the principal deity Chandika whose sound-form is famous as the nine-lettered Mantra, *nāvakṣari*. A study of these significant names will be of help to the earnest seeker. The first name is *śailaputri*, the daughter of the mountain. The mountain is the symbol of of our conscious existence with serried levels and peaks, *sānūni*. In this she takes birth, in the rock, in the hard core of inconscient Matter. At the same time, she is *brahmacāriṇi*, moving and having her existence in the Brahman, in the conscious Word, in the supreme *nāda* which creates the whole existence. The one who creates as the Word enters and takes birth in her creation, in its hardest inconscient core. She is the *nada* that spreads the Delight, the sustaining sap, *rasa*, of existence, *candraghanṭa*. She is not merely *ānanda*, the delight in the supernal ether *ākāśa*, she is the incubating Tapas, the fertile seed put into the earth, *kūṣmānda*.[1] She is *skanda-mata*, the mother of *skānda*. Skanda represents the descent of divine energy on earth. Though

---

1 *kūṣmānda* is derived from *ku* earth, *uśma* heat *tapas* and *anda* egg, seed.

firmly stationed in the supernal place, he slips down, *skanna*, as Kumara, the son of God to uplift humanity.[1] The Goddess is not only the mother of the worlds, she is also the mother of Divine Descents, *Avataras* who come to uplift humanity towards divinity. And yet she is *Katyayani*, the eternal Virgin.[2] She is *kālaratri*, the dark night carrying the luminous possibilities in her womb and she is *mahāgauri* the great Radiance, the bright day of light and knowledge. Finally, she is *siddhidātri*, the bestower of Siddhi, the one who grants and fulfills the yearning of the created towards its creator. Thus, the nine Durgas enumerated are Sailaputri, Brahmacarini, Candraghanta, Kusmanda, Skandamata, Katyayani, Kalaratri, Mahagauri and Siddhidatri.[3]

Argala means a bolt and a knowledge of its existence is necessary to open the closed door.

---

[1] न च्युतोऽपि परमान्निजधाम्न :
    स्कन्द इत्यभिधया व्यवहार: ।
    स्कन्नमेव दनुजानपहन्तुं
    देवकार्यकलितं स हि तेज: ॥

-kumārastava - Sri Kapali Sastriar

2 The Purana speaks of the goddess as the adopted daughter of the seer Katyayana and thus explains the name. The Vedic Gayatri of Durga Katyayani invokes her as the eternal virgin, *Kanya kumari* .

काल्यायनाय विद्महे कन्यकुमारि धीमहि ।
तन्नो दुर्गिः प्रचोदयात् ॥

3 Some Tantras enumerate the names of the nine Durgas as the *Vanadurga*, *Jaladurga*, *Agnidurga*, *Sthaladurga*, *Vishnudurga*, *Brahmadurga*, *Rudradurga*, *Mahadurga* and *Sulinidurga*.

A reading of the *argala stotra* is considered essential for opening up the secrets sealed in Saptasati. The verses of the stotra have a refrain, *rūpam dehi, jayam dehi, yaśo dehi, dviṣo jahi* which has been translated thus: "Give the form, give the victory, give the fame, kill the enemies."

rupam means form, the *swarupa*, the true form of oneself,[1] the distinct self of the individual which we would call his psychic being. The Divine is in all living beings, but each being has its own distinct divine element which is special to it and which is its true form. "It is the soul or spark of the Divine Fire supporting the individual evolution on the earth"[2] and the whole sadhana is to get in touch with the true form of oneself, *rupam*, and act from there. Only then will an individual being evolve as he should evolve, as per his *rupam* distinct form in this world of names and forms. The grace of the goddess alone can accomplish this and so the prayer rises forth: *rūpam dehi*. In this endeavour victory is sought at the hands of the goddess, *jayam dehi*, as well as the glory of the conquest, *yaśo dehi*. For this purpose, all the forces that are hostile to this endeavour have to be vanquished by the goddess, *dviṣo jahi*.

kīlaka is the king-pin in a machine, the pivot on which the whole thing hinges. There is a condition acting like a pivot, the fulfilment of which furnishes the key to open the hidden secrets. If the recital of Saptasati has to

---

1. '*ātma hi nama swarūpam* ' - Acharya Sankara in *Brahmasūtra* Bhasya.
2. Sri Aurobindo.

be effective, a condition has to be fulfilled and that is mentioned in the *kilaka stotra*.

The phraseology is a bit obscure and the condition is hinted at, the position of the pivot is slightly indicated in the stotra so that the knowledge may not fall in undeserving hands.

It is the doctrine of the Tantra that Siddhis result only when one does the japa of a Mantra. But it is enough if one audibly recites the seven hundred verses of Devi Mahatmyam; no Mantra is necessary; all the Siddhis will result. This is because the entire *Saptasati* is a Mantra. But mere reading of the verses will not produce the result. There is a condition which has to be fulfilled. The Sadhaka should have this feeling: "I am thy child, at thy command, thy servant, always preoccupied with thee; my thought dwells on thy name and I am employed for thy purpose." [1] He should give himself in all parts of his being unreservedly to the Divine Mother. He should offer his work, his wealth, his possession, his all, all of himself and all he has to the goddess. This is what Samadhi and Suratha did. When he consecrates himself thus, the Divine Mother gives Herself to him. To the extent he gives to Her, to that extent he receives Her into him. In no other way is she pleased. *dādāti, pratigrhnāti, nānyathaiṣā prasīdati*. This is the *kilaka*, the pivot, which turns the limited egoistic tapasya of the sadhaka into a care-free joyous waiting on the Divine Grace. A

---

[1] त्वत्प्रसूतस्त्वदाज्ञतः त्वद्दासस्त्वत्परायणः ।
त्वन्नामचिन्तनपरस्त्वदर्थेंऽइं नियोजितः ॥

knowledge of this alone leads to fulfilment *tato jnatvaiva sampannam*. But Saptasati is not a philosophical treatise; it is a practical scripture. Mere knowledge of the necessity of surrendering to the Divine will not accomplish anything. The knowledge has to be translated into action. "Knowing, one should commence and do" *jnātva prārabhya kurvita*, says the Kilaka and warns that even after knowing the secret if one does not act, one perishes *akurvāṇo vinaśyati*.

KAVACHAM

ॐ अस्य श्रीचण्डीकवचस्य ब्रह्मा ऋषिः । अनुष्टुप् छन्दः ।
चामुण्डा देवता । ॐ नमश्चण्डिकायै ॥

For the Kavacha, Brahma is the Seer, Anushtub is
the Metre and Chamunda, the Deity. Salutations to
Chandika.

मार्कण्डेय उवाच
Markandeya Said:
यद्गुह्यं परमं लोके सर्वरक्षाकरं नृणाम् ।
यन्न कस्यचिदाख्यातं तन्मे ब्रूहि पितामह ॥ १ ॥

1. Grandsire, tell me that which has not been told
to anybody, the most occult in the world, that which gives
men protection all-round.

ब्रह्मोवाच
Brhama Said:

अस्ति गुह्यतमं विप्र सर्वभूतोपकारकम् ।
देव्यास्तु कवचं पुण्यं तच्छृणुष्व महामुने ॥ २ ॥

2. Wise one, there is the most occult, the sacred
Kavacha of the Goddess, beneficial to all beings. Great
Sage, hear that.

प्रथमं शैलपुत्रीति द्वितीयं ब्रह्मचारिणी ।
तृतीयं चन्द्रघण्टेति कूष्माण्डेति चतुर्थकम् ॥ ३ ॥

3. First, the daughter of the mountain ; second the
one who moves in Brahman ; third the delightful sound;
fourth the seed of incubation on earth;

पञ्चमं स्कन्दमातेति षष्ठं कात्यायनीति च ।
सप्तमं कालरात्रिश्च महागौरीति चाष्टमम् ॥ ४ ॥

4. fifth the mother of Skanda; sixth Katyayani, the eternal virgin; seventh the dark night; eighth the great white one;

नवमं सिद्धिदात्री च नवदुर्गाः प्रकीर्तिताः ।
उक्तान्येतानि नामानि ब्रह्मणैव महात्मना ॥ ५ ॥

5. and ninth the one who grants perfection—thus are enumerated the nine Durgas. These names have been mentioned by the great Brahman himself.

अग्निना दह्यमानस्तु शत्रुमध्ये गतो रणे ।
विषमे दुर्गमे चैव भयार्ताः शरणं गताः ॥ ६ ॥

6. When consumed by fire, when in the battle field in the midst of enemies, when overtaken by fear in a crisis, in an impasse, if men take refuge (in the mother),

न तेषां जायते किंचिदशुभं रणसंकटे ।
नापदं तस्य पश्यामि शोकदुःखभयं नहि ॥ ७ ॥

7. no evil befalls them in a critical battle. I do not envisage any distress coming to them. There is absolutely no fear of grief or misery.

यैस्तु भक्त्या स्मृता नूनं तेषां सिद्धिः प्रजायते ।
प्रेतसंस्था तु चामुण्डा वाराही महिषासना ॥ ८ ॥

8. If she is remembered with devotion, surely accomplishment is effected in their cases. Stationed on the corpse is Chamunda, seated on the buffalo is Varahi.

ऐन्द्री गजसमारूढा वैष्णवी गरुडासना ।
माहेश्वरी वृषारूढा कौमारी शिखिवाहना ॥ ९ ॥

9. Aindri is mounted on the elephant, Vaishnavi seated on Garuda; Maheswari is mounted on the bull, Kaumari is borne by the peacock.

ब्राह्मी हंससमारूढा सर्वाभरणभूषिता ।
नानाभरणशोभाढ्या नानारत्नोपशोभिताः ॥ १० ॥

10. Decked with all ornaments, Brahmi is mounted on the swan. Beautiful with their varied ornaments, lustrous with their multifarious jewels,

दृश्यन्ते रथमारूढा देव्यः क्रोधसमाकुलाः ।

शङ्खं चक्रं गदां शक्तिं हलं च मुसलायुधम् ॥ ११ ॥

11. angry and agitated, the goddesses are perceived mounted on the chariots. Conch, discus, mace, lance, ploughshare and the pestle,

खेटकं तोमरं चैव परशुं पाशमेव च ।

कुन्तायुधं त्रिशूलं च शाङ्गमायुधमुत्तमम् ॥ १२ ॥

12. shield, iron club, battle axe, noose, spear, trident and the great bow Sarnga,

दैत्यानां देहनाशाय भक्तानामभयाय च ।

धारयन्त्यायुधानीत्थं देवानां च हिताय वै ॥ १३ ॥

13. Yea, these weapons they wield for destroying the bodies of the Asuras, for the weal of the Gods and for instilling fearlessness in the devotees.

महाबले महोत्साहे महाभयविनाशिनि ।

त्राहि मां देवि दुष्प्रेक्ष्ये शत्रूणां भयवर्धिनि ॥ १४ ॥

14. O thou of great strength, of great zeal, Destroyer of immense fear, Increaser of fear in our enemies, Devi, quite difficult for our perception, protect me.

प्राच्यां रक्षतु मामैन्द्री आग्नेय्यामग्निदेवता ।

दक्षिणेऽवतु वाराही नैर्ऋत्यां खड्गधारिणी ॥ १५ ॥

15. May the force of Indra protect me in the east and the goddess of Agni in the south-east. May Varahi guard me in the south and the wielder of the sword in the south-west.

प्रतीच्यां वारुणी रक्षेद्वायव्यां मृगवाहिनी ।

उदीच्यां रक्ष कौबेरी ईशान्यां शूलधारिणी ॥ १६ ॥

16. May the force of Varuna protect me in the west and the force of Vayu mounted on the deer in the north-west. May the force of Kubera protect me in the north and the wielder of the trident in the north-east.

ऊर्ध्वं ब्रह्माणी मे रक्षेदधस्ताद्वैष्णवी तथा ।

एवं दश दिशो रक्षेच्चामुण्डा शववाहना ॥ १७ ॥

17. Above, may Brahmi protect me and below may Vaishnavi afford protection. Thus may Chamunda mounted on the corpse protect in the ten quarters.

जया मे आग्रतः स्थातु विजया स्थातु पृष्ठतः ।

अजिता वामपार्श्वं तु दक्षिणे चापराजिता ॥ १८ ॥

18. Let victory (*jayā*) stand in front of me and conquest (*vijayā*) stand in the rear. Let the undefeated (*ajitā*) stand on my left and the unvanquished (*aparājitā*) on my right.

शिखां मे द्योतिनी रक्षेदुमा मूर्ध्नि व्यवस्थिता ।

मालाधरी ललाटे च भ्रुवौ रक्षेद्यशस्विनी ॥ १९ ॥

19. Let the luminous one guard the tuft of my hair, established in the head let Uma protect. May the one who wears the garland guard in the forehead and the one possessed of fame in the eye-brows;

त्रिनेत्रा च भ्रुवोर्मध्ये यमघण्टा च नासिके ।

शङ्खिनी चक्षुषोर्मध्ये श्रोत्रयोर्द्वारवासिनी ॥ २० ॥

20. the three-eyed one in the space between the eye-brows and in the nose the force of restrained sound; the bearer of the conch in the middle of the eyes and in the ears the dweller at the portals.

कपोलौ कालिका रक्षेत् कर्णमूले तु शांकरी ।

नासिकायां सुगन्धा च उत्तरोष्ठे च चर्चिका ॥ २१ ॥

21. May Kalika protect the cheeks and the force of Shankara behind the ears; the sweet smelling in the nostrils and the sweetly smeared in the upper-lip;

अधरे चामृतकला जिह्वायां च सरस्वती ।
दन्तान् रक्षतु कौमारी कण्ठमध्ये तु चण्डिका ॥ २२ ॥

22. the digit of nectar in the lower lip and Saraswati in the tongue. May the force of Kumara guard the teeth and Chandika in the middle of the neck.

घण्टिकां चित्रघण्टा च महामाया च तालुके ।
कामाक्षी चिबुकं रक्षेद्वाचं मे सर्वमंगला ॥ २३ ॥

23. May the one of varied sound protect the uvula and may Mahamaya protect the palate. May Kamakshi guard my chin and the all-auspicious my speech,

ग्रीवायां भद्रकाली च पृष्ठवंशं धनुर्धरी ।
नीलग्रीवा बहि:कण्ठे नलिकां नलकूबरी ॥ २४ ॥

24. the auspious Kali in the neck and the wielder of the bow in the back-bone; the force of Neelakanta in the outer neck and Nalakubari in the throat.

खड्गधारिण्युभौ स्कन्धौ बाहू मे वज्रधारिणी ।
हस्तयोर्दण्डिनी रक्षेदंबिका चांगुलीस्तथा ॥ २५ ॥

25. May the wielder of the sword guard my two shoulders and my arms the wielder of the thunderbolt. May the possessor of the staff guard my hands and the fingers, the mother.

नखान् शूलेश्वरी रक्षेत् कुक्षौ रक्षेन्नलेश्वरी ।
स्तनौ रक्षेन्महालक्ष्मीः मनःशोकविनाशिनी ॥ २६ ॥

26. May the goddess with the trident protect the nails. May Naleswari protect the abdomen. May

Mahalakshmi the dispeller of mental anguish guard the breasts,

हृदये ललिता देवी ह्यदरे शूलधारिणी ।
नाभौ च कामिनी रक्षेद् गुह्यं गुह्येश्वरी तथा ॥ २७ ॥

27. in the heart the goddess Lalita, in the stomach the wielder of the trident, in the navel the goddess of love. Likewise may the lady of occult secrets protect the private parts.

कट्यां भगवती रक्षेज्जानुनी चिन्ध्यवासिनी ।
भूतनाथा च मेढ्रं मे ऊरू महिषवाहिनी ॥ २८ ॥

28. Let Bhagavati guard the hips and the dweller in Vindhyas the knees. Let the head of beings guard my genital and one who mounts the buffalo my thighs.

जङ्घे महाबला प्रोक्ता सर्वकामप्रदायिनी ।
गुल्फयोर्नार्सिंही च पादौ चामिततेजसी ॥ २९ ॥

29. The giver of all desires, the goddess of immense strength has to be invoked in the shanks: in the ankles the force of Narasimha and in the feet the goddess of immeasurable lustre.

पादांगुलीः श्रीमें रक्षेत् पादाधस्तलवासिनी ।
नखान् दंष्ट्रकराली च केशांश्चैवोर्ध्वकेशिनी ॥ ३० ॥

30. May Sri guard the fingers in the feet and let the dweller in the nether regions guard the sole of the feet. May the one looking terrible with fangs guard the nails and the one with high tresses the hair.

रोमकूपेषु कौबेरी त्वचं वागीश्वरी तथा ।
रक्तमज्जावसामांसान्यस्थिमेदांसि पार्वती ॥ ३१ ॥

31. May the force of Kubera guard the pores in the skin and may the lady of speech guard the skin. Let the

daughter of the mountain guard the blood, the marrow of bone and flesh, flesh, bone and fat.

अन्त्राणि कालरात्रिश्च पित्तं च मुकुटेश्वरी ।
पद्मावती पद्मकोशे कफे चूडामणिस्तथा ॥ ३२ ॥

32. Let the goddess of dark night guard the entrails and the crowned sovereign the bile; Let the lady of the lotus guard the lungs[1] and the lady with a jewel in her crest the phlegm.

ज्वालामुखी नखज्वालामभेद्या सर्वसन्धिषु ।
शुक्रं ब्रह्माणी मे रक्षेच्छायां छत्रेश्वरी तथा ॥ ३३ ॥

33. Let the flame-faced one guard the lustre of my nails and the unbreakable one in all the joints. Let Brahma's force protect my semen and the goddess with the regal umbrella my shadow.

अहंकारं मनो बुद्धिं रक्ष मे धर्मचारिणि ।
प्राणापानौ तथा व्यानं समानोदानमेव च ॥ ३४ ॥

34. May the one whose movement is in Dharma, the law of the being, protect my mind, intellect, ego and the five vital breaths, Prana, Apana, Vyana, Samana and Udana.

यशः कीर्तिं च लक्ष्मीं च सदा रक्षतु वैष्णवी ।
गोत्रसिन्द्राणी मे रक्षेत् पशून्मे रक्ष चण्डिके ॥ ३५ ॥

35. Let the force of Vishnu always guard my name, fame and prosperity, the force of Indra my cow-pen and Chandika my cows.

पुत्रान् रक्षेन्महालक्ष्मी भार्यां रक्षतु भैरवी ।
मार्गं क्षेमकरी रक्षेद्विजया सर्वतः स्थिता ॥ ३६ ॥

---

1 Lungs representing the breath, wind, vata. The humours, wind, bile and phlegm, vata, pitta and kapha are mentioned here.

36. May Mahalakshmi guard my offsprings and Bhairavi my wife. Let the doer of good. Vijaya stand every where and protect my path.

रक्षाहीनं तु यत्स्थानं वर्जितं कवचेन तु ।

तत्सर्वं रक्ष मे देवि जयन्ती पापनाशिनी ॥ ३७ ॥

37. O Goddess, protect all those places that have been left unprotected by the Kavacha, conquering and destroying the sins on the way.

पदमेकं न गच्छेत्तु यदीच्छेच्छुभमात्मनः ।

कवचेनावृतो नित्यं यत्र यत्राधिगच्छति ॥ ३८ ॥

38. If one cares for one's welfare, one should never take a step without the armour. Wherever a man goes, constantly surrounded by the Kavacha,

तत्र तत्रार्थलाभश्च विजयः सार्वकामिकः ।

यं यं कामयते कामं तं तं प्राप्नोति निश्चितम् ॥ ३९ ॥

39. there for him the attainment of ends and an all-satisfying conquest. Whatever are his wishes he wants to be fulfilled, yea, he attains them.

परमैश्वर्यमतुलं प्राप्स्यते भूतले पुमान् ।

निर्भयो जायते मर्त्यः संग्रामेष्वपराजितः ॥ ४० ॥

40. Man in this world will acquire bounteous wealth of no comparison. Mortal though he is, unvanquished in battles, he becomes fearless.

त्रैलोक्ये तु भवेत् पूज्यः कवचेनावृतः पुमान् ।

इदं तु देव्याः कवचं देवानामपि दुर्लभम् ॥ ४१ ॥

41. The man surrounded by the Kavacha will deserve worship in all the three worlds. This Kavacha of the Goddess is difficult of acquisition even for the gods.

यः पठेत् प्रयतो नित्यं त्रिसन्ध्यं श्रद्धयान्वितः ।
देवी कला भवेत्तस्य त्रैलोक्येष्वपराजितः ॥ ४२ ॥

42. Whosoever reads this at dawn, noon or dusk, every day with faith and discipline, he becomes unvanquished in the triple world and a portion of the Divine manifests in him.

जीवेद्वर्षशतं साग्रमपमृत्युविवर्जितः ।
नश्यन्ति व्याधयः सर्वे लूता विस्फोटकादयः ॥ ४३ ॥

43. He will live for the full span of hundred years, free from unnatural or accidental death. All diseases arising out of cuts, eruptions, small-pox etc. perish.

स्थावरं जंगमं चापि कृत्रिमं चापि यद्विषम् ।
आभिचाराणि सर्वाणि मन्त्रयन्त्राणि भूतले ॥ ४४ ॥

44. Poison naturally arising out of the movable and the immovable in the world and also poison administered from outside, all charms and talismans pertaining to black magic,

भूचराः खेचराश्चैव जलजाश्चोपदेशिकाः ।
सहजाः कुलजा मालाः शाकिनी डाकिनी तथा ॥ ४५ ॥

45. those moving on earth, those moving in the sky, those born in water, those directed and induced by others, those born with oneself, those born in one's family, Mala, Sakini, Dakini and other forces,

अन्तरिक्षचरा घोरा डाकिन्यश्च महाबलाः ।
ग्रहभूतपिशाचाश्च यक्षगन्धर्वराक्षसाः ॥ ४६ ॥

46. Dakinis, possessed of immense strength, terrible, moving in mid-air, spirits that possess, elemental beings, ghosts, Yakshas, Gandharvas, Demons,

ब्रह्मराक्षसवेतालाः कूष्माण्डा भैरवादयः ।
नश्यन्ति दर्शनात्तस्य कवचे हृदि संस्थिते ॥ ४७ ॥

94

47. Brahmarakshas, Goblins, Kushmandas, Bhairavas etc.-all perish at the sight of one, when one has the Kavacha in one's heart.

मानोन्नतिर्भवेद्राज्ञस्तेजोवृद्धिकरं परम् ।
यशसा वर्धते सोऽपि कीर्तिमण्डितभूतले ॥ ४८ ॥

48. Prestige with the king will rise. This (Kavacha) is the best means of increasing one's might. He will grow in fame as well, his name spreading throughout the world.

जपेत् सप्तशतीं चण्डीं कृत्वा तु कवचं पुरा ।
यावद् भूमण्डलं धत्ते सशैलवनकाननम् ॥ ४९ ॥

49. First one should do the Kavacha and then recite the *Candi Patha* of seven hundred verses. As long as the globe of the earth stands with its hills, dales and forests,

तावत्तिष्ठति मेदिन्यां संततिः पुत्रपौत्रिकी ।
देहान्ते परमं स्थानं यत् सुरैरपि दुर्लभम् ॥ ५० ॥
प्राप्नोति पुरुषो नित्यं महामायाप्रसादतः ॥

50. his descendents of sons and grandsons last on this earth. When life in the body ends, by the grace of Mahamaya, the man attains the eternal supreme station which is difficult to be obtained even for the gods.

इति श्रीवाराहपुराणे हरिहरब्रह्मविरचितं देव्याः कवचं समाप्तम् ।

Thus ends the Kavacha of the Goddess forged by Vishnu, Siva and Brahma, in the Varaha Purana.

ARGALA STOTRAM

अस्य श्री अर्गलास्तोत्रमन्त्रस्य विष्णुर्ऋषिः । अनुष्टुप् छन्दः ।
श्री महालक्ष्मीर्देवता । ॐ नमश्चण्डिकायै ॥

For Argala Stotra, Vishnu is the seer, the metre is Anushtu and the deity is Mahalakshmi; Salutations to Chandika

जयन्ती मंगला काली भद्रकाली कपालिनी ।
दुर्गा क्षमा शिवा धात्री स्वाहा स्वधा नमोऽस्तु ते ॥ १ ॥

1. Victorious, auspicious, dark, the Bhadrakali possessed of the skull, Durga, patience, good, the upholder and sustainer, Swaha Swadha—to thee be the salutations.

मधुकैटभविद्राविा विधातृवरदे नमः ।
रूपं देहि जयं देहि यशो देहि द्विषो जहि ॥ २ ॥

2. O thou who drove away Madhu and Kaitabha, O giver of good to Brahma, Salutations. Give the form, give the victory, give the fame, kill the enemies.

महिषासुरनिर्नाशविधात्रि वरदे नमः । रूपं० ॥ ३ ॥

3. O thou who destined the destruction of Mahishasura, giver of boons, salutations. Give the form, give the victory, give the fame, kill the enemies.

वन्दितांघ्रियुगे देवि सर्वसौभाग्यदायिनि । रूपं० ॥ ४ ॥

4. Having all bowing at thy feet, O Goddess, giver of all auspicious things, give the form, give the victory, give the fame, kill the enemies.

रक्तबीजवधे देवि चण्डमुण्डविनाशिनि । रूपं० ॥ ५ ॥

5. O thou who killed Raktabija, O destroyer of Chanda and Munda, O Goddess, give the form, give the victory, give the fame, kill the enemies.

अचिन्त्यरूपचरिते सर्वेशत्रुविनाशिनि । रूपं० ॥ ६ ॥

6. O thou of form and activity beyond the ken of thought, O destroyer of all the enemies, give the form, give the victory, give the fame, kill the enemies.

नतेभ्यः सर्वदा भक्त्या चण्डिके दुरितापहे । रूपं० ॥ ७ ॥

7. O Chandika, who dispels the distress of those who always bow with devotion, give the form, give the victory, give the fame, kill the enemies.

स्तुवद्भ्यो भक्तिपूर्वं त्वां चण्डिके व्याधिनाशिनि । रूपं० ॥ ८ ॥

8. O Chandika, who destroys the disease of those who laud thee with devotion, give the form, give the victory, give the fame, kill the enemies.

चण्डिके सततं ये त्वामर्चयन्तीह भक्तितः । रूपं० ॥ ९ ॥

9. O Chandika, whoever constantly worships thee with devotion, to him give the form, give the victory, give the fame, kill the enemies.

देहि सौभाग्यमारोग्यं देहि देवि परं सुखम् । रूपं० ॥ १० ॥

10. Grant good fortune, health, Goddess, grant supreme happiness. Give the form, give the victory, give the fame, kill the enemies.

विधेहि द्विषतां नाशं विधेहि बलमुच्चकैः । रूपं० ॥ ११ ॥

11. Accomplish the destruction of enemies, create in us immense strength. Give the form, give the victory, give the fame, kill the enemies.

विधेहि देवि कल्याणं विधेहि परमां श्रियम् । रूपं० ॥ १२ ॥

12. Goddess, confer on us well-being, confer superb prosperity. Give the form, give the victory, give the fame, kill the enemies.

विद्यावन्तं यशस्वन्तं लक्ष्मीवन्तं जनं कुरु । रूपं० ॥ १३ ॥

13. Make the person endowed with knowledge endowed with fame and endowed with prosperity. Give the form, give the victory, give the fame, kill the enemies.

प्रचण्डदैत्यदर्पघ्ने चण्डिके प्रणताय मे । रूपं० ॥ १४ ॥

14. O Chandika, who destroyest the pride of the terrific Asuras, to me who has bowed down, give the form, give the victory, give the fame, kill the enemies.

चतुर्भुजे चतुर्वक्त्रसंस्तुते परमेश्वरि । रूपं० ॥ १५ ॥

15. O thou of four hands, O thou lauded by the four-faced Brahma, supreme sovereign, give the form, give the victory, give the fame, kill the enemies.

कृष्णेन संस्तुते देवि शश्वद्भक्त्या त्वमंबिके । रूपं० ॥ १६ ॥

16. O thou who art constantly lauded with devotion by the dark Vishnu, mother, give the form, give the victory, give the fame, kill the enemies.

हिमाचलसुतानाथसंस्तुते परमेश्वरि । रूपं० ॥ १७ ॥

17. O thou who art lauded by the lord of the daughter of the snow-mountain, supreme sovereign, give the form, give the victory, give the fame, kill the enemies.

सुरासुरशिरोरत्ननिघृष्टचरणेऽम्बिके । रूपं० ॥ १८ ॥

18. O Mother, whose feet get rubbed against the crest jewels of gods and asuras, give the form, give the victory, give the fame, kill the enemies.

इन्द्राणीपतिसद्भावपूजिते परमेश्वरि । रूपं० ॥ १९. ॥

19. O thou who art worshipped with true feeling by the Lord of Indrani, supreme sovereign, give the form, give the victory, give the fame, kill the enemies.

देवि भक्तजनोद्दामदत्तानन्दोदयेऽम्बिके । रूपं० ॥ २० ॥

20. Goddess who givest rise to unfettered happiness in the devotees, Mother, give the form, give the victory, give the fame, kill the enemies.

पुत्रान्देहि धनं देहि सर्वकामांश्च देहि मे । रूपं० ॥ २१ ॥

21. Bestow offsprings, bestow wealth, grant me all desires. Give the form, give the victory, give the fame, kill the enemies.

पत्नीं मनोरमां देहि मनोवृत्तानुसारिणीम् ।
तारिणीं दुर्गसंसारसागरस्य कुलोद्भवाम् ॥ २२ ॥

22. Grant me a wife, pleasing to the mind and born of a good family, one who follows the indications of my mind and ferries me across the difficult ocean of Samsara.

इदं स्तोत्रं पठित्वा तु महास्तोत्रं पठेन्नरः ।
स तु सप्तशतीसंख्यावरमाप्नोति संपदाम् ॥ २३ ॥

23. After reading this laud, a person should read the great laud, well comprised of seven hundred numbers of verses. Yea, he gets the fulfilment.

इति श्री मार्कण्डेयपुराणे अर्गलास्तोत्रम् समाप्तम् ।

Thus ends the Argala Stotra in Markandeya Purana.

K ĪLAKAM

अस्य श्री कीलकमन्त्रस्य शिव ऋषिः । अनुष्टुप् छन्दः ।
श्रीमहासरस्वती देवता । ॐ नमश्चण्डिकायै ॥

For the Kilaka, Siva is the seer, the metre is Anushtuh
and the deity is Mahasaraswati;

Salutations to Chandika.

विशुद्धज्ञानदेहाय त्रिवेदीदिव्यचक्षुषे ।
श्रेयः प्राप्तिनिमित्ताय नमः सोमार्धधारिणे ॥ १ ॥

1. Pure knowledge is his body and the three Vedas
are his eyes of divine vision. He is the cause for attaining
the supreme well-being. To him who wears the half-
moon, salutations.

सर्वमेतद्विना यस्तु मन्त्राणामपि कीलकम् ।
सोऽपि क्षेममवाप्नोति सततं जाप्यतत्परः ॥ २ ॥

2. Whosoever is intent on the recitation of these
Mantras without all this kilaka, he also acquires well
being.

सिद्ध्यन्त्युच्चाटनादीनि वस्तूनि सकलान्यपि ।
एतेन स्तुवतां नित्यं स्तोत्रमात्रेण सिद्ध्यति ॥ ३ ॥

3. All things like driving away the undesirables are
effective; but for those who laud by means of this, it is
effectuated by the mere laud.

न मन्त्रो नौषधं तत्र न किंचिदपि विद्यते ।
विना जाप्येन सिध्द्येत सर्वमुच्चाटनादिकम् ॥ ४ ॥

4. There is absolutely nothing, no charm, no medicine. All things like Uchchatana are effective without japa of mantras.

समग्राण्यपि सिध्द्यन्ति लोकसंख्यासिमां हरः ।
कृत्वा निमन्त्रयामास सर्वेमेवमिदं शुभम् ॥ ५ ॥

5. All are effectuated. Siva left this for discussion in the world and made all this laud an auspicious mantra.

स्तोत्रं वै चण्डिकायास्तु तच्च गुह्य चकार सः ।
समाप्तिनं च पुण्यस्य तां यथावन्नियन्त्रणाम् ॥ ६ ॥

6. Yea, the laud of Chandika; and he made it occult. There is no end to the merit it bestows; (and so) he put a restraint.

सोऽपि क्षेममवाप्नोति सर्वमेव न संशयः ।
कृष्णायां वा चतुर्दश्यामष्टम्यां वा समाहितः ॥ ७ ॥

7. He (Sadhaka) gets all the well-being, no doubt. Concentrated, on the fourteenth or eighth day of the dark fortnight,

ददाति प्रतिगृह्णाति नान्यथैषा प्रसीदति ।
इत्थंरूपेण कीलेन महादेवेन कीलितम् ॥ ८ ॥

8. he gives, he accepts. In no other way She is pleased. By this pivot, it is fixed by Mahadeva.

यो निष्कीलां विधायैनां नित्यं जपति सुस्फुटम् ।
स सिद्धः स गणः सोऽपि गन्धर्वो जायते ऽवने ॥ ९ ॥

9. Whoever frees this from restraint and constantly recites it clearly, he is the accomplished one, Siddha, he is in the retinue of the goddess. He becomes a Gandharva in protection.

न चैवाप्यटतस्तस्य भयं क्वापि हि जायते ।
नापमृत्युवशं याति मृतो मोक्षमवाप्नुयात् ॥ १० ॥

10. When he goes about, from nowhere does fear come to him. He does not become a victim of untimely accidental death. After death, he attains liberation.

ज्ञात्वा प्रारभ्य कुर्वांत ह्यकुर्वाणो विनश्यति ।
ततो ज्ञात्वैव संपन्नमिदं प्रारभ्यते बुधैः ॥ ११ ॥

11. Having known, one should begin and perform; if he does not perform, he perishes. The very fact of having known itself is fulfilment. This is begun by the knowers.

सौभाग्यादि च यत् किंचिद् दृश्यते ललनाजने ।
तत्सर्वं तत्प्रसादेन तेन जाप्यमिदं शुभम् ॥ १२ ॥

12. All those like auspiciousness etc. seen in the womanfolk are due to Her grace. Therefore, this auspicious laud should be recited.

शनैस्तु जप्यमानेऽस्मिन् स्तोत्रे संपत्तिरुच्चकैः ।
भवत्येव समग्रापि ततः प्रारभ्यमेव तत् ॥ १३ ॥

13. Even when this laud is recited slowly, lofty results to be the complete fulfilment. And therefore, it has to be commenced.

ऐश्वर्यं यत्प्रसादेन सौभाग्यारोग्यसंपदः ।
शत्रुहानिः परो मोक्षः स्तूयते सा न किं जनैः ॥ १४ ॥

14. Why will She not be praised by people when wealth, auspiciousness, health and other felicities, destruction of enemies and great liberation are all Her grace.

इति कीलकस्तोत्रं समाप्तम् Here ends the Kilaka stotram.

NAVĀKṢARĪ

'vak became all these worlds' *vāgeva viśvā bhuvanāni jajñe*, declares the Vedic Seer. The Tantra speaks of the *nāda brahman* as the creator of the worlds. The Tantrics hold that the Word or sound-creation precedes the creation of objects, sound first and sense next, *arthasṛṣṭeh pūrvam śabdasṛṣṭiḥ*. The Rishi, the seer when he perceives the Truth, perceives at the same time the sound embodying the Truth. He receives it in the secret depths of his being and gives expression to it in the human tongue. This is the Mantra. When the Mantra is properly uttered, the sound-force from which it has sprung is contacted, which in turn reveals the Truth it embodies. So when the Mantra of a deity is uttered, the vibrations create the sound-body of the deity and with repeated utterances, the sound-body of the deity becomes concretely formed and the powerful Presence of the deity is established. Mantra is not merely a means to contact the Divine, as is popularly imagined; it is the Devine itself it is its sound-form. So it is wrong to think of Mantra as a collection of letters. The Tantra declares: "To hell he goes who mistakes the Guru for a human, who takes the image for a piece of stone, who looks upon the Mantra as mere letters."[1]

"The Mantra is an ever-living embodiment of the Truth and Power which have found expression in it through the medium of the Rishi or Yogin who has given them that body. And when a Mantra is uttered, under

---

[1] देशिके मानवभ्रान्ति प्रतिमासु शिलामतिस् ।
मन्त्रेष्वक्षरबुद्धिं च कुर्वाणो निरयं व्रजेत् ॥

proper conditions, it is not the feeble voice of the reciter that goes forth to evoke the response of the gods to whom it is addressed but the flame of *tapasyā* and realisation, that is lying coiled up in the body of that utterance."[1] And the living touch of the Guru is needed to set the Mantra awake in the disciple. When the Guru initiates the disciple into the Mantra, he implants the Mantra along with his realisation of the Mantra and the living presence of the deity invoked. The disciple has only to tend and nurture the consciousness put into him by the Guru. The seed sown into him by the Guru will germinate, put forth shoots, blossom and yield fruits at the appropriate time. Where the Guru is a powerful personality, a great Mantra Siddha, the word of the Mantra emanating from him at the time of initiation will itself carry out the Sadhana, by constantly reverberating of its own accord in the heart of the disciple. The disciple on his part has always to relive the experience of the initiation.[2]

---

1. *Further Lights: The Veda and the Tantra* by Sri Kapali Sastriar.
2. There is a striking description of the action of Mantra in Sri Aurobindo's epic Savitri (IV.3):

"As when the mantra sinks in Yoga's ear,
Its message enters stirring the blind brain
And keeps in the dim ignorant cells its sound ;
The hearer understands a form of words
And, musing on the index thought it holds,
He strives to read it with the labouring mind,
But finds bright hints, not the embodied truth :
Then, falling silent in himself to know
He meets the deeper listening of his soul :
The Word repeats itself in rhythmic strains :
Thought, vision, feeling, sense, the body's self
Are seized unalterably and he endures
An ecstasy and an immortal change :
He feels a Wideness and becomes a Power,
All knowledge rushes on him like a sea:
Translated by the white spiritual ray
He walks in naked heavens of joy and calm,
Sees the God-face and hears transcendent speech."

The nine lettered *navārṇa* Mantra is the sound-body of Chandika composed of the nine Durgas.[1] The *Devi atharva śirṣa upaniṣad* proclaims this Mantra and extols it as *Mahadānanda dāyakaḥ*, giver of the highest Delight. "Brahmasayujya pradah" says Sri Bhaskararaya, interpreting this phrase. The Mantra grants to the Sadhaka union with the Brahman that is pure Delight, *ānanda* . "*aim hrīm klīm cāmuṇḍayai vicce*" is the Mantra. If all the vowels and consonants in the Mantra are counted, it will be twenty-four and so some acclaim this as the Gayatri of Chandi. Actually there is a sevenfold division in the Mantra *aim hrīm klīm cāmuṇḍāyai vit ca e*. *cāmuṇḍāyai* is in the dative case while the six others are in the vocative case *Aim* is the *vākbīja* , the seedsound of Mahasaraswati, knowledge that is consciousness, Cit and corresponds to *vit* in the lower triple. *hrīm* is the *māyābīja* , the seed-sound of Mahalakshmi, the all-pervasive existence *Sat* and corresponds to *ca* in the lower triple. *klīm* is *kamabija* , the seedsound of Mahakali, the all consuming delight, *ānanda* and corresponds to *e* in the lower triple. Mahasaraswati, Mahalakshmi and Mahakali represent the higher triple state of the Godhead, *Cit*. *Sat* and *Ananda* in the upper half *parārdha* and they get involved in creation, in the lower Triple worlds, *trailokyam*, physical, vital and mental, *anna, prāṇa* and *manas* through *Vijñāna*. Gnosis represented

1 There is a close correlation between the form of the deity as conceived in Dhyana and the form of the Mantra, as the Mantra is its sound-body. For example, the Mantra of Shiva, the five-faced is the five-lettered Panchakshari, that of Subrahmanya, the six-faced is the six-lettered *śaravanabhava* Mantra. The twelve manifestations of Vasudeva -Keshava, Narayana, Madhava, Govinda, Vishnu, Madhusudana, Trivikrama, Vamana, Sridhara, Hrishikesa, Padmanabha, Damodara -are represented by the twelve lettered. In the Lalita cult, it is explicitly stated that the body of Tripurasundari is made of the three *kutas* of the Mantra, *mulakutatraya kalevara*.

by Chamunda. And the lower triple in turn has to evolve into the higher triple through Chamunda. Thus in the Mantra, *Aim Hrim Klim* and *Vicce* represent the higher triple and the lower triple worlds respectively, while *camuṇḍāyai* denotes the world of Vijnana, Gnosis, the plane of light, Mahas. The Mantra is an invocation to the supreme goddess in the form of Truth-Consciousness-Bliss, made by the being circumscribed by the lower triple of physical vital and mental states. The prayer is made so that the being is freed by the grace of Chamunda from its present triple state of distortion to reach the true state of Truth-Consciousness-Bliss.

Each letter in the Mantra has to be contemplated in a definite colour.[1] The Tantra says that the first seed-sound *aim* has a moonlike lustre, the second seed-sound *hrim* has the effulgence of the sun and the third seed-sound which has to be contemplated for endless delight, *klim* blazes like the fire. The letter *ca* has the shining of pure gold and *mum* is deep red in colour; *ḍā* is deep blue dispelling the worst distress while *yai* is all black destroying the foes. *vi*, the eighth letter has the primary white colour and *cce* the ninth has a vast sweep of smoky hue.[2]

The *nāvarṇa* Mantra is always done as a limb of *saptasati* and rarely by itself.

1 The word for letter *varṇa* also means colour. It is said that Mantras have their own spectrums and they are perceived in inner contemplation on the Mantra.

पें बीजमादीन्दुसमानदीर्तिं ह्रीं सूर्यंतेजोद्युतिमद् द्वितीयम् ।
क्लीं मूर्तिर्वैश्वानरतुल्यरूपं तृतीयमानन्त्यसुखाय चिन्त्यम् ॥
चां शुद्धजाम्बूनदकान्ति तुयं मुं पञ्चमं रक्ततरं प्रकल्प्य ।
डां षट्कमुग्राततिहरं सुनीलं यैं सप्तमं कृष्णतरं रिपुघ्नम् ॥
विं पाण्डरं चाष्टममादिसिद्धं चें धूम्रवर्णं नवमं विशालम् ॥

NYĀSA

nyāsa means a pledge or a deposit that is entrusted to one's care. One must begin to identify oneself with the Mantra one worships and this is done by completely surrendering the individuality, the sense of I-ness and my-ness in all parts of one's being and entrusting it to the Mantra which is the sound-body of the Deity. One must open oneself to the Mantra-force and allow it to have its play in the being. This has to be done progressively and the process adopted is the *nyāsa*.

The Sadhaka places his fingers or palm of his right hand or of both the hands on the various parts of the body reciting the appropriate parts of the Mantra so that the Mantra is united with the body, limb by limb. This is known as *anga nyāsa*. When the parts of the Mantra are assigned to the thumbs, index fingers, middle fingers, the fourth and little fingers and the front and back of the palms, the assignment is known as *kara nyasa*. By entrusting the fingers of the hands and the other limbs of the body to the appropriate limbs of the Mantra, the whole body and through it the whole being becomes pledged to the Mantra. Once the Nyasa is done, the entire being of the *sādhaka* belongs to the Divine and the *sādhaka* has no claim over it. He deals with himself as he would with a trust property. He performs the japa of the Mantra with this attitude and no wonder Mantra done with the proper *Nyasa*, is more effective.

ekādaśa nyāsas, eleven Nyasas, are prescribed for the *saptasati* and *navārṇa* Mantra. We have already stressed that saptasati and navarna Mantra are not distinguished as separate. The Rishi, Chandas, Devatas etc. are same for both.

The first of the eleven Nyasas is the *mātṛkā* Nyasa which is said to confer on the sadhaka the same form of the deity, *devasārūpyaprada*. Matrkas are the fifty letters of the Sanskrit alphabet from *a* to *kṣa* and they are called Mothers Matrkas, because they give birth to the sound-body of the deity. Nyasa is done on different parts of the body with the letters of the alphabet which form the corresponding parts of the body of the deity. The second is the *sāraswata* nyasa, capable of dispelling inertia *jādya vināśaka*. It is done by placing the seed letters *aim hrim klim* on the fingers and limbs of the body. The third is the *mātṛgaṇa* Nyasa, seeking the protection in all directions from the hosts of mothers like Brahmi, Maheswari, etc. It is said to confer victory in the triple worlds, *trailokya vijayaprada* . The fourth is *nandajādi* Nyasa. The incarnations of the Divine Mother are called to protect the body east, west, north, south, from head to foot as well as from foot to head. This Nyasa is said to remove old age and death, *jarā mṛtyu hara*. The fifth fulfils all wishes *sarvakamprada* and goes by the name *brahmādi* Nyasa. It is also known as *abhedya panjara* the unbreakable cage. Brahma, Vishnu, Siva are invoked in the parts of the body, from foot to navel, from navel to neck and from there above, respectively. Their vehicles, the swan, the falcon and the bull are invoked in the feet, in the hands and in the eyes respectively.

Ganesha is sought to protect the whole body while the sides are left to the care of Hari who is all Delight. The sixth Nyasa is the *mahālaksmyadi* Nyasa, known also as the *vaikuntha sukha krt* conferring the bliss of Vaikuntha. Here the deities, Mahalakshmi, Mahasaraswati and Mahakali are invoked. This Nyasa is said to lead to the goal of Good, *sadgati prada*. The seventh and eighth are *mūlāksara* and *varna* Nyasas. They are done with the letters of Navaksari, from Brahmarandhra down to genitals and then in the reverse order. They are famed as destroyers of diseases and dispellers of miseries, *roga ksāyakara* and *duhkha nāśaka*. The ninth is the *mantravyapti* Nyasa. The sadhaka passes his fingers all over the body reciting the Navaksari. This he does from top to bottom, bottom to top, in all directions making *vyāpaka* eight times. This helps him to reach the Divine, *devatā prāptikara*. The tenth is the *sadanga* Nyasa acting as a charm in the triple world *trailokya vasakara*. *Navarna Mantra* is used for the *Nyasa*. Then we come to the last but not the least Nyasa. because this eleventh Nyasa is said to give the fruit of all the ten Nyasas:[1] this is known as *khatginyādi* Nyasa and extolled as the giver of all protection, all wants, remover of all undesirable things, *sarvaraksākara, sarvābhistada, sarvānistahara*. The five slokas beginning from *khatginī śūlinī ghorā* are recited and Nyasa is done on the whole body thinking of the first seed sound *Aim*, in black colour. The four slokas beginning from *śulena pāhi no devi* are recited and

---

[1] अयमेकादशन्यासो दशन्याससमो भवेत् ।
तत्फलं लभते सम्यगस्मिन्नेकादशे कृते ॥

Nyasa is done on the whole body thinking of the second seed-sound *Hrim* as effulgent as the rising Sun. The five slokas beginning from *Sarvaswarūpe sarveśe* are recited and *Nyasa* is done on the whole body, thinking of the third seed-sound *Klim* as white crystal.

Having done these elevan Nyasas, one proceeds to perform the Anga Nyasa and Kara Nyasa of the Navarna Mantra fences the quarters and tells the three Dhyana slokas beginning with *khadgam cakra gadeṣu*, *akṣasrak paraśūgadeṣu* and *ghanṭā sulahalāni*.[1] Then he does the japa and dedicates it to the Divine Mother by the following verse :

"Thou art the protector of the most occult secrets. Pray accept the japa done by me. O Supreme Sovereign, May accomplishment come to me by Thy Grace."

---

1 These are explained at the beginning of the three episodes of the text.

एकादशन्यासाः ॥

आदौ मातृकान्यासः ॥

सर्वेत्रादौ प्रणवोच्चारः । अं नमो ललाटे । आं नमो मुखवृत्ते । इं नमो दक्षिणनेत्रे । ईं नमो वामनेत्रे । उं नमो दक्षिणकर्णे । ऊं नमो वामकर्णे । ऋं नमो दक्षिणनासायां । ॠं नमो वामनासायां । लृं नमो दक्षिणगण्डे । लॄं नमो वाम- गण्डे । एं नम ऊर्ध्वौष्ठे । ऐं नमोऽधरोष्ठे । ओं नम ऊर्ध्वदन्त- पङ्क्तौ । औं नमोऽधोदन्तपङ्क्तौ । अं नमः शिरसि । अः नमो मुखे । कं नमो दक्षबाहुमूले । खं नमो दक्षकूर्परे । गं नमो दक्षमणिबन्धे । घं नमो दक्षाङ्गुलिमूले । ङं नमो दक्षाङ्गुल्यग्रे । चं नमो वामबाहुमूले । छं नमो वामकूर्परे । जं नमो वाममणि- बन्धे । झं नमो वामाङ्गुलिमूले । ञं नमो वामाङ्गुल्यग्रे । टं नमो दक्षपादमूले । ठं नमो दक्षजानुनि । डं नमो दक्षगुल्फे । ढं नमो दक्षपादाङ्गुलिमूले । णं नमो दक्षपादाङ्गुल्यग्रे । तं नमो वामपादमूले । थं नमो वामजानुनि । दं नमो वामगुल्फे । धं नमो वामपादाङ्गुलिमूले । नं नमो वामपादाङ्गुल्यग्रे । पं नमो दक्षपार्श्वे । फं नमो वामपार्श्वे । बं नमः पृष्ठे । भं नमो नाभौ । मं नमो जठरे । यं नमो हृदि । रं नमो दक्षांसे । लं नमः ककुदि । वं नमो वामांसे । शं नमो हृदादिदक्षहस्तान्ते । षं नमो हृदादि- वामहस्तान्ते । सं नमो हृदादिदक्षपादान्ते । हं नमो हृदादि- वामपादान्ते । ळं नमो जठरे । क्षं नमो मुखे ॥

द्वितीयः सारस्वतन्यासः ॥

ऐं ह्रीं क्लीं नमः कनिष्ठयोः । ऐं ह्रीं क्लीं नमः अनामिकयोः । ऐं ह्रीं क्लीं नमः मध्यमयोः । ऐं ह्रीं क्लीं नमः तर्जन्योः । ऐं ह्रीं क्लीं

नमः अङ्गुष्ठयोः । ऐं ह्रीं क्लीं नमः करमध्ये । ऐं ह्रीं क्लीं नमः करपृष्ठे । ऐं ह्रीं क्लीं नमः मणिबन्धयोः । ऐं ह्रीं क्लीं नमः कूर्परयोः । ऐं ह्रीं क्लीं नमः हृदयाय नमः । ऐं ह्रीं क्लीं नमः शिरसे स्वाहा । ऐं ह्रीं क्लीं नमः शिखायै वषट् । ऐं ह्रीं क्लीं नमः कवचाय हुं । ऐं ह्रीं क्लीं नमः नेत्रत्रयाय वौषट् । ऐं ह्रीं क्लीं नमः अस्त्राय फट् ॥

तृतीयः मातृगणन्यासः ॥

ह्रीं ब्राह्मी पूर्वस्यां मां पातु । ह्रीं माहेश्वरी आग्नेय्यां मां पातु । ह्रीं कौमारी दक्षिणस्यां मां पातु । ह्रीं वैष्णवी नैर्ऋत्यां मां पातु । ह्रीं वाराही पश्चिमायां मां पातु । ह्रीं इन्द्राणी वायव्यां मां पातु । ह्रीं चामुण्डा उत्तरस्यां मां पातु । ह्रीं महालक्ष्मीरैशान्यां मां पातु । ह्रीं व्योमेश्वरी ऊर्ध्वं मां पातु । ह्रीं सप्तद्वीपेश्वरी भूमौ मां पातु । ह्रीं कामेश्वरी पाताले मां पातु ॥

चतुर्थः नन्दजादिन्यासः ॥

कमलाङ्कुशमण्डिता नन्दजा पूर्वाङ्गं मे पातु ।

खड्गपाशधरा रक्तदन्तिका दक्षिणाङ्गं मे पातु ।

पुष्पपल्लवसंयुता शाकंभरी पश्चिमाङ्गं मे पातु ।

धनुर्बाणकरा दुर्गा वामाङ्गं मे पातु ।

शिरःपात्रकरा भीमा मस्तकात् चरणावधि मां पातु ।

चित्रकान्तिभृद् भ्रामरी पादादिमस्कान्तं मे पातु ॥

पञ्चमः ब्रह्मादिन्यासः ॥

पादादिनाभिपर्यन्तं ब्रह्मा मां पातु । नाभेर्विशुद्धिपर्यन्तं जनार्दनो मां पातु । विशुद्धे ब्रह्मरन्ध्रान्तं रुद्रो मां पातु । हंसो मे

पद्द्वयं पातु । वैनतेयः करद्वयं मे पातु । वृषभध्वजरूपी मे पातु ।
गजाननः सर्वाङ्गं मे पातु । आनन्दमयो हरिः परापरौ देहभागौ
मे पातु ॥

षष्ठः महालक्ष्म्यादिन्यासः ॥

अष्टादशभुजा महालक्ष्मी मध्यभागं मे पातु ।
अष्टभुजा महासरस्वती ऊर्ध्वभागं मे पातु ।
दशभुजा महाकाली अधोभागं मे पातु ।
सिंहो हस्तद्वयं मे पातु । परहंसोऽक्षियुगं मे पातु ।
महिषारूढो यमः पदद्वयं मे पातु । महेशः चण्डिकायुक्तः
सर्वाङ्गं मे पातु ॥

सप्तमः मूलाक्षरन्यासः ॥

ऐं नमो ब्रह्मरन्ध्रे । ह्रीं नमो दक्षिणनेत्रे । क्लीं नमो वामनेत्रे ।
चां नमो दक्षिणकर्णे । सुं नमो वामकर्णे । डां नमो दक्षिणनासा-
पुटे । यैं नमो वामनासापुटे । विं नमो मुखे । च्चें नमो गुह्ये ॥

अष्टमः वर्णन्यासः ॥

च्चें नमो गुह्ये । विं नमो मुखे । यैं नमो वामनासापुटे ।
डां नमो दक्षिणनासापुटे । सुं नमो वामकर्णे । चां नमो दक्षिण-
कर्णे । क्लीं नमो वामनेत्रे । ह्रीं नमो दक्षिणनेत्रे । ऐं नमो
ब्रह्मरन्ध्रे ॥

नवमः मन्त्रव्यापकन्यासः ॥

मूलमुच्चार्य मस्तकाच्चरणान्तं चरणान्मस्तकान्तं अष्टवारं व्यापकं
कुर्यात् । प्रथमं पुरतो मूलेन मस्तकाच्चरणावधि । ततश्चरणात् ।
मस्तकावधि मूलोच्चारेण व्यापकम् । पश्च दक्षिणतः पश्चाद् वाम

114

भागे चेति प्रतिदिग्भागेऽनुलोमविलोमतया द्विर्द्विरिति अग्रबाहं व्यापकं भवति ॥

दशमः मूलपङ्कन्यासः ॥

मूलमुद्वायं हृदयाय नमः । एधं सर्वत्र मूलमुद्वायं शिरसे स्वाहा । शिखायै वषट् । कवचाय हुं । नेत्रत्रयाय वौषट् । अस्त्राय फट् ॥

एकादशः सूक्तादिबीजत्रयन्यासः ।

खड्गिनी शूलिनी घोरा गदिनी चक्रिणी तथा ।
शङ्खिनी चापिनी बाणभुशुण्डीपरिघायुधा ॥
सौम्या सौम्यतराशेषसौम्येभ्यस्त्वतिसुन्दरी ।
परापराणां परमा त्वमेव परमेश्वरी ॥
यच्च किञ्चित्क्वचिद्वस्तु सदसद्वाखिलात्मिके ।
तस्य सर्वस्य या शक्तिः सा त्वं किं स्तूयते मया ॥
यया त्वया जगत्स्रष्टा जगत्पात्यत्ति यो जगत् ।
सोऽपि निद्रावशं नीतः कस्त्वां स्तोतुमिहेश्वरः ॥
विष्णुः शरीरग्रहणमहमीशान एव च ।
कारितास्ते यतोऽतस्त्वां कः स्तोतुं शक्तिमान् भवेत् ।

आद्यं वाग्बीजं क्षणतरं ध्यात्वा सर्वाङ्गे विन्यसामि ।

शूलेन पाहि नो देवि पाहि खड्गेन चाम्बिके ।
घण्टास्वनेन नः पाहि चापज्यानिःस्वनेन च ॥
प्राच्यां रक्ष प्रतीच्यां च चण्डिके रक्ष दक्षिणे ।
भ्रामणेनात्मशूलस्य उत्तरस्यां तथेश्वरि ॥

सौम्यानि यानि रूपाणि त्रैलोक्ये विचरन्ति ते ।
यानि चात्यन्तघोराणि तै रक्षास्तांस्तथा भुवम् ॥
खड्गशूलगदादीनि यानि चास्त्राणि तेऽम्बिके ।
करपल्लवसङ्गीनि तैरस्मान् रक्ष सर्वतः ॥

द्वितीयं मायाबीजं सूर्यसदृशं ध्यात्वा सर्वाङ्गे विन्यसामि ।

सर्वस्वरूपे सर्वेशे सर्वशक्तिसमन्विते ।
भयेभ्यस्त्राहि नो देवि दुर्गे देवि नमोऽस्तु ते ॥
एतत्ते वदनं सौम्यं लोचनत्रयभूषितम् ।
पातु नः सर्वभूतेभ्यः कात्यायनि नमोऽस्तु ते ॥
ज्वालाकरालमत्युग्रमशेषासुरसूदनम् ।
त्रिशूलं पातु नो भीते भद्रकालि नमोऽस्तु ते ॥

हिनस्ति दैत्यतेजांसि स्वनेनापूर्य या जगत् ।
सा घण्टा पातु नो देवि पापेभ्योऽनः सुतानिव ॥
असुरासृग्वसापङ्कचर्चितस्ते करोज्ज्वलः ।
शुभाय खड्गो भवतु चण्डिके त्वां नता वयम् ॥

तृतीयं कामबीजं स्फटिकाभं ध्यात्वा सर्वाङ्गे विन्यसामि ॥

अथ मूलषडङ्गन्यासः ॥

ऐं अङ्गुष्ठाभ्यां नमः । ह्रीं तर्जनीभ्यां नमः । क्लीं मध्यमा-
भ्यां नमः । चामुण्डायै अनामिकाभ्यां नमः । विच्चे कनिष्ठिकाभ्यां
नमः । ऐं ह्रीं क्लीं चामुण्डायै विच्चे करतलकरपृष्ठाभ्यां नमः ॥
एवं हृदयादि ॥ ध्यानम् - खड्गं चक्रगदेषु ······ अक्षस्रक् परशू
गदेषु ······ घण्टाशूलहलानि ······ ॥ लमित्यादि पञ्चपूजां कृत्वा
जपान्ते उत्तरन्यासान् विधाय जपं देव्यै समर्पयेत् ।
गुह्यातिगुह्यगोप्त्री त्वं गृहाणास्मत्कृतं जपम् ।
सिद्धिर्भवतु मे देवि त्वत्प्रसादान्महेश्वरि ॥

RATRI SUKTA

One should read Ratri Sukta before reciting the text of the three episodes and read Devi Sukta immediately after. These two are the 127th and 125th Suktas in the tenth Mandala of the Rig Veda. The very fact that *Saptasati*, the cream of Tantric literature, has to be recited, prefixed and suffixed by two Vedic Suktas shows the great importance the Tantra attaches to Vedic wisdom and tradition.

The Seer of Ratri Sukta is Kusika and *rātri* Night is the Deity.

The Vedic Seers worshipped the Sun as the Godhead of the supreme Truth and knowledge dispelling falsehood and ignorance by his rays of illumination. Dawn, Ushas, is his precursor and she is symbolic of the awakening of the Divine in Man. She opens out vistas of illumination in him and brings him face to face with Surya, the God of Truth. But light has no meaning if there has been no darkness, its counter-part. "For the world as we see it has come out of the darkness concealed in darkness, the deep and abysmal flood that covered all things, the inconscient ocean, *apraketam sallilam*; in that non-existence the seers have found by desire in the heart and thought in the mind that which builds up the true existence. This non-existence of the truth of things *asat* is the first aspect of them that emerges from the inconscient ocean; and its great darkness is the Vedic Night, *rātrim jagato niveśanīm* which holds the world and all its unrevealed potentialities in her obscure bosom."[1]

"Out of this non-existence, existence is born" says the Upanishad.[2] From the inconscient, all the consciousness has sprung up ; from the deluge and dissolution, *laya* , the creation, is manifested ; from darkness light has come and from the Night the day dawns. If day is the symbol of divine illumination, night is the symbol of the force of manifestation of that illumination which she keeps in her hidden. All the creation she holds in her as the seed and helps the world towards manifestation; and she is the base, the repository of all the unmanifested worlds.[3]

The Tantra proclaims her as the great Mother, the Mother who heads the creation and bears in her womb the seed of manifestation. She is the dark night, the great night, the terrible night of delusion *kālarātrir mahārātrir moharātrisca dāruṇā*. She patiently bears Dawn, the divine illuminiation in her womb and waits for the appropriate time, *kāla* to deliver her so that she (Dawn) in turn may deliver up to the worlds ridden by falsehood and ignorance, the Sun of Truth and knowledge. So she

---

1 *On the Veda* - Sri Aurobindo.

2 असद्धा इदमग्र आसीत् ।   ततो वै सदजायत ।

3 अन्तर्निहितसर्वसृष्टिगर्भा जगदाविष्कारप्रयोजिका अनाविष्कृतसमस्तजगदाधारभूता

Sri Kapali Sastriar in Veda Guptartha *siddhānjana bhāsya* (R.V.I,35-1)

is called *kāli*, She is the Yoga Nidra of Vishnu, the all-pervasive primordeal principle who withdraws into superconscient sleep on his couch of Infinity, *ananta*, spread on the waters of the inconscient ocean, *apraketam salilam*. This sleep is the precursor of the great awakening, this withdrawal is the harbinger of a powerful projection of the Godhead in creation and this delusion brings in its wake the supreme enlightment. She is the first, the eldest of all creation. *jyesthā* of the *dasa mahāvidyās*. She is the dark mother but not absolutely dark as she bears the light within her. She is *dhūmāvati* of smoky hue.

Night is the symbol of the ordinary consciousness in man while the day signified by dawn is the symbol of the divine consciousness. All that is lit up in the day is in the womb of the night; and all that is lit up in the divine consciousness is in the womb of the human consciousness.[1] *ratri* by her darkness creates fear in the minds of ordinary men. She is terrible *dārunā* with the thieves at large and the beasts of prey like the wolf prowling around. She lets loose all the *niśācaras*-the Daityas, the sons of division, the Rakshasas, the Pisachas, the offsprings of strife and falsehood. But for the aspirant, the night is not so terrible. "The divine flame of the seer-will Agni burns through the dense murk giving light

---

[1] राित्रशब्देन अस्माकं साधारणी मानुषी प्रज्ञा, उपोलक्षितेन अह्ना देवी प्रज्ञा च सङ्केतिते । दिने प्रकाशमानं सर्वं राित्रगर्भे वर्तते । देवप्रज्ञायां प्रकाशमानं सर्वं मानुषप्रज्ञागर्भे वर्तते ॥

Sri Kapali Sastriar in Veda Guptartha *siddhānjana bhāsya* (RV.1.13-7).

to him who sits afar in its shadow, though not yet kindled, as it shall be at dawn, on a sacrificial altar, yet even so it fulfils on our earth as the lowest and greatest of the gods the will and works of the hidden light in spite of all this enveloping smoke of passion and desire. And the stars shine out and the moon comes at night making manifest the invincible workings of the infinite King."[1]

Knowledge and Ignorance are the two facets of the Supreme who transcends both. Day and Night are the obverse and reverse sides of the same eternal infinite. "There is a constant rhythm and alteration of night and dawn, illuminations of the Light and periods of exile from it, openings up of our darkness and its settling upon us once more, till the celestial Birth is accomplished."[2] If this is understood, the significance of the Upanishadic saying will be clear: "One who knows knowledge and ignorance, both together, crosses death by ignorance and attains immortality by knowledge."[3]

It is quite common in the Veda that the seer extols Ushas in the Riks ascribed to Ratri and extols Ratri in turn in the Riks ascribed to Ushas. He acclaims both as sisters, daughters of Heaven, "Kutsa hymns the two sisters, 'Immortal with a common lover, agreeing, they move over heaven and earth forming the hue of the light; common is the path of the sisters, infinite; and they range

---

1 *On the veda* - Sri Aurobindo.

2 *On the Veda* - Sri Aurobindo.

3 विद्यां चाविद्यां च यस्तद्वेदोभयं सह ।
अविद्यया मृत्युं तीर्त्वा विद्ययाऽमृतमश्नुते ॥

it, the one and the other, taught by the gods; common they, though different their forms.' (R. V. I. 113-2-3) For one is the bright mother of the herds, the other the dark cow, the black, infinite who can yet be made to yield us the shining milk of heaven."[1]

---

1 *On the Veda* - Sri Aurobindo.

RATRI SUKTAM

रात्रिसूक्तम् ॥

ॐ रात्री व्यख्यदायती पुरुत्रा देव्यक्षभिः ।
विश्वा अधिश्रियोधित ॥ १ ॥

1. The goddess Night that comes, saw with eyes
of vision in many planes. She holds high all the splendours.

ओर्वेप्रा अमर्त्या निवतो देव्युद्धतः ।
ज्योतिषा बाधते तमः ॥ २ ॥

2. The goddess immortal, she fills the vast, the high
and the low places. She repels darkness with light.

निरु खसारमस्कृतोषसं देव्यायती ।
अपेदुहासते तमः ॥ ३ ॥

3. The goddess that comes, prepared her sister
Ushas. And the darkness leaves.

सा नो अद्य यस्या वयं नि ते यामन्नविक्ष्महि ।
वृक्षे न वसतिं वयः ॥ ४ ॥

4. She is ours now. May we find refuge in her
movements as a bird its dwelling on the tree.

नि ग्रामासो अविक्षत नि पद्वन्तो नि पक्षिणः ।
नि इयेनासश्चिदर्थिनः ॥ ५ ॥

5. The hosts of men had refuge in her. The footed,

the feathered and the hawks as well seek her intensely.

यावया वृक्यं वृकं यवयस्तेनमूर्ग्ये ।
अथा नः सुतरा भव ॥ ६ ॥

6. Assail the she-wolf. Separate from us the he-wolf[1], and the thief. Then in the billowings ferry us with ease.

उप मा पेपिशत्तमः कृष्णं व्यक्तमस्थित ।
उप ऋणेव यातय ॥ ७ ॥

7. She has come near to me giving clear shapes to the black darkness. O Dawn, absolve me as from debts.

उप ते गा इवाकरं वृणीष्व दुहितर्दिवः ।
रात्रि स्तोमं न जिग्युषे ॥ ८ ॥

8. I have offered to thee like kine. Accept O Night, daughter of Heaven, the laud as for a conqueror.

---

1 The Supreme is infinite. The force that limits it, makes it finite is the Asura's. The *akhaṇḍa* becomes *khaṇḍita*, torn to pieces. This is the act of *vṛka* the tearer the wolf.

THE THREE EPISODES

THE FIRST EPISODE
अथ प्रथमचरित्रम् ॥

प्रथमचरित्रस्य ब्रह्मा ऋषिः । महाकाली देवता । गायत्री
छन्दः । नन्द्रा शक्तिः । रक्तदन्तिका बीजम् । अग्निस्तत्त्वम् । ऋग्वेदः
स्वरूपम ॥

For the first episode Brahma is the seer, Mahakali
the deity and Gayatri the metre. The force is Nanda, the
seed Raktadantika and the principle Fire. The form is Rig
Veda.

श्रीमहाकालीप्रीत्यर्थं धर्मार्थे जपे विनियोगः ॥

The application in Japa is for Dharma, for pleasing
Sri Mahakali.

खड्गं चक्रगदेषुचापपरिघान् शूलं भुशुण्डीं शिरः
शङ्खं सन्दधतीं करैस्त्रिनयनां सर्वाङ्गभूषावृताम् ।
नीलाइमद्युतिमास्यपाददशकां सेवे महाकालिकां
यामस्तौत् स्वपिते हरौ कमलजो हन्तुं मधुं कैटभम् ।

Wielding in her hands the sword, discus, mace,
arrow, bow, iron club, trident, sling, human head and
conch, she has three eyes and ornaments decked on all
her limbs. She shines like a blue stone and has ten faces
and ten feet. That Mahakali I worship whom the lotus-
born Brahma lauded in order to slay Madhu and Kaitabha
when Hari was asleep.

ॐ नमश्चण्डिकायै ।

OM Salutations to Chandika.

ॐ ऐं मार्कण्डेय उवाच ॥ १ ॥

1. OM AIM Markendeya said :

सावर्णिः सूर्यतनयो यो मनुः कथ्यतेऽष्टमः ।
निशामय तदुत्पत्तिं विस्तराद्गदतो मम ॥ २ ॥
महामायानुभावेन यथा मन्वन्तराधिपः ।
स बभूव महाभागः सावर्णिस्तनयो रवेः ॥ ३ ॥

2-3. sāvarṇi, son of Surya, is said to be the eighth Manu[1]. Hear from me about his birth, while I narrate in detail, how Savarni, the offspring of the Sun, highly fortunate, became the head of a Manvantara by the grace of Mahamaya.

स्वारोचिषेऽन्तरे पूर्वं चैत्रवंशसमुद्भवः ।
सुरथो नाम राजाभूत् समस्ते क्षितिमण्डले ॥ ४ ॥

4. Formerly, in the period of Manu Svarochisha, for the whole globe of earth, there was a king by name Suratha, born in the family of Chaitra.

तस्य पालयतः सम्यक् प्रजाः पुत्रानिवौरसान् ।
बभूवुः शत्रवो भूपाः कोलाविध्वंसिनस्तदा ॥ ५ ॥

5. When he was protecting his subjects well as he would his own legitimate sons, the kings who were destroyers of Kolas became his enemies.

---

1 "If we examine the profound legendary tradition of India, we see that its idea of the Manu is more a symbol than anything else. His name means man, the mental being. He is the divine legislator, the mental demi-god in humanity who fixes the lines upon which the race or people has to govern its evolution. In the Purana, he or his sons are said to reign in subtle earths or worlds or, as we may say, they reign in the larger mentality which to us is subconscient and from there have power to determine the lines of development of the conscious life of man" - Sri Aurobindo.

तस्य तैरभवद् युद्धमतिप्रबलदण्डिनः ।
न्यूनैरपि स तैर्युद्धे कोलाविध्वंसिभिर्जितः ॥ ६ ॥

6. There was a battle between him, possessed of very strong forces and them. But he was conquered in battle by the destroyers of Kolas though they were inferior to him.

ततः स्वपुरमायातो निजदेशाधिपोऽभवत् ।
आक्रान्तः स महाभागस्तैस्तदा प्रबलारिभिः ॥ ७ ॥

7. Then, he returned to his city and became the head of his own country. There again that illustrious one was attacked by powerful enemies.

अमात्यैर्बलिभिर्दुष्टै दुर्बलस्य दुरात्मभिः ।
कोशो बलं चापहृतं तत्रापि स्वपुरे ततः ॥ ८ ॥

8. The treasury and army of the weak king were seized by his strong wicked ministers of evil designs, that too in his own city.

ततो मृगयाव्याजेन हृतस्वाम्यः स भूपतिः ।
एकाकी हयमारुह्य जगाम गहनं वनम् ॥ ९ ॥

9. Then the king, deprived of authority, on the pretext of hunting, mounted on a horse and proceeded to the dense forest, all alone.

स तत्राश्रममद्राक्षीद् द्विजवर्यस्य मेधसः ।
प्रशान्तश्वापदाकीर्णं मुनिशिष्योपशोभितम् ॥ १० ॥

10. There he saw the hermitage of Medhas, the supreme among the twice-born, -the place littered with

beasts of prey, tamed of their ferocity and radiant with the disciples of the sage.

तस्थौ कञ्चित् स कालं च मुनिना तेन सत्कृतः ।
इतश्चेतश्च विचरंस्तस्मिन् मुनिवराश्रमे ॥ ११ ॥

11. Receiving the hospitality of the sage, he remained there for some time, moving about hither and thither in the hermitage of the great sage.

सोऽचिन्तयत् तदा तत्र ममत्वाकृष्टमानसः ॥ १२ ॥

12. At that time he fell into the thought, his mind gravitating towards the sense of 'my'ness.

मत्पूर्वैः पालितं पूर्वं मया हीनं पुरं हि तत् ।
मद्भृत्यैस्तैरसद्वृत्तैर्धर्मतः पाल्यते न वा ॥ १३ ॥

13. "Ah, I have deserted the city formerly gaurded by my forefathers. Is it being gaurded righteously or not by my bearers of evil conduct?

न जाने स प्रधानो मे शूरो हस्ती सदामदः ।
मम वैरिवशं यातः कान् भोगानुपलप्स्यते ॥ १४ ॥

14. "I do not know. My chief elephant, valorous and always in rut, has fallen in the hands of my enemies. What experiences is it going to get?

ये ममानुगता नित्यं प्रसादधनभोजनैः ।
अनुवृत्तिं ध्रुवं तेऽद्य कुर्वन्त्यन्यमहीभृताम् ॥ १५ ॥

15. "Those who were my constant followers for the sake of my favour, money and food are now surely rendering service to other monarchs.

असम्यग्व्ययशीलैस्तैः कुर्वेद्भिः सततं व्ययम् ।
सञ्चितः सोऽतिदुःखेन क्षयं कोशो गमिष्यति ॥ १६ ॥

16. "The treasury, accumulated with great difficulty, will be depleted, with these spend-thrifts spending ceaselessly."

एतच्चान्यच्च सततं चिन्तयामास पार्थिवः ।
तत्र विप्राश्रमाभ्याशे वैश्यमेकं ददर्श सः ॥ १७ ॥

17. The lord of the earth was constantly thinking of these and other things. There, in the vicinity of the Brahman's hermitage, he saw a Vaishya.

स पृष्टस्तेन कस्त्वं भो हेतुश्चागमनेऽत्र कः ।
सशोक इव कस्मात्त्वं दुर्मना इव लक्ष्यसे ॥ १८ ॥

18. He asked him : "Who are you, Sir ? What is the reason of your coming here ? Why do you appear to be sad and ill at ease ?"

इत्याकर्ण्य वचस्तस्य भूपतेः प्रणयोदितम् ।
प्रत्युवाच स तं वैश्यः प्रश्रयावनतो नृपम् ॥ १९ ॥

19. Hearing the words of the king uttered with consideration, the Vaishya bowed in courtesy to the king and replied.

वैश्य उवाच ॥ २० ॥

20. Vaishya said :

समाधिर्नाम वैश्योऽहमुत्पन्नो धनिनां कुले ।
पुत्रदारैर्निरस्तश्च धनलोभादसाधुभिः ॥ २१ ॥

132

21. "I am a Vaishya named Samadhi, born in a family of monied men; and now cast away by unworthy sons and wife, out of greed for my wealth."

विह्लीनश्च धनैर्दारैः पुत्रैरादाय मे धनम् ।
वनमभ्यागतो दुःखी निरस्तश्चाप्तबन्धुभिः ॥ २२ ॥

22. "My sons and my wife took from me all the money and made me devoid of wealth; I have come to the forest in sorrow abandoned by my trusted kinsmen."

सोऽहं न वेद्मि पुत्राणां कुशलाकुशलात्मिकाम् ।
प्रवृत्ति स्वजनानां च दाराणां चात्र संस्थितः ॥ २३ ॥

23. "Stationed here I do not know the state of affairs, good or bad, of my sons, wife and kinsmen."

किं नु तेषां गृहे क्षेममक्षेमं किं नु साम्प्रतम् ॥ २४ ॥

24. "At the present moment, are things well or not well with them at home?"

कथं ते किं नु सद्वृत्ता दुर्वृत्ताः किं नु मे सुताः ॥ २५ ॥

25. "How are they, my sons? Are they of good conduct or of evil ways?"

राजोवाच ॥ २६ ॥

26. The king said:

यैर्निरस्तो भवाँल्लुब्धैः पुत्रदारादिभिर्धनैः ॥ २७ ॥
तेषु किं भवतः स्नेहमनुबध्नाति मानसम् ॥ २८ ॥

27-28. "Why is your mind bound in endearment to that crowd, the covetous sons and wife who deprived you of your wealth?"

वैश्य उवाच ॥ २९ ॥

29. The Vaishya said :

एवमेतद् यथा प्राह भवानसद्गतं वचः ।
किं करोमि न बध्नाति मम निष्ठुरतां मनः ॥ ३० ॥

30. "The same thought struck me exactly as you have uttered; but what can I do? My mind does not entertain harshness.

यैः सन्त्यज्य पितृस्नेहं धनलुब्धैर्निराकृतः ।
पतिस्वजनहार्दं च हार्दि तेष्वेव मे मनः ॥ ३१ ॥

31. "Throwing away filial attachment and affection towards one's husband and one's kinsmen, they spurned me out of greed for my wealth; but yet my mind goes to them in affection."

किमेतन्नाभिजानामि जानन्नपि महामते ।
यत् प्रेमप्रवणं चित्तं विगुणेष्वपि बन्धुषु ॥ ३२ ॥

32. "O great-minded king! though knowing, I do not understand how it is that the mind is prone to love even towards worthless relations."

तेषां कृते मे निःश्वासो दौर्मनस्यं च जायते ॥ ३३ ॥

33. "For their sake comes forth my sigh and dejection in my mind."

करोमि किं यन्न मनस्तेष्वप्रीतिषु निष्ठुरम् ॥ ३४ ॥

34. "What can I do as my mind does not become harsh towards those unloving ones?"

मार्कण्डेय उवाच ॥ ३५ ॥

35. Markendeya said :

ततस्तौ सहितौ विप्र तं मुनिं समुपस्थितौ ॥ ३६ ॥

समाधिर्नाम वैश्योऽसौ स च पार्थिवसत्तमः ॥ ३७ ॥

36-37. O Brahman, they then jointly approached the sage-the Vaishya named Samadhi and that noble monarch.

कृत्वा तु तौ यथान्यायं यथार्हं तेन संविदम् ।
उपविष्टौ कथाः काश्चिच्चक्रतुर्वैश्यपार्थिवौ ॥ ३८ ॥

38. The Vaishya and the king, observing due and proper etiquette towards him, seated themselves and conversed on some topics.

राजोवाच ॥ ३९ ॥

39. The king said :

भगवंस्त्वामहं प्रष्टुमिच्छाम्येकं वदस्व तत् ॥ ४० ॥

40. "Sire, I wish to ask you something. Pray, reply to it."

दुःखाय यन्मे मनसः स्वचित्तायत्ततां विना ॥ ४१ ॥

41. "Without any dependece on my thoughts, my mind gives itself to grief."

ममत्वं गतराज्यस्य राज्याङ्गेष्वखिलेष्वपि ।
जानतोऽपि यथाऽज्ञस्य किमेतन्मुनिसत्तम ॥ ४२ ॥

42. "I have lost my kingdom; but yet this sense of 'mine' in all the limbs of the government! What is this that happens to me, though knowing as though to an ignorant man, O Sage Supreme!"

अयं च निकृतः पुत्रैदरिैिभृत्यैस्तथोज्झितः ।
खजनेन च सन्त्यक्तस्तेषु हार्दीं तथाप्यति ॥ ४३ ॥

43. "And this one is spurned by his sons and wife, abandoned by his bearers and forsaken by his own people; even then, he is very much affectionate towards them."

एवमेष तथाहं च द्वावप्यत्यन्तदुःखितौ ।
दृष्टदोषेऽपि विषये ममत्वाकृष्टमानसौ ॥ ४४ ॥

44. "Thus, he and I, though we perceive the defects in a thing, are still attracted in mind towards it by the sense of "my"-ness and hence we both are exceedingly unhappy."

तत् किमेतन्महाभाग यन्मोहो ज्ञानिनोरपि ।
ममास्य च भवत्येषा विवेकान्धस्य मूढता ॥ ४५ ॥

45. "O illustrious one! How is it that even to the knowledgeable, the delusion comes? This ignorance has fallen on him and me, blind to the sense of discrimination."

ऋषिरुवाच ॥ ४६ ॥

46. The Sage said :

ज्ञानमस्ति समस्तस्य जन्तोर्विषयगोचरे ।
विषयाश्च महाभाग यान्ति चैवं पृथक् पृथक् ॥ ४७ ॥

47. O illustrious one! There is a knowledge amongst all beings appertaining to their senses; and these senses operate in distinct fields.

दिवान्धाः प्राणिनः केचिद्रात्रावन्धास्तथाऽपरे ।
केचिद्दिवा तथा रात्रौ प्राणिनस्तुल्यदृष्टयः ॥ ४८ ॥

48. Some beings are blind by day, some blind by night : and some beings have equal vision by day as well as by night.

ज्ञानिनो मनुजाः सत्यं किन्नु ते न हि केवलम् ।
यतो हि ज्ञानिनः सर्वं पशुपक्षिमृगादयः ॥ ४९ ॥

49. It is true that men have knowledge; but are they the only ones? Birds, cattle and other animals—all have knowledge.

ज्ञानं च तन्मनुष्याणां यत्तेषां मृगपक्षिणाम् ।
मनुष्याणां च यत्तेषां तुल्यमन्यत् तथोभयोः ॥ ५० ॥

50. The knowledge that beasts and birds have, men also have; and what the men have, they too have; it is same for both.

ज्ञानेऽपि सति पश्यैतान् पतङ्गाञ्छावचञ्चुषु ।
क्षणमोक्षाट्टतान् मोहात्पीड्यमानानपि क्षुधा ॥ ५१ ॥

51. Look at these birds. They have the knowledge that they are afflicted by hunger; yet by delusion they go on feeding grains into the beaks of their young ones.

मानुषा मनुजव्याघ्र साभिलाषाः सुतान् प्रति ।
लोभात् प्रत्युपकाराय नन्वेतान् किं न पश्यसि ॥ ५२ ॥

52. O Valorous among men! Men love their children coveting for a return. Do you not perceive this from these birds ?

तथापि ममतावर्तं मोहगर्तं निपातिताः ।
महामायाप्रभावेण संसारस्थितिकारिणा ॥ ५३ ॥

53. Even so, men are hurled into the whirlpool of "my"ness, into the hollow of delusion by the power of

Mahamaya who institutes the continuance of the world.

तस्मात विस्मयः कार्यो योगनिद्रा जगत्पतेः ।
महामाया हरेश्चेया तया सम्मोह्यते जगत् ॥ ५४ ॥

54. You need not be surprised. This Mahamaya is
Yoganidra[1] (Superconscious sleep)[1] of Hari, the Lord of
the world. The world is deluded by her.

ज्ञानिनामपि चेतांसि देवी भगवती हि सा ।
बलादाकृष्य मोहाय महामाया प्रयच्छति ॥ ५५ ॥

55. She, the Goddess, the Divine Mahamaya draws
by force the minds of even the knowing ones and yea,
makes them over to delusion.

तया विसृज्यते विश्वं जगदेतच्चराचरम् ।
सैया प्रसन्ना वरदा नृणां भवति मुक्तये ॥ ५६ ॥

56. This revolving universe, containing all that is
mobile and immobile, is cast out from her. She, gracious,
grants the best and shows the way for men's release.

सा विद्या परमा मुक्तेर्हेतुभूता सनातनी ॥ ५७ ॥

57. She is the supreme knowledge, the Eternal, the
cause for liberation.

संसारबन्धहेतुश्च सैव सर्वेश्वरेश्वरी ॥ ५८ ॥

58. The Goddess of all the gods, she too is the cause
for bondage in *samasara*[2]

---

1. Ordinary sleep is largely subconscious. In yoga-nidra there is a
self-gathering luminous poise of super conscience.

2. Continuous movement (s to move); cycle of births and deaths.

138

राजोवाच ॥ ५९ ॥

59. The king said :

भगवन् का हि सा देवी महामायेति यां भवान् ।
ब्रवीति कथमुत्पन्ना सा कर्मास्याश्च किं द्विज ॥ ६० ॥

60. "Sire, who is that Goddess whom you speak
of as Mahamaya ? How is she born ? O, twice-born, what
is her work?"

यत्प्रभावा च सा देवी यत्स्वरूपा यदुद्भवा ॥ ६१ ॥

61. "What power has she, what form, what source,
the Goddess?"

तत्सर्वं श्रोतुमिच्छामि त्वत्तो ब्रह्मविदां वर ॥ ६२ ॥

62. "Eminent amongst knowers of Brahman! I
desire to hear all this from you."

ऋषिरुवाच ॥ ६३ ॥

63. The Sage said :

नित्यैव सा जगन्मूर्तिस्तया सर्वमिदं ततम् ॥ ६४ ॥

64. She is eternal ; the world is her embodiment;
all this is pervaded by her.

तथापि तत्समुत्पत्तिर्बहुधा श्रूयतां मम ॥ ६५ ॥

65. Even so, her birth is in many ways. Hear from
me.

देवानां कार्यसिद्ध्यर्थमाविर्भवति सा यदा ।
उत्पन्नेति तदा लोके सा नित्याप्यभिधीयते ॥ ६६ ॥

66. Whenever She manifests herself for the accomplishment of Divine purpose, she, though eternal, is said
to be born in the world.

योगनिद्रां यदा विष्णुर्जगत्येकार्णवीकृते ।
आस्तीर्य शेषमभजत् कल्पान्ते भगवान् प्रभुः ॥ ६७ ॥

67. At the end of a Kalpa[1] when the world was made
into one vast stretch of ocean, the mighty Lord spread
his couch of Sesha and sank into a super-conscious sleep.

तदा द्वावसुरौ घोरौ विख्यातौ मधुकैटभौ ।
विष्णुकर्णमलोद्भूतौ हन्तुं ब्रह्माणमुद्यतौ ॥ ६८ ॥

68. Then two terrible Asuras, the famed Madhu and
Kaitabha, came into being out of the ear-wax of Vishnu
and sought to kill Brahma.

स नाभिकमले विष्णोः स्थितो ब्रह्मा प्रजापतिः ।
दृष्ट्वा तावसुरौ चोग्रौ प्रसुप्तं च जनार्दनम् ॥ ६९ ॥

तुष्टाव योगनिद्रां तामेकाग्रहृदयः स्थितः ।
विबोधनार्थाय हरेर्हरिनेत्रकृतालयाम् ॥ ७० ॥

69-70. Brahma, the lord of beings was stationed in
the navel-lotus of Vishnu. Perceiving those fierce Asuras
and Vishnu sleeping, in order to awaken Hari, he praised
Yoganidra , abiding in the eyes of Hari, with concentration in the heart.

---

1 *kalpa* is the *sankalpa* , resolution of the Lord to create and
denotes a perlod of time during which the resolution is operative. The
kalpa comes to an end with dissolution, *pralaya* , and then there is a fresh
resolution to create. The successive resolutions and dissolutions are
denoted by the terms *kalpa* and *pralaya* . The ocean is the image of
infinite and eternal existence. At the time of *pralaya* all finite things
disappear, only the Infinite remains. Vishnu, the all-pervading Deity,
rests on his serpent *ananta* , the Infinite, on *sesa* , the remnant.

विश्वेश्वरीं जगद्धात्रीं स्थितिसंहारकारिणीम् ।
निद्रां भगवतीं विष्णोरतुलां तेजसः प्रभुः ॥ ७१ ॥

71. The Lord of Light (extolled) the Sovereign of
the Universe, the upholder and sustainer of the worlds,
the cause of preservation as well as destruction, the
unparalleled Sleep Divine of Vishnu.

ब्रह्मोवाच ॥ ७२ ॥

72. Brahma said :

त्वं स्वाहा त्वं स्वधा त्वं हि वषट्कारः स्वरात्मिका ।
सुधा त्वमक्षरे नित्ये त्रिधामात्रात्मिका स्थिता ॥ ७३ ॥

73. Thou art *svāhā*. Thou art *svadhā*. Thou, yea,
the word of Vashat;[1] the soul of sound. Thou art well-
borne. In the eternal immutable Omkara, thou standest
in the form of the three fold *mātrā*[2].

अर्धमात्रा स्थिता नित्या यानुच्चार्या विशेषतः ।
त्वमेव सन्ध्या सावित्री त्वं देवि जननी परा ॥ ७४ ॥

74. Thou standest as half the *mātrā*. The eternal,
thou art that which cannot be specifically uttered. Thou
only art the *sandhyā*, thou art Savitri. Goddess! thou art
Mother Supreme.

त्वयैतद्धार्यते विश्वं त्वयैतत् सृज्यते जगत् ।
त्वयैतत् पाल्यते देवि त्वमत्स्यन्ते च सर्वदा ॥ ७५ ॥

75. The universe is held and sustained by thee. This
world is created by thee, Goddess! This is protected by
thee. Finally, thou consumest this always.

---

1 *svāhā* is the mantra of offering to the Devas while *svadhā* is the
mantra of offering to the pitris. *vaṣaṭ* is used in *yajna*, Sacrifice.

2 A,U,M of *omkara*.

विसृष्टौ सृष्टिरूपा त्वं स्थितिरूपा च पालने ।
तथा संहतिरूपाऽन्ते जगतोऽस्य जगन्मये ॥ ७६ ॥

76. O thou who hast become the world! When casting out, thou takest the form of creation; when protecting, the form of preservation. Similarly at the termination of the world thou takest the form of destruction.

महाविद्या महामाया महामेधा महास्मृतिः ।
महामोहा च भवती महादेवी महेश्वरी ॥ ७७ ॥

77. Great knowledge, great illusion, great intellect, great remembrance, great delusion, thou art great goddess, great sovereign.

प्रकृतिस्त्वं च सर्वस्य गुणत्रयविभाविनी ।
कालरात्रिर्महारात्रिर्मोहरात्रिश्च दारुणा ॥ ७८ ॥

78. Thou art the Prakriti (nature) of everything manifesting the three Gunas. Thou, the dark night the great night, the terrible night of delusion.

त्वं श्रीस्त्वमीश्वरी त्वं ह्रीः त्वं बुद्धिर्बोधलक्षणा ।
लज्जा पुष्टिस्तथा तुष्टिस्त्वं शान्तिः क्षान्तिरेव च ॥ ७९ ॥

79. Thou art beauty, sovereignty ; thou art modesty, intellect the sign of knowledge. Bashfulness, nourishment, contentment art Thou, also tranquillity and forbearance.

खड्गिनी शूलिनी घोरा गदिनी चक्रिणी तथा ।
शङ्खिनी चापिनी बाणभुशुण्डीपरिघायुधा ॥ ८० ॥

80. Thou hast the sword, thou hast the spear : Terrible, thou hast the mace and the discus. Thou hast the conch, the bow, the arrows, the sling and the iron club.

सौम्या सौम्यतराशेषसौम्येभ्यस्त्वतिसुन्दरी ।
परापराणां परमा त्वमेव परमेश्वरी ॥ ८१ ॥

81. Thou art pleasing; more pleasing than all the pleasing things; thou art exceedingly beautiful. The lofty one beyond the superior and inferior, thou alone art the Supreme Sovereign.

यच्च किञ्चित्कचिद्वस्तु सदसद्वाऽखिलात्मिके ।
तस्य सर्वस्य या शक्तिः सा त्वं किं स्तूयसे मया ॥ ८२ ॥

82. O Soul of all! Whatever may be a thing, existent or non-existent, the power, *sakti*, in all those things is thyself. How can I praise thee?

यया त्वया जगत्स्रष्टा जगत्पाल्यत्ति यो जगत् ।
सोपि निद्रावशं नीतः कस्त्वां स्तोतुमिहेश्वरः ॥ ८३ ॥

83. By thee has been put to sleep the one who creates the world, preserves the world and consumes the world. So, who here has the capacity to extol thee ?

विष्णुः शरीरग्रहणमहमीशान एव च ।
कारितास्ते यतोऽतस्त्वां कः स्तोतुं शक्तिमान् भवेत् ॥ ८४ ॥

84. By thee, Vishnu, myself and Ishvara have been made to take an embodied form. Therefore, who has the power to praise thee ?

सा त्वमित्थं प्रभावैः स्वैरुदारैर्देवि संस्तुता ।
मोहयैतौ दुराधर्षावसुरौ मधुकैटभौ ॥ ८५ ॥

85. O Devi, lauded thus by thine own eloquent powers, delude these two unassailable Asuras, Madhu and Kaitabha.

प्रबोधं च जगत्स्वामी नीयतामच्युतो लघु ॥ ८६ ॥

86. Let Achyuta, the master of the world, be speedily brought to the waking state.

बोधश्च क्रियतामस्य हन्तुमेतौ महासुरौ ॥ ८७ ॥

87. Make him wise for slaying these great Asuras.

ऋषिरुवाच ॥ ८८ ॥

88. The Sage said :

एवं स्तुता तदा देवी तामसी तत्र वेधसा ।
विष्णोः प्रबोधनार्थाय निहन्तुं मधुकैटभौ ॥ ८९ ॥

नेत्रास्यनासिकाबाहुहृदयेभ्यस्तथोरसः ।
निर्गम्य दर्शने तस्थौ ब्रह्मणोऽव्यक्तजन्मनः ॥ ९० ॥

89-90. Thus lauded by Brahma in order to awaken Vishnu for killing Madhu and Kaitabha, the Goddess of inertia emerged out of (Vishnu's) eyes, mouth, nose, arms, heart and chest and came to the vision of Brahma, who takes birth from the Unmanifest.

उत्तस्थौ च जगन्नाथस्तया मुक्तो जनार्दनः ।
एकार्णवेऽहिशयनात्ततः स ददृशे च तौ ॥ ९१ ॥

91. Released by her, Vishnu, the lord of the world, got up from his bed of snake on the Absolute Ocean. There he saw them.

मधुकैटभौ दुरात्मानावतिवीर्यपराक्रमौ ।
क्रोधरक्तेक्षणावन्तुं ब्रह्माणं जनितोद्यमौ ॥ ९२ ॥

92. Madhu and Kaitabha, the wicked ones of exceeding valour and prowess, red in the eyes with anger, endeavouring to eat up Brahma.

समुत्थाय ततस्ताभ्यां युयुधे भगवान् हरिः ।
पञ्चवर्षसहस्राणि बाहुप्रहरणो विभुः ॥ ९३ ॥

93. Rising up, the Lord Hari fought with them for five thousand years with his bare arms as weapon.

तावप्यतिबलोन्मत्तौ महामायाविमोहितौ ॥ ९४ ॥
उक्तवन्तौ वरोऽस्मत्तो व्रियतामिति केशवम् ॥ ९५ ॥

94-95. Intoxicated with their excessive power, deluded by Mahamaya, they told Vishnu "Choose a boon from us."

श्रीभगवानुवाच ॥ ९६ ॥

96. The Lord said :

भवेतामद्य मे तुष्टौ मम वध्यावुभावपि ॥ ९७ ॥
किमन्येन वरेणात्र एतावद्धि वृतं मया ॥ ९८ ॥

97-98. May you two be slain by me, if you are pleased with me. What other boon is there to ask? This much have I chosen.

ऋषिरुवाच ॥ ९९ ॥

99. The Sage said :

वञ्चिताभ्यामिति तदा सर्वमापोमयं जगत् ।
विलोक्य ताभ्यां गदितो भगवान् कमलेक्षणः ॥ १०० ॥

100. Deceived thus, those two, seeing the whole world full of water, said to the lotus-eyed Lord.

आवां जहि न यत्रोर्वीं सलिलेन परिप्लुता ॥ १०१ ॥

101. Kill us where the earth is not inundated with water.

ऋषिरुवाच ॥ १०२ ॥

102. The Sage said :

तथेत्युक्त्वा भगवता शङ्खचक्रगदाभृता ।
कृत्वा चक्रेण वै छिन्ने जघने शिरसी तयोः ॥ १०३ ॥

103. "So be it" said the Lord, the wielder of the conch, the discus and the mace. Taking them on his loins, he severed their heads with his discus.

एवमेषा समुत्पन्ना ब्रह्मणा संस्तुता स्वयम् ।
प्रभावमस्या देव्यास्तु भूयः श्रृणु वदामि ते ॥ १०४ ॥

104. Thus lauded by Brahma, she was born of her own accord. Listen, I shall tell you more of the glory of the Goddess.

ऐं ओं श्रीमार्कण्डेयपुराणे सावर्णिके मन्वन्तरे देवीमाहात्म्ये प्रथमः ॥ १ ॥

AIM.OM. Here ends the first of Devi Mahatmya in Markandeya Purana during the period of *sāvarṇi*, the Manu.

THE SECOND EPISODE

अथ मध्यमचरित्रम् ॥

मध्यमचरितस्य विष्णुऋषिः । महालक्ष्मीः देवता । उष्णिक्
छन्दः । शाकंभरी शक्तिः । दुर्गा बीजम् । वायुस्तत्त्वम् ।
यजुर्वेदः स्वरूपम् ॥

For the middle episode Vishnu is the seer, Mahalakshmi the deity and Ushnik the metre. The force is Sakambhari, the seed Durga and the principle wind. The form is Yajur Veda.

श्रीमहालक्ष्मीप्रीत्यर्थे अर्थिर्थे जपे विनियोगः ॥

The application in Japa, is for Artha, for pleasing Sri Mahalakshmi.

अक्षस्रकपरशू गदेषुकुलिशं पद्मं धनुः कुण्डिकां
दण्डं शक्तिमसिं च चर्म जलजं घण्टां सुराभाजनम् ।
शूलं पाशसुदर्शने च दधतीं हस्तैः प्रवालप्रभां
सेवे सैरिभमर्दिनीमिह महालक्ष्मीं सरोजस्थिताम् ॥

Wielding in her hands the string of beads, battle axe, mace, arrow, thunderbolt, lotus, bow, water-pot, cudgel, lance, sword, shield, conch, bell, wine-cup, trident, noose and the discus *sudarsana* , she has a complextion of coral and is seated on a lotus. I worship here that Mahalakshmi, the vanquisher of the asura, Mahisha.

148

ॐ ह्रीं ऋषिरुवाच ॥ १ ॥

1. OM HRIM, the Sage said :

देवासुरमभूद् युद्धं पूर्णमब्दशतं पुरा ।
महिषेऽसुरगणामधिपे देवानां च पुरन्दरे ॥ २ ॥

2. Long ago, when Mahisha was the lord of the Asuras and Indra, of the gods, there was a war between the gods and the Asuras for a full hundred years.

तत्रासुरैर्महावीर्यं देवसैन्यं पराजितम् ।
जित्वा च सकलान् देवानिन्द्रोऽभून्महिषासुरः ॥ ३ ॥

3. In that, the army of the gods was vanquished by Asuras of great valour. Having conquered all the gods, Mahishasura became Indra.[1]

ततः पराजिता देवाः पद्मयोनिं प्रजापतिम् ।
पुरस्कृत्य गतास्तत्र यत्रेशगरुडध्वजौ ॥ ४ ॥

4. Then, the vanquished gods led by Brahma, the lotus-born, the lord of beings went to the place where were Shiva and the Garuda-bannered God.

यथावृत्तं तयोस्तद्वन्महिषासुरचेष्टितम् ।
त्रिदशाः कथयामासु देवाभिभवविस्तरम् ॥ ५ ॥

5. The gods narrated to both of them the activities of Mahishasura and the details of insults heaped upon the gods, just as they happened:

सूर्येन्द्राग्न्यनिलेन्दूनां यमस्य वरुणस्य च ।
अन्येषां चाधिकारान् सः स्वयमेवाधितिष्ठति ॥ ६ ॥

---

1 It is a post conferring lordship over the Gods. A person who has performed a hundred horse-sacrifices is eligible for Indrahood.

6. "He himself now wields the authority of the sun, Indra, the fire, the wind, the moon, Yama, Varuna and of other gods.

स्वर्गान्निराकृताः सर्वे तेन देवगणा भुवि ।
विचरन्ति यथा मर्त्या महिषेण दुरात्मना ॥ ७ ॥

7. The entire hosts of gods, expelled by the wicked Mahisha from Heaven wander across the earth as mortals do.

एतद्वः कथितं सर्वममरारिविचेष्टितम् ।
शरणं च प्रपन्नाः स्मो वधस्तस्य विचिन्त्यताम् ॥ ८ ॥

8. We have narrated in full the deeds of the enemy of gods. We seek refuge in you. Pray think about slaying him.

इत्थं निशम्य देवानां वचांसि मधुसूदनः ।
चकार कोपं शम्भुश्च भ्रुकुटीकुटिलाननौ ॥ ९ ॥

9. Thus, having heard the words of the gods, the slayer of Madhu got angry and so also Shiva, their faces frowning with knit eye-brows.

ततोऽति कोपपूर्णस्य चक्रिणो वदनात्ततः ।
निश्चक्राम महत्तेजो ब्रह्मणः शङ्करस्य च ॥ १० ॥

10. Then, from the face of the wielder of discus, which was brimming with fury and from the faces of Brahma and Shankara, a great effulgence emerged.

अन्येषां चैव देवानां शक्रादीनां शरीरतः ।
निर्गतं सुमहत्तेजः तच्चैक्यं समगच्छत ॥ ११ ॥

11. From the bodies of other gods like Indra, a great effulgence emerged as well and it all became a united mass.

अतीव तेजसः कूटं ज्वलन्तमिव पर्वतम् ।
ददृशुस्ते सुरास्तत्र ज्वालाव्याप्तदिगन्तरम् ॥ १२ ॥

12. The gods saw there a lofty peak of effulgence looking like a blazing volcano, pervading the quarters with its flames.

अतुलं तत्र तत्तेजः सर्वदेवशरीरजम् ।
एकस्थं तदभून्नारी व्याप्तलोकत्रयं त्विषा ॥ १३ ॥

13. Born out of the bodies of all the gods, that unique effulgence, combined into one mass of light, took the form of a woman, pervading the triple worlds with its lustre.

यदभूच्छाम्भवं तेजः तेनाजायत तन्मुखम् ।
याम्येन चाभवन् केशा बाहवो विष्णुतेजसा ॥ १४ ॥

14. In that effulgence, what was the light of Shiva from that was formed the face. The tresses were formed from the light of Yama and the arms from the light of Vishnu.

सौम्येन स्तनयोर्युग्मं मध्यं चैन्द्रेण चाभवत् ।
वारुणेन च जङ्घोरू नितम्बस्तेजसा भुवः ॥ १५ ॥

15. The two breasts were formed from the light of the moon, the middle portion from the light of Indra, the legs and thighs from the light of Varuna and the hips from the light of the earth.

ब्रह्मणस्तेजसा पादौ तदङ्गुल्योऽर्कतेजसा ।
वसूनां च कराङ्गुल्यः कौबेरेण च नासिका ॥ १६ ॥

16. The feet from the light of Brahma and its fingers from the sun's light. The fingers of the hand from that of the Vasus and the nose from the light of Kubera.

तस्यास्तु दन्ताः सम्भूताः प्राजापत्येन तेजसा ।
नयनत्रितयं जज्ञे तथा पावकतेजसा ॥ १७ ॥

17. Her teeth were formed from the light of Prajapati,
the lord of beings; likewise, the triad of her eyes was born
from the light of fire.

भ्रुवौ च सन्ध्ययोस्तेजः श्रवणावनिलस्य च ।
अन्येषां चैव देवानां सम्भवस्तेजसां शिवा ॥ १८ ॥

18. The eyebrows from the two Sandhyas; her ears
from the light of the wind. From the light of other gods as
well, the auspicious Goddess was formed.

ततः समस्तदेवानां तेजोराशिसमुद्भवाम् ।
तां विलोक्य मुदं प्रापुरमरा महिषार्दिताः ॥ १९ ॥

19. Then, on seeing her born out of the lights heaped
up from all the gods, the immortals, afflicted by Mahisha,
became happy.

ततो देवा ददुस्तस्यै स्वानि स्वान्यायुधानि च ।
शूलं शूलाद्विनिष्कृष्य ददौ तस्यै पिनाकधृक् ॥ २० ॥

20. Then the gods gave individually to her their
respective weapons. The wielder of *pinaka* gave to her the
trident drawing it out of his trident.

चक्रं च दत्तवान् कृष्णः समुत्पाट्य स्वचक्रतः ।
शङ्खं च वरुणः शक्तिं ददौ तस्यै हुताशनः ॥ २१ ॥

21. The dark God also gave the discus, whirling it
forth from his own discus. Varuna gave her the conch,
Agni the lance.

मारुतो दत्तवांश्चापं बाणपूर्णे तथेषुधी ।

वज्रमिन्द्रः समुत्पाह्य कुलिशादमराधिपः ॥ २२ ॥

ददौ तस्यै सहस्राक्षो घण्टां ऐरावताद् गजात् ।

कालदण्डाद्यमो दण्डं पाशं चाम्बुपतिर्ददौ ॥ २३ ॥

22-23. Vayu gave her a bow and a pair of quivers filled with arrows. Indra, the thousand-eyed, lord of the gods, gave her the thunderbolt, taking it out of his thunderbolt and the bell from his elephant *airāvata* . Yama gave a cudgel out of his cudgel of death and the lord of waters the noose.

प्रजापतिश्चाक्षमालां ददौ ब्रह्मा कमण्डलुम् ।

समस्तरोमकूपेषु निजरश्मीन् दिवाकरः ॥ २४ ॥

24. Brahma, the lord of beings, gave her the rosary of beads and the water-pot. Surya placed his own rays on all the pores of her skin.

कालश्च दत्तवान् खड्गं तस्यै चर्मे च निर्मलम् ।

क्षीरोदश्चामलं हारमजरे च तथाम्बरे ॥ २५ ॥

चूडामणिं तथा दिव्यं कुण्डले कटकानि च ।

अर्धचन्द्रं तथा शुभ्रं केयूरान् सर्वेबाहुषु ॥ २६ ॥

नूपुरौ विमलौ तद्वद् ग्रैवेयकमनुत्तमम् ।

अङ्गुलीयकरत्नानि समस्तास्वङ्गुलीषु च ॥ २७ ॥

25-27. Kala gave her a sword and a spotless shield. The milky ocean gave her an unsullied garland, a pair of unaging garments, a brilliant crest-jewel, a pair of ear-pendants, bangles, a luminous half-moon ornament, bracelets in all arms, a pair of shining anklets, likewise a unique necklace and bejewelled rings on all the fingers.

विश्वकर्मा ददौ तस्यै परशुं चातिनिर्मलम् ।
अस्त्राण्यनेकरूपाणि तथाऽभेद्यं च दंशनम् ॥ २८ ॥

28. Vishwakarma gave her a brilliant axe, missiles of various forms as well as an unbreakable armour.

अम्लानपङ्कजां मालां शिरस्युरसि चापराम् ।
अददद्उज्जलधिस्तस्यै पङ्कजं चातिशोभनम् ॥ २९ ॥

29. The ocean gave her an unfading lotus-garland to wear on the head, another one to wear on the breast and a very beautiful lotus to be held in her hand.

हिमवान् वाहनं सिंहं रत्नानि विविधानि च ।
ददावशून्यं सुरया पानपात्रं धनाधिपः ॥ ३० ॥

30. Himavan gave her the lion as the vehicle and various gems. The lord of wealth gave her a drinking cup always full of wine.

शेषश्च सर्वनागेशो महामणिविभूषितम् ।
नागहारं ददौ तस्यै धत्ते यः पृथिवीमिमाम् ॥ ३१ ॥

31. The king of all serpents, Shesha, who bears this world, gave her a snake garland bedecked with huge jewels.

अन्यैरपि सुरैर्देवी भूषणैरायुधैस्तथा ।
सम्मानिता ननादोच्चैः साट्टहासं मुहुर्मुहुः ॥ ३२ ॥

32. Honoured with ornaments and weapons by the other remaining gods as well, the Goddess roared with loud laughter again and again.

तस्या नादेन घोरेण कृत्स्नमापूरितं नभः ।
अमायतातिमहता प्रतिशब्दो महानभूत् ॥ ३३ ॥

33. The entire sky was filled up with her immeasurable stupendous terrible roar and great was the echo that arose.

चुक्षुभुः सकला लोकाः समुद्राश्च चकम्पिरे ।
चचाल वसुधा चेलुः सकलाश्च महीधराः ॥ ३४ ॥

34. All the worlds were agitated and the oceans raged. The earth quaked and all the mountains rocked.

जयेति देवाश्च मुदा तामूचुः सिंहवाहिनीम् ।
तुष्टुवुर्मुनयश्चैनां भक्तिनम्रात्ममूर्तयः ॥ ३५ ॥

35. 'Victory to thee' exclaimed the Gods in joy to her, mounted on the lion. And the sages lauded her, their bodies bowed in devotion.

दृष्ट्वा समस्तं संक्षुब्धं त्रैलोक्यममरारयः ।
सन्नद्धाखिलसैन्यास्ते समुत्तस्थुरुदायुधाः ॥ ३६ ॥

36. Seeing the entire triple world agitated, the enemies of the immortals marshalled all their forces and rose up with weapons uplifted.

आः किमेतदिति क्रोधादाभाष्य महिषासुरः ।
अभ्यधावत तं शब्दमशेषैरसुरैर्वृतः ॥ ३७ ॥

37. "Ah, what is this!" exclaimed Mahishasura in wrath and rushed towards that sound, surrounded by all the Asuras.

स ददर्श ततो देवीं व्याप्तलोकत्रयां त्विषा ।
पादाक्रान्त्या नतभुवं किरीटोल्लिखिताम्बराम् ॥ ३८ ॥
क्षोभिताशेषपातालां धनुर्ज्यानिःस्वनेन ताम् ।
दिशो भुजसहस्रेण समन्ताद् व्याप्य संस्थिताम् ॥ ३९ ॥

38-39. Then, he saw the Goddess pervading the three worlds with her effulgence. The tread of her feet bent the earth low, the top of her crown scraped the welkin high. With the twang of her bow-string, she shook the entire nether-world and with a thousand arms, she stood covering all the quarters.

ततः प्रववृते युद्धं तथा देव्या सुरद्विषाम् ।
शस्त्रास्त्रैर्बहुधा मुक्तैरादीपितदिगन्तरम् ॥ ४० ॥

40. Then began the battle between the Goddess and the enemies of gods, where the quarters were illumined by various arrows and missiles thrown at each other.

महिषासुरसेनानीश्चिक्षुराख्यो महासुरः ।
युयुधे चामरश्चान्यैश्चतुरङ्गबलान्वितः ॥ ४१ ॥

41. The general of Mahishasura, a great Asura Chikshura, by name, and Chamara fought with the opponents, equipped with the fourfold complement of forces.[1]

रथानामयुतैः षड्भिरुदग्राख्यो महासुरः ।
अयुध्यतायुतानां च सहस्रेण महाहनुः ॥ ४२ ॥

42. A great Asura, Udagra by name, with sixty thousand chariots and Mahahanu with a crore waged the battle.

पञ्चाशद्भिश्च नियुतैरसिलोमा महासुरः ।
अयुतानां शतैः षड्भिर्गर्णकलो युयुधे रणे ॥ ४३ ॥

43. The great Asiloma fought in that battle with hundred and fifty lakhs while Bhashkala fought with sixty lakhs (of chariots).

---

1 *ratha-gaja-turaga-padāti*: Chariot, elephant, horse and soldier on foot.

गजवाजिसहस्रौघैरनेकैः परिवारितः ।
वृतो रथानां कोट्या च युद्धे तस्मिन्नयुध्यत ॥ ४४ ॥

44. Parivarita surrounded by many thousands of elephants and horses and crores of chariots fought in that battle.

बिडालाख्योऽयुतानां च पञ्चाशद्भिरथायुतैः ।
युयुधे संयुगे तत्र रथानां परिवारितः ॥ ४५ ॥

45. One named Bidala fought in that battle surrounded by five hundred crores of chariots.

अन्ये च तत्रायुतशो रथनागहयैर्वृताः ।
युयुधुः संयुगे देव्या सह तत्र महासुराः ॥ ४६ ॥

46. Other great Asuras, tens of thousands in number encircled by chariots elephants and horses fought in the war-front with the Goddess.

कोटिकोटिसहस्रैस्तु रथानां दन्तिनां तथा ।
हयानां च वृतो युद्धे तत्राभून्महिषासुरः ॥ ४७ ॥

47. In that battle, Mahishasura stood encircled by thousands crores and crores of chariots, elephants and horses.

तोमरैर्भिन्दिपालैश्च शक्तिमिर्मुसलैस्तथा ।
युयुधुः संयुगे देव्या खड्गैः परशुपट्टिशैः ॥ ४८ ॥

48. With iron maces and javelins, with lances and pestles, with swords, battle-axes and halberds they fought with the Goddess in the fronts.

केचिच्च चिक्षिपुः शक्तीः केचित् पाशांस्तथापरे ।
देवीं खड्गप्रहारैस्तु ते तां हन्तुं प्रचक्रमुः ॥ ४९ ॥

49. Some hurled lances. Some others threw nooses. They began to attack the Goddess by striking her with swords.

सापि देवी ततस्तानि शस्त्राण्यस्त्राणि चण्डिका ।
लीलयैव प्रचिच्छेद निजशस्त्रास्त्रवर्षिणी ॥ ५० ॥

50. The Goddess Chandika also, quite playfully, cut into pieces those arrows and missiles by pouring on them her own arrows and missiles.

अनायस्तानना देवी स्तूयमाना सुरर्षिभिः ।
मुमोचासुरदेहेषु शस्त्राण्यस्त्राणि चेश्वरी ॥ ५१ ॥

51. Praised by the gods and the sages, the Goddess Ishvari, showing no fatigue in her face cast arrows and missiles on the bodies of the Asuras.

सोऽपि क्रुद्धो धुतसटो देव्या वाहनकेसरी ।
चचारासुरसैन्येषु वनेष्विव हुताशनः ॥ ५२ ॥

52. And the lion also, the mount of Devi, shook its mane in fury and roamed amidst the armies of the Asuras like fire in the forests.

निःश्वासान् मुमुचे यांश्च युध्यमाना रणेऽम्बिका ।
त एव सद्यः सम्भूताः गणाः शतसहस्रशः ॥ ५३ ॥

53. The sighs that the Mother fighting on the battle-front heaved became immediately her hosts in hundreds and thousands.

युयुधुस्ते परशुभिर्भिन्दिपालासिपट्टिशैः ।
नाशयन्तोऽसुरगणान् देवीशक्त्युपबृंहिताः ॥ ५४ ॥

54. Aggrandised by the force of the Goddess, these hosts fought destroying the hosts of Asuras with battle-axes, javelins, swords and halberds.

अवादयन्त पटहान् गणाः शङ्खांस्तथापरे ।
मृदङ्गांश्च तथैवान्ये तस्मिन् युद्धमहोत्सवे ॥ ५५ ॥

55. In that festival of war, some of the hosts beat the drums, some blew conches and others played on mridangas.

ततो देवी त्रिशूलेन गदया शक्तिऋष्टिभिः ।
खड्गादिभिश्च शतशो निजघान महासुरान् ॥ ५६ ॥

56. Then the Goddess killed the great Asuras in hundreds by means of trident, mace, Iance, double-edged swords and ordinary swords.

पातयामास चैवान्यान् घण्टास्वनविमोहितान् ।
असुरान् भुवि पाशेन बध्वा चान्यानकर्षयत् ॥ ५७ ॥

57. She felled certain Asuras to the ground by making them stunned with the sound of her bell. Certain others she dragged along the ground by binding them with the noose.

केचिद् द्विधाकृतास्तीक्ष्णैः खड्गपातैस्तथापरे ।
विपोथिता निपातेन गदया भुवि शेरते ॥ ५८ ॥

58. Some were split in two by the sharp fall of swords; others smashed by the blow of her mace were laid on the ground.

वेमुश्च केचिद्रुधिरं मुसलेन भृशं हताः ।
केचिन्निपतिता भूमौ भिन्नाः शूलेन वक्षसि ॥ ५९ ॥

59. Severely struck by the pestle, some vomitted blood. Rent by the trident in the chest, some were felled on the ground.

निरन्तराः शरौघेण कृताः केचिद् रणाजिरे ।
शल्यानुकारिणः प्राणान् मुमुचुस्त्रिदशार्दनाः ॥ ६० ॥

60. In the battlefield, some of those who afflicted the gods were caught in a flood of arrows, leaving no space in their bodies unstruck. Resembling porcupines, they breathed their last.

वेषाञ्चिद् बाहवः छिन्नाः छिन्नग्रीवाः तथापरे ।
शिरांसि पेतुरन्येषामन्ये मध्ये विदारिताः ॥ ६१ ॥

61. Some had their arms cut, some others their necks. Heads of some fell and others were rent asunder in the middle.

विच्छिन्नजङ्घास्त्वपरे पेतुरुर्व्यां महासुराः ।
एकबाह्वक्षिचरणाः केचिद् देव्या द्विधाकृताः ॥ ६२ ॥

62. Some other great Asuras, their legs cut off, fell on the ground. Some rendered one-armed, one-eyed, and one-legged were again rent into two by the Goddess.

छिन्नेऽपि चान्ये शिरसि पतिताः पुनरुत्थिताः ।
ननृतुश्चापरे तत्र युद्धे तूर्यलयाश्रिताः ॥ ६३ ॥

63. A few, their heads cut off, fell and rose again. Others danced in the battlefield in tune with the battle drums.

कबन्धाश्छिन्नशिरसः खड्गशक्त्यृष्टिपाणयः ।
तिष्ठ तिष्ठेति भाषन्तो देवीमन्ये महासुराः ॥ ६४ ॥

160

64. The trunks of other great Asuras, with swords, lances and double edged swords still in their hands, their heads just cut off shouted at the Goddess "Stop, Stop."

पातिते रथनागाश्वैरसुरैश्च वसुन्धरा ।
अगम्या साभवत्तत्र यत्राभूत् स महारणः ॥ ६५ ॥

65. The place on the earth where the great battle took place became impassable on account of the chariots, elephants, horses and Asuras felled on the ground.

शोणितौघा महानद्यस्सद्यस्तत्र प्रसुस्रुबुः ।
मध्ये चासुरसैन्यस्य वारणासुरवाजिनाम् ॥ ६६ ॥

66. Streams of blood from the Asuras, elephants and horses became in no time huge rivers and flowed amidst the army of the Asuras.

क्षणेन तन्महासैन्यमसुराणां तथाम्बिका ।
निन्ये क्षयं यथा वह्निस्तृणदारुमहाचयम् ॥ ६७ ॥

67. Thus, the Mother, in a moment's time, led to destruction the great army of the Asuras just as fire would, a huge stalk of wood and grass.

स च सिंहो महानादमुत्सृजन् धुतकेसरः ।
शरीरेभ्योऽमरारीणामसूनिव विचिन्वति ॥ ६८ ॥

68. That lion also, shaking its mane and making a terrible roar prowled about, searching as it were the life-breaths in the bodies of the enemies of the immortals.

देव्या गणैश्च तैस्तत्र कृतं युद्धं तथासुरैः ।
यथैषां तुतुषुर्देवाः पुष्पवृष्टिमुचो दिवि ॥ ६९ ॥

69. The Goddess with her hosts fought with the Asuras in such a manner that the gods were pleased and showered flowers from Heaven.

इति श्रीमार्कण्डेयपुराणे सावर्णिके मन्वन्तरे देवीमहात्म्ये द्वितीयः ॥ २ ॥

Here ends the second of *devi mahatmya* in Markendeya Purana during the period of *savarni*, the Manu.

THIRD CHAPTER

ऋषिरुवाच ॥ १ ॥

1. The Sage said

निघ्न्यमानं तत्सैन्यमवलोक्य महासुरः ।
सेनानीश्चिक्षुरः कोपादययौ योद्धुमथाम्बिकाम् ॥ २ ॥

2. Seeing that army being slain, the great Asura, Chikshura, the Commander-in-chief proceeded in anger to fight the Mother.

स देवीं शरवर्षेण ववर्ष समरेऽसुरः ।
यथा मेरुगिरेः श्रृङ्गं तोयवर्षेण तोयदः ॥ ३ ॥

3. The Asura rained showers of arrows on the Goddess in battle just as a cloud would pour in showers of rain on the peak of the Meru Mountain.

तस्य छित्वा ततो देवी लीलयैव शरोत्करान् ।
जघान तुरगान्बाणैर्यन्तारं चैव वाजिनाम् ॥ ४ ॥

4. Then the Goddess playfully cutting asunder the volley of arrows, killed his horses and their driver with her arrows.

चिच्छेद च धनुः सद्यो ध्वजं चातिसमुच्छ्रितम् ।
विव्याध चैव गात्रेषु छिन्नधन्वानमाशुगैः ॥ ५ ॥

5. Immediately, she broke his bow and his banner flying aloft; and with swift shafts struck in the limbs of him whose bow had been broken.

स छिन्नधन्वा विरथो हताश्वो हतसारथिः ।
अभ्यधावत तां देवीं खड्गचर्मधरोऽसुरः ॥ ६ ॥

6. His bow broken, his chariot smashed, his horse killed and his charioteer slain, the Asura wielding a sword and a shield jumped at the Goddess.

सिंहमाहत्य खड्गेन तीक्ष्णधारेण मूर्धनि ।
आजघान भुजे सव्ये देवीमप्यतिवेगवान् ॥ ७ ॥

7. With terrific speed he struck the lion on the head with a sharp-edged sword and hit the Goddess on her left arm.

तस्याः खड्गो भुजं प्राप्य पफाल नृपनन्दन ।
ततो जग्राह शूलं स कोपादरुणलोचनः ॥ ८ ॥

8. O Delight of kings! the sword, the moment it touched her arm, broke into pieces. Red in the eyes with anger, he took the spear.

चिक्षेप च ततस्तत् तु भद्रकाल्यां महासुरः ।
जाज्वल्यमानं तेजोभी रविबिम्बमिवाम्बरात् ॥ ९ ॥

9. The great Asura hurled the weapon, resplendent with lustre, at *bhadrakāli*, as though he was hurling the orb of the Sun from the skies.

दृष्ट्वा तदापतच्छूलं देवी शूलममुञ्चत ।
तेन तत् शतधा नीतं शूलं स च महासुरः ॥ १० ॥

10. Seeing the spear coming upon her, the Goddess released her spear. It broke his spear into a hundred pieces, as well as the great Asura.

हते तस्मिन् महावीर्ये महिषस्य चमूपतौ ।
आजगाम गजारूढश्चामरस्त्रिदशार्दनः ॥ ११ ॥

11. When that General of Mahisha, of great valour, was slain, Chamara, the afflicter of the gods came forward mounted on an elephant.

सोऽपि शक्तिं मुमोचाथ देव्यास्तामम्बिका द्रुतम् ।
हुङ्काराभिहतां भूमौ पातयामास निष्प्रभाम् ॥ १२ ॥

12. He hurled his lance at the Devi. And the Mother immediately with a grunt, made it fall to the ground lustreless.

भग्नां शक्तिं निपतितां दृष्ट्वा क्रोधसमन्वितः ।
चिक्षेप चामरः शूलं बाणैस्तदपि साऽच्छिनत् ॥ १३ ॥

13. Seeing his lance broken and fallen, Chamara, filled with anger, hurled the spear. She broke it as well with her arrows.

ततः सिंहः समुत्पत्य गजकुम्भान्तरे स्थितः ।
बाहुयुद्धेन युयुधे तेनोच्चैस्त्रिदशारिणा ॥ १४ ॥

14. Then, the lion leaped upwards, seated itself between the temples of the elephant and engaged itself in a hand to hand fight with that enemy of the gods.

युध्यमानौ ततस्तौ तु तस्मान्नागान्महीं गतौ ।
युयुधातेऽतिसंरब्धौ प्रहारैरतिदारुणैः ॥ १५ ॥

15. In the course of fighting, they came down from the elephant to the ground and fought quite excited, dealing each other terrible blows.

ततो वेगात् खमुत्पत्य निपत्य च मृगारिणा ।
करप्रहारेण शिरश्चामरस्य पृथक् कृतम् ॥ १६ ॥

16. Then, the foe of beasts leaped to the sky with force and from there sprang on Chamara, severing his head with a blow of its paw.

उद्ग्रथ रणे देव्या शिलावृक्षादिभिर्हतः ।
दन्तमुष्टितलैश्चैव करालश्च निपातितः ॥ १७ ॥

17. Udagra was killed in battle of the Devi by means of rocks, trees and the like. Karala was brought down by biting with her teeth, hitting with her fist and slapping with her palm.

देवी क्रुद्धा गदापातैश्चूर्णयामास चोद्धतम् ।
बाष्कलं भिन्दिपालेन बाणैस्ताम्रं तथान्धकम् ॥ १८ ॥

18. The Devi in wrath pulverised Uddhata with strokes of her mace. She slew Bhaskala with a javelin, Tamra and Andhaka with arrows.

उग्रास्यमुग्रवीर्यं च तथैव च महाहनुम् ।
त्रिनेत्रा च त्रिशूलेन जघान परमेश्वरी ॥ १९ ॥

19. The great Goddess, possessed of three eyes, smote and slew Ugrasya, Ugravirya and Mahahanu with her trident.

बिडालस्यासिना कायात् पातयामास वै शिरः ।
दुर्धरं दुर्मुखं चोभौ शरैर्निन्ये यमक्षयम् ॥ २० ॥

20. By her sword, she made the head of Bidala fall from his body and sent Durdhara and Durmukha to the abode of death by her arrows.

एवं संक्षीयमाणे तु स्वसैन्ये महिषासुरः ।
माहिषेण स्वरूपेण त्रासयामास तान् गणान् ॥ २१ ॥

21. Seeing his own army being demolished thus Mahishasura terrified the hosts of the Devi with his buffalo form.

कांश्चित् तुण्डप्रहारेण खुरक्षेपैस्तथापरान् ।
लाङ्गूलताडितांश्चान्यान् श्रृङ्गाभ्यां च विदारितान् ॥ २२ ॥
वेगेन कांश्चिदपरान्नादेन भ्रमणेन च ।
निःश्वासपवनेनान्यान् पातयामास भूतले ॥ २३ ॥

22-23. Hitting by the muzzle some, trampling by the hooves some others, lashing by his tail some, tearing by his horns some others, with sheer speed some, with bellowing and whirling about some others and with the blast of his breath the rest, he laid the hosts on the ground.

निपात्य प्रमथानीकमभ्यधावत सोऽसुरः ।
सिंहं हन्तुं महादेव्याः कोपं चक्रे ततोऽम्बिका ॥ २४ ॥

24. After laying low the hosts of Pramathas, that Asura leaped to slay the lion of the great Goddess. Seeing this, the Mother became angry.

सोऽपि कोपान्महावीर्यः खुरक्षुण्णमहीतलः ।
श्रृङ्गाभ्यां पर्वतानुच्चांश्चिक्षेप च ननाद च ॥ २५ ॥

25. He too, of great valour, pounded the terrain with his hooves in rage, threw about the mountains with his horns and roared.

वेगभ्रमणविक्षुण्णा मही तस्य व्यशीर्यत ।
लाङ्गूलेनाहतश्चाब्धिः प्लावयामास सर्वतः ॥ २६ ॥

26. Crushed by his whirling speed, the earth crumbled to pieces; lashed by his tail the ocean flooded everywhere.

धुतश्रृङ्गविमिश्राश्च खण्डं खण्डं ययुर्घनाः ।
श्वासानिलास्ताः शतशो निपेतुर्नभसोऽचलाः ॥ २७ ॥

27. Broken by his moving horns, the clouds went into pieces. His heaving breath lifted up mountains in the sky and brought them down.

इति क्रोधसमाधातमापतन्तं महासुरम् ।
दृष्ट्वा सा चण्डिका कोपं तद्वधाय तदाकरोत् ॥ २८ ॥

28. Seeing the great Asura bloated with rage advancing towards her, she Chandika, assumed an angry mood in order to kill him.

सा क्षिप्त्वा तस्य वै पाशं तं बबन्ध महासुरम् ।
तत्याज माहिषं रूपं सोऽपि बद्धो महामृधे ॥ २९ ॥

29. She threw the noose over the great Asura and bound him. Thus bound in the great battle, he left off his buffalo form.

ततः सिंहोऽभवत् सद्यो यावत्तस्याम्बिका शिरः ।
छिनत्ति तावत् पुरुषः खड्गपाणिरदृश्यत ॥ ३० ॥

30. Then immediately he became a lion. No sooner the Mother cut the head off than a man appeared with a sword in hand.

तत एवाशु पुरुषं देवी चिच्छेद सायकैः ।
तं खड्गचर्मणा सार्धं ततः सोऽभून्महागजः ॥ ३१ ॥

31. Soon the Goddess cut the man asunder along with his sword and shield, by means of her arrows. Then he became a huge elephant.

करेण च महासिंहं तं चकर्ष जगर्ज च ।
कर्षतस्तु करं देवी खड्गेन निरकृन्तत ॥ ३२ ॥

32. The elephant pulled the lion with its trunk and roared. As it pulled, the Goddess cut off the trunk with her sword.

ततो महासुरो भूयो माहिषं वपुराश्थितः ।
तथैव क्षोभयामास त्रैलोक्यं सचराचरम् ॥ ३३ ॥

33. The great Asura resumed the body of a buffalo and as before shook the three worlds along with their mobile and immobile things.

ततः क्रुद्धा जगन्माता चण्डिका पानमुत्तमम् ।
पपौ पुनः पुनश्चैव जहासारुणलोचना ॥ ३४ ॥

34. Enraged at this, Chandika, the Mother of the worlds, quaffed again and again a superb drink and laughed, her eyes becoming red.

ननर्द चासुरः सोऽपि बलवीर्यमदोद्धतः ।
विषाणाभ्यां च चिक्षेप चण्डिकां प्रति भूधरान् ॥ ३५ ॥

35. The Asura too intoxicated with his strength and valour roared and threw mountains at Chandika with his horns.

सा च तान्प्रहितांस्तेन चूर्णयन्ती शरोत्करैः ।
उवाच तं मदोद्धूतमुखरागाकुलाक्षरम् ॥ ३६ ॥

36. And she, with a volley of arrows, reduced to powder those that were hurled at her and said to him, her words faltering and colour mounting up her face due to the intoxication of the drinks.

देव्युवाच ॥ ३७ ॥

37. The Goddess said :

गर्ज गर्ज क्षणं मूढ मधु यावत्पिबाम्यहम् ।
मया त्वयि हतेऽत्रैव गर्जिष्यन्त्याशु देवताः ॥ ३८

38. Roar, roar, O fool, for a moment till I drink this wine. Soon the gods are going to roar here when you are slain by me.

ऋषिरुवाच ॥ ३९ ॥

39. The sage said :

एवमुक्त्वा समुत्पत्य सारूढा तं महासुरम् ।
पादेनाक्रम्य कण्ठे च शूलेनैनमताडयत् ॥ ४० ॥

40. Exclaiming thus, she jumped and climbed on the great Asura. Crushing his neck under her foot, she hit him with the trident.

ततः सोऽपि पदाक्रान्तस्तया निजमुखात्तदा ।
अर्धनिष्क्रान्त एवासीद्देव्या वीर्येण संवृतः ॥ ४१ ॥

41. Then, crushed by her foot, he was able to emerge only as half of his self from his own mouth, overpowered by the valour of the Goddess.

अर्धनिष्क्रान्त एवासौ युध्यमानो महासुरः ।
तया महासिना देव्या शिरश्छिर्त्वा निपातितः ॥ ४२ ॥

42. Continuing to fight as half of his self, the great Asura was beheaded by the Goddess with the sword and slain.

ततो हाहाकृतं सर्वं दैत्यसैन्यं ननाश तत् ।
प्रहर्षं च परं जग्मुः सकला देवतागणाः ॥ ४३ ॥

43. Then, crying in consternation, the entire army of the Asuras perished; and the entire hosts of gods derived immense delight.

तुष्टुवुस्तां सुरा देवीं सह दिव्यैर्महर्षिभिः ।
जगुर्गन्धर्ववैपतयो ननृतुश्चाप्सरोगणाः ॥ ४४ ॥

44. The gods along with the divine seers, lauded the Goddess. The Gandharva kings sang and the hosts of Apsaras danced.

इति श्रीमार्कण्डेयपुराणे सावर्णिके मन्वन्तरे देवीमाहात्म्ये
तृतीयः ॥ ३ ॥

Here ends the third of Devi Mahatmyam in Markendeya Purana during the period of Savarni, the Manu.

FOURTH CHAPTER

ऋषिरुवाच ॥ १ ॥

1. The Sage said :

शक्रादयः सुरगणा निहतेऽतिवीर्ये
तस्मिन्दुरात्मनि सुरारिबले च देव्या ।
तां तुष्टुवुः प्रणतिनम्रशिरोधरांसा
वाग्भिः प्रहर्षपुलकोद्गमचारुदेहाः ॥ २ ॥

2. When the most valiant and wicked Asura and the army of the enemies of gods were slain by the Goddess, the hosts of gods headed by Indra lauded her, their necks and shoulders bowed in salutation and their bodies charming with horripilations of delight.

देव्या यया ततमिदं जगतात्मशक्त्या
निःशेषदेवगणशक्तिसमूहमूर्त्या ।
तामम्बिकामखिलदेवमहर्षिपूज्यां
भक्त्या नताः स्म विदधातु शुभानि सा नः ॥ ३ ॥

3. All this world has been pervaded by the Goddess, through her Soul-Force which has embodied itself in the form of the joint forces of the entire hosts of gods. To her, the mother, worthy of worship by all the gods and seers we bow in devotion. May she arrange for us auspicious things !

यस्याः प्रभावमतुलं भगवाननन्तो
ब्रह्मा हरश्च न हि वक्तुमलं बलं च ।
सा चण्डिकाऽखिलजगत्परिपालनाय
नाशाय चाशुभभयस्य मतिं करोतु ॥ ४ ॥

4. The infinite Lord,[1] Brahma and Siva cannot
adequately describe her unparalleled glory and strength.
May she, Chandika, be pleased to give thought to the
protection of the entire world and to the destruction of the
fear of evil.

या श्रीः स्वयं सुकृतिनां भवनेष्वलक्ष्मीः
पापात्मनां कृतधियां हृदयेषु बुद्धिः ।
श्रद्धा सतां कुलजनप्रभवस्य लज्जा
तां त्वां नताः स्म परिपालय देवि विश्वम् ॥ ५ ॥

5. Thou art prosperity and beauty in the mansions
of those who perform good deeds, poverty and ugliness
in the case of those disposed towards evil, intelligence in
the heart of those who possess a cultivated mind; faith in
the good folk and modesty in those born in a noble family.
We bow down to thee, O Devi, protect the universe.

किं वर्णयाम तव रूपमचिन्त्यमेतत्
किंश्चातिवीर्यमसुरक्षयकारि भूरि ।
किं चाहवेषु चरितानि तवाति यानि
सर्वेषु देव्यसुरदेवगणादिकेषु ॥ ६ ॥

---

1 *Ananta* : endless, infinite. Here it denotes Vishnu. It is the middle
one of the triad Achyuta, Ananta and Govinda, the manifestations of Vishnu,
presiding over heaven, the mid-regions, *antariksa* and the earth respectively.
Ananta is also a synonym of Shesha, the Lord's couch who is reputed to have
thousand heads. The import is that Adishesha though possessed of thousand
tongues cannot adequately describe the glory of the Devi.

6. O Devi, how can we describe thy form! It cannot be grasped by the mind. And how to extol thy excessive valour playing havoc amongst the Asuras! And those exploits of thine in battles surpassing all those of the divine and the *asuric* hosts.

हेतुः समस्तजगतां त्रिगुणापि दोषै-
र्न ज्ञायसे हरिहरादिभिरप्यपारा ।
सर्वाश्रयाखिलमिदं जगदंशभूत-
मव्याकृता हि परमा प्रकृतिस्त्वमाद्या ॥ ७ ॥

7. Thou art the cause of all the worlds. Thou art made up of the three gunas, yet a stranger to their attendant defects. Thou art beyond the ken of preception of even Vishnu, Shiva and others. Refuge of all art thou. This whole world is a portion of thine. Yea, thou art the primordeal, unmanifest, supreme Prakriti.

यस्याः समस्तसुरता समुदीरणेन
तृप्तिं प्रयाति सकलेषु मखेषु देवि ।
स्वाहासि वै पितृगणस्य च तृप्तिहेतु-
रुच्चार्यसे त्वमत एव जनैः स्वधा च ॥ ८ ॥

8. O Devi, thou art *swāhā*, by uttering which all the godheads get satisfaction in all the sacrifices. Thou art also the cause of satisfaction to the Pitris. That is why thou art called *swadhā* as well by people.

या मुक्तिहेतुरविचिन्त्यमहाव्रता त्वं
अभ्यस्यसे सुनियतेन्द्रियतत्त्वसारैः ।
मोक्षार्थिभिर्मुनिभिरस्तसमस्तदोषै-
र्विद्याऽसि सा भगवती परमा हि देवि ॥ ९ ॥

9. O Devi, thou art supreme knowledge, the cause of liberation. Thou, Bhagavati, constituting great unthinkable austerities art practised by sages who reject all their short-comings, keep their senses well under restraint, know the essence of truth and seek liberation.

शब्दात्मिका सुविमलर्ग्यजुषां निधान-
मुद्गीथरम्यपदपाठवतां च साम्नाम् ।
देवि त्रयी भगवती भवभावनाय
वार्तासि सर्वजगतां परमार्तिहन्त्री ॥ १० ॥

10. Soul of sound, Treasure-trove of immaculate Rik, Yajus and Saman whose arrangement of words is beautiful with the resonance of Omkara, thou, Bhagavati, art the three Vedas. O Devi, thou who destroyest the great distress of all the worlds, art the common speech for carrying on in the work-a-day world.

मेधासि देवि विदिताखिलशास्त्रसारा
दुर्गासि दुर्गभवसागरनौरसङ्गा ।
श्रीः कैटभारिहृदयैककृताधिवासा
गौरी त्वमेव शशिमौलिकृतप्रतिष्ठा ॥ ११ ॥

11. O Devi, thou art verily Gowri, established by the moon-crested Shiva; Lakshmi who has taken abode solely in the heart of Vishnu, the enemy of Kaitabha; Sarasvati, the intellect, knowing the essence of all Sastras; Durga, seated unattached, the boat for crossing the unfordable sea of existence.

ईषत्सहासममलं परिपूर्णचन्द्र-
बिम्बानुकारि कनकोत्तमकान्तिकान्तम् ।
अत्यद्भुतं प्रहृतमात्तरुषा तथापि
वक्त्रं विलोक्य सहसा महिषासुरेण ॥ १२ ॥

12. Slightly smiling and spotless, resembling the orb of a full moon, glowing like pure shining gold was thy face. Yet, it is very strange that on seeing it, Mahishasura became furious and struck it with violence.

दृष्ट्वा तु देवि कुपितं भ्रुकुटीकराल-
मुद्यच्छशाङ्कसदृशच्छवि यन्न सद्यः ।
प्राणान् मुमोच महिषस्तदतीव चित्रं
कैर्जीव्यते हि कुपितान्तकदर्शनेन ॥ २३ ॥

13. O Devi, Even more strange was the fact that Mahishasura did not breathe his last immediately he saw thy angry face, terrible with eye-brows knit and crimson, like the rising moon. Who lives after beholding the enraged Lord of Death?

देवि प्रसीद परमा भवति भवाय
सद्यो विनाशयसि कोपवती कुलानि ।
विज्ञातमेतदधुनैव यदस्तमेत-
न्नीतं बलं सुविपुलं महिषासुरस्य ॥ १४ ॥

14. Devi, thou art supreme. Be gracious for the existence here. Enraged, thou destroyest forthwith the families. We have known this now that the huge army of Mahishasura has been vanquished.

ते सम्मता जनपदेषु धनानि तेषां
तेषां यशांसि न च सीदति धर्मवर्गः ।
धन्यास्त एव निभृतात्मजभृत्यदाराः
येषां सदाऽभ्युदयदा भवती प्रसन्ना ॥ १५ ॥

15. To whomsoever thou art gracious, thou ever grantest them prosperity. They are well esteemed in the countries, theirs is the wealth, theirs the fame and their

pursutis of Dharma perish not. They are the fortunate ones who have devoted children, servants and wives.

धर्म्याणि देवि सकलानि सदैव कर्मा-
ण्यत्याद्दत: प्रतिदिनं सुकृती करोति ।
स्वर्गं प्रयाति च ततो भवतीप्रसादा-
ल्लोकत्रयेऽपि फलदा ननु देवि तेन ॥ १६ ॥

16. Devi, by Thy grace,[1] the doer of good acts does daily with great faith all the deeds conducive to Dharma and always doing so, reaches Heaven. O Devi, art thou not therefore the giver of the fruit in all the three worlds?

दुर्गे स्मृता हरसि भीतिमशेषजन्तो:
स्वस्थै: स्मृता मतिमतीव शुभां ददासि ।
दारिद्र्यदु:खभयहारिणि का त्वदन्या
सर्वोपकारकरणाय सदार्द्रचित्ता ॥ १७ ॥

17. When thou art remembered in a crisis, thou removest the fear of all beings. When remembered by those stationed in themselves, thou grantest the most auspicious thought. O Dispeller of poverty, suffering, and fear! who else, except thee, has an ever compassionate heart to render help to everybody ?

एभिर्हतैर्जगदुपैति सुखं तथैते
कुर्वन्तु नाम नरकाय चिराय पापम् ।
संग्राममृत्युमधिगम्य दिवं प्रयान्तु
मत्वेति नूनमहितान्विनिहंसि देवि ॥ १८ ॥

---

1 It is generally said that by doing good acts, one gets Her grace: rather it is Her grace that makes one do the good acts. One who chooses the Divine is already chosen by Him. *yamaivesa vṛnute tena labhyaḥ.*

18. If these are slain, the world will attain happiness. Let them be committing sins for a long stay in Hell. But they can go to Heaven by meeting their death in battle. O Devi, thinking thus, thou hast slain the enemies : this is certain.

दृष्ट्वैव किं न भवती प्रकरोति भस्म
सर्वासुरानरिषु यत्प्रहिणोपि शस्त्रम् ।
लोकान् प्रयान्तु रिपवोऽपि हि शस्त्रपूता
इत्थं मातिर्भवति तेष्वहितेषु साध्वी ॥ १९ ॥

19. Why dost thou not reduce all the Asuras to ashes by a look ? The fact that thou employest weapons to fight the foes in order that even those enemies, purified by weapons, may attain higher worlds, shows the kind thought thou hast towards those unkind ones.

खड्गप्रभानिकरबिस्फुरणैस्तथोग्रैः
शूलाग्रकान्तिनिवहेन दृशोऽसुराणाम् ।
यन्नागता विलयमंशुमदिन्दुखण्ड -
योग्याननं तव विलोकयतां तदेतत् ॥ २० ॥

20. The eyes of the Asuras have not been put out by the fierce lightning flashes of shining swords and the mass of light emerging from the points of the trident. This is so because they were seeing thy face adorned with the crescent moon emitting cool rays.

दुर्वृत्तवृत्तशमनं तव देवि शीलं
रूपं तथैतदविचिन्त्यमतुल्यमन्यैः ।
वीर्यं च हन्तृ हृतदेवपराक्रमाणां
वैरिष्वपि प्रकटितैव दया त्वयेत्थम् ॥ २१ ॥

21. O Devi, thy nature is to subdue the deeds of the wicked. Likewise, this thy form cannot be grasped by thought and has no parallel with other things. And thy valour destroys those who take away the gods' prowess. Thus, mercy has been exhibited even to enemies by thee.

केनोपमा भवतु तेऽस्य पराक्रमस्य
रूपं च शत्रुभयकार्यतिहारि कुत्र ।
चित्ते कृपा समरनिष्ठुरता च दृष्टा
त्वय्येव देवि वरदे भुवनत्रयेऽपि ॥ २२ ॥

22. What can be the comparison to this thy prowess? And where can one find a form like thine very captivating and at the same time striking fear in the enemies? O Devi, giver of the best, in all the triple world, only in thee have been seen compassion in the heart and harshness in the battle.

त्रैलोक्यमेतदखिलं रिपुनाशनेन
त्रातं त्वया समरमूर्धनि तेऽपि हत्वा ।
नीता दिवं रिपुगणा भयमप्यपास्त-
मस्माकमुन्मदसुरारिभवं नमस्ते ॥ २३ ॥

23. The entire triple world has been saved by thee by the destruction of foes. And the hosts of foes have been led to Heaven by being killed in the battle front. Our fear rising out of the haughty Asuras has been dispelled. Salutations to thee.

शूलेन पाहि नो देवि पाहि खड्गेन चाम्बिके ।
घण्टास्वनेन नः पाहि चापज्यानिस्वनेन च ॥ २४ ॥

24. O Devi, guard us with spear, Mother, guard us

with the sword. With the ring of the bell, guard us, and so with the twang of the bow-string.

प्राच्यां रक्ष प्रतीच्यां च चण्डिके रक्ष दक्षिणे ।
भ्रामणेनात्मशूलस्य उत्तरस्यां तथेश्वरि ॥ २५ ॥

25. Protect us in the east, in the west, Chandika! protect us in the south, Ishvari, likewise in the north whirling thy spear.

सौम्यानि यानि रूपाणि त्रैलोक्ये विचरन्ति ते ।
यानि चात्यन्तघोराणि तै रक्षास्मांस्तथा भुवम् ॥ २६ ॥

26. Whatever are thy auspicious forms and whatever thy terrible forms that move about in the triple world, with them protect us and the earth as well.

खड्गशूलगदादीनि यानि चास्त्राणि तेऽम्बिके ।
करपल्लवसङ्गीनि तैरस्मान् रक्ष सर्वतः ॥ २७ ॥

27. Mother, protect us from everything with whatever weapons thy tender hand contacts, the sword, the trident, the mace and the like.

ऋषिरुवाच ॥ २८ ॥

28. The Sage said :

एवं स्तुता सुरैर्दिव्यैः कुसुमैर्नन्दनोद्भवैः ।
अर्चिता जगतां धात्री तथा गन्धानुलेपनैः ॥ २९ ॥

29. Thus the upholder and sustainer of the worlds was lauded by the gods and worshipped with flowers produced in the garden Nandana and with fragrant sandal paste.

भक्त्या समस्तैस्त्रिदशैर्दिव्यैर्धूपैः सुधूपिता ।
प्राह प्रसादसुमुखी समस्तान् प्रणतान् सुरान् ॥ ३० ॥

30. She was offered with devotion by all the gods the divine incense. Gracious and benign in countenance she spoke to all the gods, bowing in salutation.

देव्युवाच ॥ ३१ ॥

31. The Goddess said :

व्रियतां त्रिदशाः सर्वं यदस्मत्तोऽभिवाञ्छितम् ॥ ३२ ॥

32. Let the gods choose whatever they desire from me.

देवा ऊचुः ॥ ३३ ॥

33. The gods said :

भगवत्या कृतं सर्वं न किञ्चिदवशिष्यते ।
यदयं निहतः शत्रुरस्माकं महिषासुरः ॥ ३४ ॥

34. Thy eminence has done everything. Nothing is left to be done, as our enemy Mahishasura has been killed.

यदि चापि वरो देयस्त्वयास्माकं महेश्वरि ।
संस्मृता संस्मृता त्वं नो हिंसेथाः परमापदः ॥ ३५ ॥

35. Great Goddess! If a boon has to be conferred on us by thee, whenever we think of thee, destroy our great sufferings.

यश्च मर्त्यः स्तवैरेभिस्त्वां स्तोष्यत्यमलानने ।
तस्य वित्तर्द्धिविभवैर्धनदारादिसम्पदाम् ॥ ३६ ॥
वृद्धयेऽस्मत्प्रसन्ना त्वं भवेथाः सर्वदाम्बिके ॥ ३७ ॥

36-37. Mother of immaculate face! Whosoever is the mortal who praises thee with these lauds, may thou, who art gracious to us be so to him all the time for the plenitude of knowledge, growth, glory along with opulence in wealth and household comforts like wife etc.

ऋषिरुवाच ॥ ३८ ॥

38. The Sage said :

इति प्रसादिता देवैर्जंगतोऽर्थं तथात्मनः ।
तथेत्युक्त्वा भद्रकाली बभूवाऽन्तर्हिता नृप ॥ ३९ ॥

39. O King, thus propitiated by the gods for the sake of the world and for their own sake, Bhadrakali said "yes" and vanished.

इत्येतत् कथितं भूप सम्भूता सा यथा पुरा ।
देवी देवशरीरेभ्यो जगत्त्रयहितैषिणी ॥ ४० ॥

40. O Protector of the earth! Thus far has been said how the Goddess desiring the weal of the three worlds was born long ago from the bodies of the gods.

पुनश्च गौरीदेहात् सा समुद्भूता यथाभवत् ।
वधाय दुष्टदैत्यानां तथा शुम्भनिशुम्भयोः ॥ ४१ ॥

रक्षणाय च लोकानां देवानामुपकारिणी ।
तच्छृणुष्व मयाऽऽख्यातं यथावत् कथयामि ते ॥ ४२ ॥

41-42. Again how, as a helper of the gods, she manifested out of Gowri's body for the protection of the world and for the destruction of wicked Asuras as well as Shumbha and Nishumbha, I shall relate. Listen to it. I shall tell as it happened.

ह्रीं ओं
HRIM. OM.

श्रीमार्कण्डेयपुराणे सावर्णिके मन्वन्तरे देवीमाहात्म्ये
चतुर्थः ॥ ४ ॥

Here ends the fourth of Devi Mahatmya in Markendeya Purana, during the period of Savarni, the Manu.

THE THIRD EPISODE
अथ उत्तमचरितम् ॥

उत्तमचरितस्य रुद्र ऋषि: । महासरस्वती देवता । अनुष्टुप्
छन्द: । भीमा शक्ति: । भ्रामरी बीजम् । सूर्यस्तत्त्वम् । सामवेद:
स्वरूपम् ॥

For the final episode Rudra is the seer, Mahasaraswati
the deity and Anushtub the metre. The force is Bhima,
the seed Bhramari and the principle sun. The form is Sama
Veda.

श्रीमहासरस्वतीप्रीत्यर्थे कामार्थे जपे विनियोग: ॥

The application in Japa is for Kama, for pleasing
Sri Mahasaraswati.

घण्टाशूलहलानि शङ्खमुसले चक्रं धनु: सायकं
हस्ताब्जैर्दधतीं घनान्तविलसच्छीतांशुतुल्यप्रभाम् ।
गौरीदेहसमुद्भवां त्रिजगतामाधारभूतां महा-
पूर्वामत्र सरस्वतीमनुभजे शुम्भादिदैत्यार्दिनीम् ॥

Wielding in her lotus-hands the bell, trident,
ploughshare, conch, pestle, discus, bow, and arrow, her
lustre is like that of a moon shining in autumn sky. She
is born from the body of Gowri and is the sustaining base
of the three worlds. That Mahasaraswati I worship here
who destroyed Sumbha and other Asuras.

FIFTH CHAPTER

ॐ क्लीं ऋषिरुवाच ॥ १ ॥

1. OM KLIM, the Sage said :

पुरा शुम्भनिशुम्भाभ्यामसुराभ्यां शचीपतेः ।
त्रैलोक्यं यज्ञभागाश्च हृता मदबलाश्रयात् ॥ २ ॥

2. Long ago, Indra's shares in the sacrifices and his authority over the triple world were captured by the Asuras, Shumbha and Nishumbha, by resorting to their strength and pride.

तावेव सूर्यतां तद्वदधिकारं तथैन्दवम् ।
कौबेरमथ याम्यं च चक्राते वरुणस्य च ॥ ३ ॥

3. They two, themselves, took over the authority of the sun, the moon, Kubera, Yama and Varuna.

तावेव पवनर्द्धिं च चक्रतुर्वेह्निकर्म च ।
ततो देवा विनिर्धूताः भ्रष्टराज्याः पराजिताः ॥ ४ ॥

4. They two captured the glory of Vayu and performed the acts of Agni. Their kingdoms lost, the vanquished gods were expelled.

हृताधिकारास्त्रिदशास्ताभ्यां सर्वे निराकृताः ।
महासुराभ्यां तां देवीं संस्मरन्त्यपराजिताम् ॥ ५ ॥

5. All the gods whose authority has been captured

and who were spurned by the two great Asuras remembered that Goddess who is invincible.

तयास्माकं वरो दत्तो यथापत्सु स्मृताखिलाः ।
भवतां नाशयिष्यामि तत्क्षणात्परमापदः ॥ ६ ॥

6. A boon was given to us by her as follows : "If you remember me in distress, that very moment I shall destroy all your worst sufferings."

इति कृत्वा मतिं देवा हिमवन्तं नगेश्वरम् ।
जग्मुस्तत्र ततो देवीं विष्णुमायां प्रतुष्टुवुः ॥ ७ ॥

7. Resolving thus, the gods went to Himavan the Lord of the mountains. There they praised the divine Vishnu Maya.

देवा ऊचुः ॥ ८ ॥

8. The gods said :

नमो देव्यै महादेव्यै शिवायै सततं नमः ।
नमः प्रकृत्यै भद्रायै नियताः प्रणताः स्म ताम् ॥ ९ ॥

9. Salutations to the Goddess, to the great Goddess; our constant salutations to the auspicious. Salutations to Prakriti, to the good. With restraint, we have bowed down to her.

रौद्रायै नमो नित्यायै गौर्यै धात्र्यै नमो नमः ।
ज्योत्स्नायै चेन्दुरूपिण्यै सुखायै सततं नमः ॥ १० ॥

10. Salutations to her who is terrible, to her who is eternal. Saluatations, salutations to Gowri, to her who upholds and sustains. Our constant salutations to her who is the form of the moon, who is moonlight and who is delight.

कल्याण्यै प्रणतामृद्धयै सिद्धयै कुर्मो नमो नमः ।
नैर्क्रत्यै भूभृतां लक्ष्म्यै शर्वाण्यै ते नमो नमः ॥ ११ ॥

11. We make our obeisance to her who is auspicious to the obeisant, to growth and prosperity, to accomplishment. Salutations to thee, consort of Shiva, to the misfortune, to the good fortune of kings.

दुर्गायै दुर्गपारायै सारायै सर्वकारिण्यै ।
ख्यात्यै तथैव कृष्णायै धूम्रायै सततं नमः ॥ १२ ॥

12. To Durga who fords us across difficulties, to the essence, to the doer of all, to the discriminating knowledge, to the dark one, to the smoky one[1] our constant salutations.

अतिसौम्यातिरौद्रायै नतास्तस्यै नमो नमः ।
नमो जगत्प्रतिष्ठायै देव्यै कृत्यै नमो नमः ॥ १३ ॥

13. We have prostrated before the exceedingly beautiful, before the extremely terrible. Salutations, salutations to her. To the mainstay of the world, to the Goddess, workmanship, we bow, we bow.

[2] या देवी सर्वभूतेषु विष्णुमायेति शब्दिता ।
नमस्तस्यै नमस्तस्यै नमस्तस्यै नमो नमः ॥ १४-१६ ॥

14-16. To the Goddess who in all beings is resonant as Vishnu Maya, to her salutations, to her salutations, to her salutations, salutations, salutations.

या देवी सर्वभूतेषु चेतनेत्यभिधीयते ।
नमस्तस्यै नमस्तस्यै नमस्तस्यै नमो नमः ॥ १७-१९ ॥

1 When ignorance is changed to knowledge, when darkness is changed to light, the intermediate stage which is hazy, is denoted by *dhūmāvati*, the smoky one. She is counted amongst the ten *mahāvidyas*.

2. The following 21 slokas have to be repeated thrice. See Introduction.

17-19. To the Goddess who in all beings is called consciousness, to her salutations, to her salutations, to her salutations, salutations, salutations.

या देवी सर्वभूतेषु बुद्धिरूपेण संस्थिता ।
नमस्तस्यै नमस्तस्यै नमस्तस्यै नमो नमः ॥ २०-२२ ॥

20-22. To the Goddess who in all beings abides in the form of intelligence, to her salutations, to her salutations, to her salutations, salutations, salutations.

या देवी सर्वभूतेषु निद्रारूपेण संस्थिता ।
नमस्तस्यै नमस्तस्यै नमस्तस्यै नमो नमः ॥ २३-२५ ॥

23-25. To the Goddess who in all beings abides in the form of sleep, to her salutations, to her salutations, to her salutations, salutations, salutations.

या देवी सर्वभूतेषु क्षुधारूपेण संस्थिता ।
नमस्तस्यै नमस्तस्यै नमस्तस्यै नमो नमः ॥ २६-२८ ॥

26-28. To the Goddess who in all beings abides in the form of hunger, to her salutations, to her salutations, to her salutations, salutations, salutations.

या देवी सर्वभूतेषु छायारूपेण संस्थिता ।
नमस्तस्यै नमस्तस्यै नमस्तस्यै नमो नमः ॥ २९-३१ ॥

29-31. To the Goddess who in all beings abides in the form of shadow, to her saluations, to her salutatios, to her salutations, salutations, salutations.

या देवी सर्वभूतेषु शक्तिरूपेण संस्थिता ।
नमस्तस्यै नमस्तस्यै नमस्तस्यै नमो नमः ॥ ३२-३४ ॥

32-34. To the Goddess who in all beings abides in the form of force, to her salutations, to her salutations, to her salutations, salutations, salutations.

या देवी सर्वभूतेषु तृष्णारूपेण संस्थिता ।
नमस्तस्यै नमस्तस्यै नमस्तस्यै नमो नमः ॥ ३५-३७ ॥

35-37. To the Goddess who in all beings abides in the form of thirst, to her salutations, to her salutations, to her salutations, salutations, salutations.

या देवी सर्वभूतेषु क्षान्तिरूपेण संस्थिता ।
नमस्तस्यै नमस्तस्यै नमस्तस्यै नमो नमः ॥ ३८-४० ॥

38-40. To the Goddess who in all beings abides in the form of patience, to her salutations, to her salutations, to her salutations, salutations, salutations.

या देवी सर्वभूतेषु जातिरूपेण संस्थिता ।
नमस्तस्यै नमस्तस्यै नमस्तस्यै नमो नमः ॥ ४१-४३ ॥

41-43. To the Goddess who in all beings abides in the form of genus, to her salutations, to her salutations, to her salutations, salutations, salutations.

या देवी सर्वभूतेषु लज्जारूपेण संस्थिता ।
नमस्तस्यै नमस्तस्यै नमस्तस्यै नमो नमः ॥ ४४-४६ ॥

44-46. To the Goddess who in all beings abides in the form of modesty, to her salutations, to her salutations, to her salutations, salutations, salutations.

या देवी सर्वभूतेषु शान्तिरूपेण संस्थिता ।
नमस्तस्यै नमस्तस्यै नमस्तस्यै नमो नमः ॥ ४७-४९ ॥

47-49. To the Goddess who in all beings abides in the form of peace, to her salutations, to her salutations, to her salutations, salutations, salutations.

या देवी सर्वभूतेषु श्रद्धारूपेण संस्थिता ।
नमस्तस्यै नमस्तस्यै नमस्तस्यै नमो नमः ॥ ५०-५२ ॥

50-52. To the Goddess who in all beings abides in the form of faith, to her salutations, to her salutations, to her salutations, salutations, salutations.

या देवी सर्वभूतेषु कान्तिरूपेण संस्थिता ।
नमस्तस्यै नमस्तस्यै नमस्तस्यै नमो नमः ॥ ५३-५५ ॥

53-55. To the Goddess who in all beings abides in the form of glowing charm, to her salutations, to her salutations, to her salutations, salutations, salutations.

या देवी सर्वभूतेषु लक्ष्मीरूपेण संस्थिता ।
नमस्तस्यै नमस्तस्यै नमस्तस्यै नमो नमः ॥ ५६-५८ ॥

56-58. To the Goddess who in all beings abides in the form of good fortune to her salutations, to her salutations, to her salutations, salutations, salutations.

या देवी सर्वभूतेषु वृत्तिरूपेण संस्थिता ।
नमस्तस्यै नमस्तस्यै नमस्तस्यै नमो नमः ॥ ५९-६१ ॥

59-61. To the Goddess who in all beings abides in the form of activity, to her salutations, to her salutations, to her salutations, salutations, salutations.

या देवी सर्वभूतेषु स्मृतिरूपेण संस्थिता ।
नमस्तस्यै नमस्तस्यै नमस्तस्यै नमो नमः ॥ ६२-६४ ॥

62-64. To the Goddess who in all beings abides in the form of remembrance, to her salutations, to her salutations, to her salutations, salutations, salutations.

या देवी सर्वभूतेषु दयारूपेण संस्थिता ।
नमस्तस्यै नमस्तस्यै नमस्तस्यै नमो नमः ॥ ६५-६७ ॥

65-67. To the Goddess who in all beings abides in

the form of mercy, to her salutations, to her salutations, to her salutations, salutations, salutations.

या देवी सर्वभूतेषु तुष्टिरूपेण संस्थिता ।
नमस्तस्यै नमस्तस्यै नमस्तस्यै नमो नमः ॥ ६८-७० ॥

68-70. To the Goddess who in all beings abides in the form of contentment, to her salutations, to her salutations, to her salutations, salutations, salutations.

या देवी सर्वभूतेषु मातृरूपेण संस्थिता ।
नमस्तस्यै नमस्तस्यै नमस्तस्यै नमो नमः ॥ ७१-७३ ॥

71-73. To the Goddess who in all being abides in the form of mother, to her salutations, to her salutations, to her salutations, salutations, salutations.

या देवी सर्वभूतेषु भ्रान्तिरूपेण संस्थिता ।
नमस्तस्यै नमस्तस्यै नमस्तस्यै नमो नमः ॥ ७४-७६ ॥

74-76. To the Goddess who in all beings abides in the form of mistake, to her salutations, to her salutations, to her salutations, salutations, salutations.

इन्द्रियाणामधिष्ठात्री भूतानां चाखिलेषु या ।
भूतेषु सततं तस्यै व्याप्त्यै देव्यै नमो नमः ॥ ७७ ॥

77. To her who presides over the senses and over the beings and also permeates into all beings, to that ever-pervasive Goddess, salutations, salutations.

चितिरूपेण या कृत्स्नमेतद्व्याप्य स्थिता जगत् ।
नमस्तस्यै नमस्तस्यै नमस्तस्यै नमो नमः ॥ ७८-८० ॥

78-80. To the Goddess who pervading this entire world abides in the form of consciousness, to her salutations, to her salutations, to her salutations, salutations, salutations.

स्तुताः सुरैः पूर्वमभीष्टसंश्रयात्
तथा सुरेन्द्रेण दिनेषु सेविता ।
करोतु सा नः शुभहेतुरीश्वरी
शुभानि भद्राण्यभिहन्तु चापदः ॥ ८१ ॥

81. Lauded by the gods, formerly for attaining the desired object and then served for days together by the king of gods, may she Ishvari, the cause of auspiciousness do us the auspicious good and destroy the miseries.

या साम्प्रतं चोद्धतदैत्यतापितै
रस्माभिरीशा च सुरैर्नमस्यते ।
या च स्मृता तत्क्षणमेव हन्ति नः
सर्वापदो भक्तिविनम्रमूर्तिभिः ॥ ८२ ॥

82. And who is at the present moment offered salutations by us gods, tormented by the haughty sons of Diti and who when remembered by us with bodies bent with devotion, destroys that very moment all our miseries.

ऋषिरुवाच ॥ ८३ ॥

83. The Sage said :

एवं स्तवामियुक्तानां देवानां तत्र पार्वती ।
स्नातुमभ्याययौ तोये जाह्नव्या नृपनन्दन ॥ ८४ ॥

84. O the delight of kings! Thus while the gods were engaged in the laud, Parvati, the daughter of the mountain came to bathe in the waters of the Ganges.

साब्रवीत् तान् सुरान् सुभ्रूर्भवद्भिः स्तूयतेऽत्र का ।
शरीरकोशतश्चास्याः समुद्भूताऽब्रवीच्छिवा ॥ ८५ ॥

85. She of pretty eye-brows asked those gods : "Who is she that is being lauded here ?" From her body-sheath an auspicious form emerged and replied.

स्तोत्रं ममैतत् क्रियते शुग्मभदैत्यनिराकृतैः ।
देवैः समेतैः समरे निशुम्भेन पराजितैः ॥ ८६ ॥

86. This laud is done to me by the gods assembled
here, who have been vanquished by Nishumbha in battle
and spurned by the Asura Shumbha.

शरीरकोशाद् यत् तस्याः पार्वत्या निःसृताम्बिका ।
कौशिकीति समस्तेषु ततो लोकेषु गीयते ॥ ८७ ॥

87. As the Mother emerged, from the physical
sheath of the daughter of the mountain, henceforth she is
extolled as Kowshiki in all the worlds.

तस्यां विनिर्गतायां तु कृष्णाऽभूत् सापि पार्वती ।
कालिकेति समाख्याता हिमालयकृताश्रया ॥ ८८ ॥

88. After she emerged, Parvati, the daughter of the
mountain, became dark and was called *kālikā* (dark). She
took her abode in the Himalayas.

ततोऽम्बिकां परं रूपं बिभ्राणां सुमनोहरम् ।
ददर्श चण्डो मुण्डश्च भृत्यौ शुम्भनिशुम्भयोः ॥ ८९ ॥

89. Then Chanda and Munda, the bearers of Shumbha and
Nishumbha espied the Mother who had taken a most charming
form.

ताभ्यां शुम्भाय चाख्याता सातीव सुमनोहरा ।
काप्यास्ते स्त्री महाराज भासयन्ती हिमाचलम् ॥ ९० ॥

90. Shumbha was informed by them : "O great king!
Some woman resides there, exceedingly charming, shed-
ding lustre on the mountain *himavān*.

नैव ताहक् कचिद्रूपं दृष्टं केनचिदुत्तमम् ।
ज्ञायतां काप्यसौ देवी गृह्यतां चासुरेश्वर ॥ ९१ ॥

91. Nobody has ever seen such an exquisite form anywhere. O King of Asuras, please ascertain who that Goddess is and take possession of her.

स्त्रीरत्नमतिचार्वङ्गी द्योतयन्ती दिशस्त्विषा ।
सा तु तिष्ठति दैत्येन्द्र तां भवान् द्रष्टुमर्हति ॥ ९२ ॥

92. A gem among women, of exceedingly lovely limbs, she stands, making the quarters luminous by her lustre. You ought to see her.

यानि रत्नानि मणयो गजाश्वादीनि वै प्रभो ।
त्रैलोक्ये तु समस्तानि साम्प्रतं भान्ति ते गृहे ॥ ९३ ॥

93. O Lord, whatever things are there in the three worlds, all of them, gems, jewels, elephants, horses etc. are now appearing in your mansion.

ऐरावतः समानीतो गजरत्नं पुरन्दरात् ।
पारिजाततरुश्चायं तथैवोच्चैः श्रवा हयः ॥ ९४ ॥

94. From Indra, Airavata, the gem amongst elephants has been brought, likewise this Parijata tree and the horse Ucchaihshravas.

विमानं हंससंयुक्तमेतत् तिष्ठति तेऽङ्गणे ।
रत्नभूतमिहानीतं यदासीद् वेधसोऽद्भुतम् ॥ ९५ ॥

95. Here stands in your courtyard the aerial chariot yoked with swans. This wonderful thing originally belonged to Brahma and has been brought as a gem of its class.

निधिरेष महापद्मः समानीतो धनेश्वरात् ।
किञ्जल्किनीं ददौ चाब्धिर्मालामम्लानपङ्कजाम् ॥ ९६ ॥

194

96. This treasure Mahapadma has been brought from Kubera, the lord of wealth. The ocean has given the garland of unfading lotuses, full of filaments.

छत्रं ते वारुणं गेहे काञ्चनस्रावि तिष्ठति ।
तथाऽयं स्यन्दनवरो यः पुरासीत् प्रजापतेः ॥ ९७ ॥

97. The umbrella of Varuna, showering gold is now in your mansion. Similarly this nice chariot which belonged once to the lord of beings.

मृत्योरुत्क्रान्तिदा नाम शक्तिरीश त्वया हृता ।
पाशः सलिलराजस्य भ्रातुस्तव परिग्रहे ॥ ९८ ॥

98. O Lord, you have seized the lance of Yama, the famous *utkrāntidā*. [1]The noose of Varuna, the king of waters, is in the possession of your brother.

निशुम्भस्याधिजगताश्च समस्ता रत्नजातयः ।
बहिरपि ददौ तुभ्यमग्निशौचे च वाससी ॥ ९९ ॥

99. All classes of gems born out of the ocean have become Nishumbha's. Agni too has granted you a pair of garments, purified by fire.

एवं दैत्येन्द्र रत्नानि समस्तान्याहृतानि ते ।
क्षीररत्नमेषा कल्याणी त्वया कस्मान्न गृह्यते ॥ १०० ॥

100. O Lord of the sons of division! Thus, all gems have been seized by you. Why this auspicious lady, a gem of women, has not been taken by you?

---

1 The lance is so called because it grants exit *utkrāntim dadāti*, out of the body.

ऋषिरुवाच ॥ १०१ ॥

101. The Sage said:

निशम्येति वचः शुम्भः स तदा चण्डमुण्डयोः ।
प्रेषयामास सुग्रीवं दूतं देव्या महासुरम् ॥ १०२ ॥

102. On hearing these words of Chanda and Munda, Shumbha sent the great Asura Sugriva as messenger to the Goddess.

इति चेति च वक्तव्या सा गत्वा वचनान्मम ।
यथा चाभ्येति सम्प्रीत्या तथा कार्यं त्वया लघु ॥ १०३ ॥

103. Go and tell her such and such according to what I say. You have to finish the work speedily in such a way that she comes forward in love.

स तत्र गत्वा यत्रास्ते शैलोद्देशेऽतिशोभने ।
तां च देवीं ततः प्राह श्लक्ष्णं मधुरया गिरा ॥ १०४ ॥

104. He went to the very lovely spot in the mountain where the Goddess was seated and spoke to her nicely sweet words.

दूत उवाच ॥ १०५ ॥

105. The messenger said :

देवि दैत्येश्वरः शुम्भस्त्रैलोक्ये परमेश्वरः ।
दूतोऽहं प्रेषितस्तेन त्वत्सकाशमिहागतः ॥ १०६ ॥

106. O Goddess, Shumbha, the lord of the sons of Diti, is the supreme sovereign in the three worlds. I am sent by him as messenger and have come here to your presence.

अव्याहताज्ञः सर्वासु यः सदा देवयोनिषु ।
निर्जिताखिलदैत्यारिः स यदाह श्रृणुष्व तत् ॥ १०७ ॥

107. None of the divine births has ever transgressed his commands and he has defeated all the foes of the Asuras. Listen to what he says!

मम त्रैलोक्यमखिलं मम देवा वशानुगाः ।
यज्ञभागानहं सर्वानुपाश्नामि पृथक् पृथक् ॥ १०८ ॥

108. Mine is the entire triple world. The gods are under my control. I partake each one of all their shares in the sacrifices.

त्रैलोक्ये वररत्नानि मम वश्यान्यशेषतः ।
तथैव गजरत्नं च हृतं देवेन्द्रवाहनम् ॥ १०९ ॥

109. All the best gems in the three worlds, without exception, are under my control. Likewise, Indra's vehicle, the gem of elephants has been taken by me.

क्षीरोदमथनोद्भूतमश्वरत्नं ममामरैः ।
उच्चैःश्रवससंज्ञं तत् प्रणिपत्य समर्पितम् ॥ ११० ॥

110. That gem of a horse, Ucchaishravas by name, produced out of the churning of the milky ocean was offered to me with salutations by the gods.

यानि चान्यानि देवेषु गन्धर्वेषूरगेषु च ।
रत्नभूतानि भूतानि तानि मय्येव शोभने ॥ १११ ॥

111. O beautiful one, whatever things were, like rare gems, with the gods, Gandharvas and Nagas they are all now with me only.

क्षीररत्नभूतां त्वां देवि लोके मन्यामहे वयम् ।
सा त्वमस्मानुपागच्छ यतो रत्नभुजो वयम् ॥ ११२ ॥

112. O Goddess, we in the world esteem you, a gem

among women, So, you come to us as we are the enjoyers of rare gems.

मां वा ममानुजं वापि निशुम्भमुरुविक्रमम् ।
भज त्वं चञ्चलापाङ्गि रत्नभूतासि वै यतः ॥ ११३ ॥

113. You come to me or to my brother Nishumbha of vast prowess, O lady of wavering glance, as you are really a gem.

परमैश्वर्यमतुलं प्राप्स्यसे मत्परिग्रहात् ।
एतद्बुद्ध्या समालोच्य मत्परिग्रहतां व्रज ॥ ११४ ॥

114. By accepting me you will get huge wealth of no comparison. Think over this in your mind and become my spouse.

ऋषिरुवाच ॥ ११५ ॥

115. The Sage said :

इत्युक्ता सा तदा देवी गम्भीरान्तःसिता जगौ ।
दुर्गा भगवती भद्रा ययेदं धार्यते जगत् ॥ ११६ ॥

116. Thus spoken to, the Goddess Durga, adorable and auspicious, by whom this world is upheld and sustained, said seriously, laughing within herself.

देव्युवाच ॥ ११७ ॥

117. The Goddess said :

सत्यमुक्तं त्वया नात्र मिथ्या किञ्चित् त्वयोदितम् ।
त्रैलोक्याधिपतिः शुम्भो निशुम्भश्चापि तादृशः ॥ ११८ ॥

118. You have spoken the truth. No falsehood has been uttered by you in this connection. Shumbha is the overlord of the triple world and Nishumbha too is likewise.

किं त्वत् यत् प्रतिज्ञातं मिथ्या तत् क्रियते कथम् ।
श्रूयतामल्पबुद्धित्वात् प्रतिज्ञा या कृता पुरा ॥ ११९ ॥

119. But how to falsify the promise formerly made out of immaturity in mind ? Hear the promise I made long ago.

यो मां जयति सङ्ग्रामे यो मे दर्पं व्यपोहति ।
यो मे प्रतिबलो लोके स मे भर्ता भविष्यति ॥ १२० ॥

120. He alone will become my husband who conquers me in battle, who vanquishes my pride and who is equal to me in strength in the world.

तदागच्छतु शुम्भोऽत्र निशुम्भो वा महाबलः ।
मां जित्वा किं चिरेणात्र पाणिं गृह्णातु मे लघु ॥ १२१ ॥

121. And so let Shumbha come here or Nishumbha of great strength. Let them conquer me easily and win my hand in marriage; why delay?

दूत उवाच ॥ १२२ ॥

122. The messenger said :

अवलिप्तासि मैवं त्वं देवि ब्रूहि ममाग्रतः ।
त्रैलोक्ये कः पुमांस्तिष्ठेदग्रे शुम्भनिशुम्भयोः ॥ १२३ ॥

123. O Goddess, you are haughty. Do not say like this in front of me. In all the three worlds, which male dare stand before Shumbha and Nishumbha?

अन्येषामपि दैत्यानां सर्वे देवा न वै युधि ।
तिष्ठन्ति सम्मुखे देवि किं पुनः स्त्री त्वमेकिका ॥ १२४ ॥

124. Also before other Asuras even all the gods assembled cannot stand in battle. Then what about you, all alone and that too a woman?

इन्द्राद्याः सकला देवास्तस्थुर्येषां न संयुगे ।
शुम्भादीनां कथं तेषां स्त्री प्रयास्यसि सम्मुखम् ॥ १२५ ॥

125. How can you, a woman, confront Shumbha
and others whom all the Gods headed by Indra cannot
stand in battle ?

सा त्वं गच्छ मयैवोक्ता पार्श्वं शुम्भनिशुम्भयोः ।
केशाकर्षणनिर्धूतगौरवा मा गमिष्यसि ॥ १२६ ॥

126. On my word alone, you go to the vicinity of
Shumbha and Nishumbha. There is no need of your going
to them dragged by your tresses and your dignity lost.

देव्युवाच ॥ १२७ ॥

127. The Goddess said :

एवमेतद् बली शुम्भो निशुम्भश्चापि तादृशः ।
किं करोमि प्रतिज्ञा मे यदनालोचिता पुरा ॥ १२८ ॥

128. It is true. Shumbha is strong and Nishumbha
is likewise. What can I do? My promise made in an
unthinking moment is there.

स त्वं गच्छ मयोक्तं ते यदेतत्सर्वमादृतः ।
तदाचक्ष्वासुरेन्द्राय स च युक्तं करोतु यत् ॥ १२९ ॥

129. You go and tell the lord of Asuras carefully
all that I have said. Let him do what is proper.

इति श्रीमार्कण्डेयपुराणे सावर्णिके मन्वन्तरे देवीमाहात्म्ये
पञ्चमः ॥ ५ ॥

Here ends the fifth of Devi Mahatmya in Markendeya
Purana during the period of Savarni, the Manu.

SIXTH CHAPTER

ऋषिरुवाच ॥ १ ॥

1. The Sage said :

इत्याकर्ण्य वचो देव्याः स दूतोऽमर्षपूरितः ।
समाचष्ट समागम्य दैत्यराजाय विस्तरात् ॥ २ ॥

2. Hearing the words of the Goddess thus, the messenger, full of impatience, went to the King of Asuras and told him in detail.

तस्य दूतस्य तद्वाक्यमाकर्ण्यासुरराट् ततः ।
सक्रोधः प्राह दैत्यानामधिपं धूम्रलोचनम् ॥ ३ ॥

3. Then, hearing those words of that messenger, the Asura monarch, with anger, told Dhumralochana, a chieftain of the Asuras.

हे धूम्रलोचनाशु त्वं स्वसैन्यपरिवारितः ।
तामानय बलाद् दुष्टां केशाकर्षणविह्वलाम् ॥ ४ ॥

4. O Dhumralochana, surrounded by your army, you speed up and bring by force that wicked one here unnerving her by dragging her by the hair.

तत्परित्राणदः कश्चिद्यदि वोत्तिष्ठते परः ।
स हन्तव्योऽमरो वापि यक्षो गन्धर्व एव वा ॥ ५ ॥

5. If any one else stands up to give her protection, he should be slain, be he a god, Yaksha or Gandharva.

ऋषिरुवाच ॥ ६ ॥

6. The Sage said :

तेनाज्ञप्तस्ततः शीघ्रं स दैत्यो धूम्रलोचनः ।
वृतः षष्ट्या सहस्राणामसुराणां द्रुतं ययौ ॥ ७ ॥

7. Then ordered by him quickly, the Asura Dhumralochana past surrounded by sixty thousand Asuras.

स दृष्ट्वा तां ततो देवीं तुहिनाचलसंस्थिताम् ।
जगादोच्चैः प्रयाहीति मूलं शुम्भनिशुम्भयोः ॥ ८ ॥

8. On seeing the Goddess seated on the snowy mountain, he shouted : "Set out to the presence of Shumbha and Nishumbha.

न चेत्प्रीत्याद्य भवती मद्भर्तारमुपैष्यति ।
ततो बलान्नयाम्येष केशाकर्षणविह्वलाम् ॥ ९ ॥

9. If you do not go to my master now with love, I shall take you by force, unnerving you by dragging you by the hair."

देव्युवाच ॥ १० ॥

10. The Goddess said :

दैत्येश्वरेण प्रहितो बलवान् बलसंवृतः ।
बलान्नयसि मामेवं ततः किं ते करोम्यहम् ॥ ११ ॥

11. You are sent by the lord of the Asuras. You are strong, are surrounded by an army. If you thus take me by force, what can I do to you?

ऋषिरुवाच ॥ १२ ॥

12. The Sage said :

इत्युक्तः सोऽभ्यधावत् तामसुरो धूम्रलोचनः ।
हुङ्कारेणैव तं भस्म सा चकाराम्बिका तदा ॥ १३ ॥

13. Spoken to thus, the Asura Dhumralochana rushed towards her. The mother reduced him to ashes by a mere grunt (*humkāra*).

अथ क्रुद्धं महासैन्यमसुराणां तथाम्बिका ।
बवर्ष सायकैस्तीक्ष्णैस्तथा शक्तिपरश्वधैः ॥ १४ ॥

14. Then the great army of the Asuras enraged showered on the mother sharp arrows, lances and hatchets.

ततो धुतसटः कोपात् कृत्वा नादं सुभैरवम् ।
पपाताSसुरसेनायां सिंहो देव्याः खवाहनः ॥ १५ ॥

15. Then the lion, the mount of the Goddess, shook its mane in anger, made a terrible noise and fell on the army of the Asuras.

कांश्चित् करप्रहारेण दैत्यानास्येन चापरान् ।
आक्रान्त्या चाधरेणान्यान् स जघान महासुरान् ॥ १६ ॥

16. Some Asuras with a blow of its paw, others with its mouth and some others with a stampede of its hind legs, it slaughtered.

केषांश्चित् पाटयामास नखैः कोष्ठानि केसरी ।
तथा तलप्रहारेण शिरांसि कृतवान् पृथक् ॥ १७ ॥

17. The lion tore with its claws the bellies of some Asuras and striking with its paw it severed their heads.

विच्छिन्नबाहुशिरसः कृतास्तेन तथा परे ।
पपौ च रुधिरं कोष्ठादन्येषां धुतकेसरः ॥ १८ ॥

18. It cut asunder the arms and heads of others; and shaking its mane, it drank the blood from the bellies of some others.

क्षणेन तद्बलं सर्वं क्षयं नीतं महात्मना ।
तेन केसरिणा देव्या वाहनेनातिकोपिना ॥ १९ ॥

19. In a moment, the entire army was destroyed by
that enraged lion, the noble vehicle of the Goddess.

श्रुत्वा तमसुरं देव्या निहतं धूम्रलोचनम् ।
बलं च क्षयितं कृत्स्नं देवीकेसरिणा ततः ॥ २० ॥

चुक्रोप दैत्याधिपतिः शुम्भः प्रस्फुरिताधरः ।
आज्ञापयामास च तौ चण्डमुण्डौ महासुरौ ॥ २१ ॥

20-21. Hearing that the Asura Dhumralochana was
slain by the Goddess and the entire army was destroyed
by the lion of the Goddess, Shumbha, the lord of the
Asuras, became furious. With his lips quivering, he ordered the great Asuras, Chanda and Munda.

हे चण्ड हे मुण्ड बलैर्बहुभिः परिवारितौ ।
तत्र गच्छत गत्वा च सा समानीयतां लघु ॥ २२ ॥

केशेष्वाकृष्य बध्द्वा वा यदि वः संशयो युधि ।
तदाशेषायुधैः सर्वैरसुरैर्विनिहन्यताम् ॥ २३ ॥

22-23. O Chanda, O Munda, You two go there
accompanied by a huge army and bring her here easily
by dragging by the hair or binding her. If you have doubts
about doing this, then strike her in battle with all the
weapons and all the Asuras.

तस्यां हतायां दुष्टायां सिंहे च विनिपातिते ।
शीघ्रमागम्यतां बध्द्वा गृहीत्वा तामथाम्बिकाम् ॥ २४ ॥

24. When that wicked one is struck and the lion felled, capture the Ambika, bind her and come with her quickly.

इति श्रीमार्कण्डेयपुराणे सावर्णिके मन्वन्तरे देवीमाहात्म्ये
षष्ठः ॥ ६ ॥

Here ends the sixth of the *Devi Mahatmya* in Markandeya Purana during the period of *Savarni* , the Manu.

SEVENTH CHAPTER

ऋषिरुवाच ॥ १ ॥

1. The Sage said :

आज्ञप्तास्ते ततो दैत्याश्चण्डमुण्डपुरोगमाः ।
चतुरङ्गबलोपेता ययुरभ्युद्यतायुधाः ॥ २ ॥

2. Then receiving the command, the Asuras headed by Chanda and Munda, fully equipped with arms, marched with the full fourfold complement of the armies.

दृदृशुस्ते ततो देवीमीषद्धासां व्यवस्थिताम् ।
सिंहस्योपरि शैलेन्द्रशृङ्गे महति काञ्चने ॥ ३ ॥

3. They saw the Goddess on a lofty golden peak of the Himalayas, seated on her lion, smiling.

ते दृष्ट्वा तां समादातुमुद्यमञ्चक्रुरुद्यताः ।
आकृष्टचापासिधरास्तथाऽन्ये तत्समीपगाः ॥ ४ ॥

4. Seeing her, they got excited and made effort to capture her. Some went near her with swords drawn and bows bent in readiness.

ततः कोपं चकारोच्चैरम्बिका तानरीन् प्रति ।
कोपेन चास्या वदनं मषीवर्णमभूत् तदा ॥ ५ ॥

5. Thereupon, the Mother became exceedingly angry towards those foes; and her face then became dark as ink, with anger.

भ्रुकुटीकुटिलात् तस्या ललाटफलकाद् द्रुतम् ।
काली करालवदना विनिष्क्रान्तासिपाशिनी ॥ ६ ॥

6. From the plane of her forehead, furrowed with
knitted eyebrows, immediately emerged forth Kali of the
terrible face, having the sword and the noose.

विचित्रखट्वाङ्गधरा नरमालाविभूषणा ।
द्वीपिचर्मपरीधाना शुष्कमांसातिभैरवा ॥ ७ ॥

7. She held a strange skull-topped staff, a garland
of human skeletons, her ornament. Wearing for her garment a tiger skin she looked terrible with her body, all
skin and bone.

अतिविस्तारवदना जिह्वाललनभीषणा ।
निमग्नारक्तनयना नादापूरितदिङ्मुखा ॥ ८ ॥

8. A wide gaping mouth and her lolling tongue
striking fear, with sunken eyes, all red, she filled the
quarters with her roar.

सा वेगेनाभिपतिता घातयन्ती महासुरान् ।
सैन्ये तत्र सुरारीणामभक्षयत तद् बलम् ॥ ९ ॥

9. She fell on the army, on the great Asuras fast,
slaughtering them. And she devoured the army of the foes
of the gods.

पार्ष्णिग्राहाङ्कुशग्राहायोधघण्टासमन्वितान् ।
समादायैकहस्तेन मुखे चिक्षेप वारणान् ॥ १० ॥

10. With one hand, she took and put into her mouth
the elephants, along with their guards on both the sides,
the drivers with their spikes, the warrior-riders and the
hanging bells.

तथैव योधं तुरगे रथं सारथिना सह ।
निक्षिप्य वक्त्रे दशनैश्चर्वयन्त्यतिभैरवम् ॥ ११ ॥

11. Likewise, putting into her mouth the cavalry with their horses and the chariots with the charioteers she chewed them most frightfully with her teeth.

एकं जग्राह केशेषु ग्रीवायामथ चापरम् ।
पादेनाक्रम्य चैवान्यमुरसाऽन्यमपोथयत् ॥ १२ ॥

12. She caught one by the hair, the other by the neck. She assaulted one with her foot and crushed the other by hugging to her chest.

तैर्मुक्तानि च शस्त्राणि महास्त्राणि तथासुरैः ।
मुखेन जग्राह रुषा दशनैर्मथितान्यपि ॥ १३ ॥

13. She caught in her mouth the arrows and the great missiles hurled by those Asuras and gnashed them in fury with her teeth.

बलिनां तद् बलं सर्वमसुराणां दुरात्मनाम् ।
ममर्दाभक्षयच्चान्यानन्यांश्चाताडयत् तदा ॥ १४ ॥

14. She pounded the entire army of the mighty wicked Asuras, devoured some and beat others.

असिना निहताः केचित् केचित् खट्वाङ्गताडिताः ।
जग्मुर्विनाशमसुरा दन्ताग्राभिहतास्तथा ॥ १५ ॥

15. Some were struck by the sword; some were beaten by the staff with skull-top. Other Asuras perished lacerated by the edge of her teeth.

क्षणेन तद् बलं सर्वमसुराणां निपातितम् ।
दृष्ट्वा चण्डोऽभिदुद्राव तां कालीमतिभीषणाम् ॥ १६ ॥

16. Seeing that the entire army of the Asuras was
in a moment laid to the ground, Chanda ran towards the
terrible Kali.

शरवर्षैर्महाभीमैर्भीमाक्षीं तां महासुरः ।
छादयामास चक्रैश्च मुण्डः क्षिप्तैः सहस्रशः ॥ १७ ॥

17. The great Asura with terrific showers of arrows
and Munda with discuses hurled in thousands covered her
of terrific eyes.

तानि चक्राण्यनेकानि विशमानानि तन्मुखम् ।
बभुर्यथार्कबिम्बानि सुबहूनि घनोदरम् ॥ १८ ॥

18. Those numerous discuses entering her mouth
shone like so many orbs of the Sun entering into the belly
of a cloud.

ततो जहासातिरुषा भीमं भैरवनादिनी ।
काली करालवदना दुर्दर्शदशनोज्ज्वला ॥ १९ ॥

19. Then Kali of terrible face, laughed fiercely in
wrath making a frightful noise, her gleaming teeth daz-
zling the eyes.

उत्थाय च महासिंहं देवी चण्डमधावत ।
गृहीत्वा चास्य केशेषु शिरस्तेनासिनाच्छिनत् ॥ २० ॥

20. Mounting on the great lion, the Devi rushed at
Chanda. Catching him by the hair, she severed the head
with her sword.

अथ मुण्डोऽभ्यधावत् तां दृष्ट्वा चण्डं निपातितम् ।
तमप्यपातयद् भूमौ सा खड्गाभिहतं रुषा ॥ २१ ॥

21. Seeing Chanda fallen, Munda rushed at her. She felled him too to the ground, striking him with the sword in her wrath.

हतशेषं ततः सैन्यं दृष्ट्वा चण्डं निपातितम् ।
मुण्डं चसुमहावीर्यं दिशो भेजे भयातुरम् ॥ २२ ॥

22. Seeing Chanda and the great warrior Munda vanquished, the remaining army left unslain, striken with terror, fled in every direction.

शिरश्चण्डस्य काली च गृहीत्वा मुण्डमेव च ।
प्राह प्रचण्डाट्टहासमिश्रमभ्येत्य चण्डिकाम् ॥ २३ ॥

23. And Kali bearing the heads of Chanda and Munda went up to Chandika and said laughing all the while frightfully loudly.

मया तवात्रोपहृतौ चण्डमुण्डौ महापशू ।
युद्धयज्ञे स्वयं शुम्भं निशुम्भं च हनिष्यसि ॥ २४ ॥

24. In this sacrifice of battle I have brought to you here two victims, Chanda and Munda. You yourself will slay Shumbha and Nishumbha.

ऋषिरुवाच ॥ २५ ॥

25. The Sage said :

तावानीतौ ततो दृष्ट्वा चण्डमुण्डौ महासुरौ ।
उवाच कालीं कल्याणी ललितं चण्डिका वचः ॥ २६ ॥

26. Then seeing the two great Asuras Chanda and

Munda brought to her, the auspicious Chandika spoke
nice words to Kali.

यस्माच्चण्डं च मुण्डं च गृहीत्वा त्वमुपागता ।
चामुण्डेति ततो लोके ख्याता देवी भविष्यसि ॥ २७ ॥

27. As you have come to me bringing Chanda and
Munda, you will henceforth become famous in the world
as Goddess Chamunda.

इति श्रीमार्कण्डेयपुराणे सावर्णिके मन्वन्तरे देवीमाहात्म्ये
सप्तमः ॥ ७ ॥

Here ends the seventh of Devi Mahatmya in
Markendeya Purana during the period of Savarni, the
Manu.

EIGHTH CHAPTER

ऋषिरुवाच ॥ १ ॥

1. The Sage said :

चण्डे च निहते दैत्ये मुण्डे च विनिपातिते ।
बहुलेषु च सैन्येषु क्षयितेष्वसुरेश्वरः ॥ २ ॥
ततः कोपपराधीनचेताः शुम्भः प्रतापवान् ।
उद्योगं सर्वसैन्यानां दैत्यानामादिदेश ह ॥ ३ ॥

2-3. When Chanda was killed and the Asura Munda was felled and when most of the armies were destroyed, the valorous Shumbha, the lord of the Asuras, with mind subjugated by wrath commanded the marshalling of all Asura armies.

अद्य सर्वबलैर्दैत्याः षडशीतिरुदायुधाः ।
कम्बूनां चतुराशीतिर्निर्यान्तु स्वबलैर्वृताः ॥ ४ ॥

4. Now, let the eighty-six Asuras with all their forces and uplifted weapons and the eightyfour of Kambu clan along with their forces set out for battle.

कोटिवीर्याणि पञ्चाशदसुराणां कुलानि वै ।
शतं कुलानि धौम्राणां निर्गच्छन्तु ममाज्ञया ॥ ५ ॥

5. Let fifty of the Kotivirya Asura families and hundred of the Dhowmra families come out by my command.

कालका दौर्हृदा मौर्याः कालिकेयास्तथासुराः ।
युद्धाय सज्जा निर्यान्तु आज्ञया त्वरिता मम ॥ ६ ॥

6. Likewise, let the Asura clans, Kalaka, Dowrhrida, Mowrya and Kalikeya hasten and start ready for battle, by my command.

इत्याज्ञाप्यासुरपतिः शुम्भो भैरवशासनः ।
निर्जगाम महासैन्यसहस्रैर्बहुभिर्वृतः ॥ ७ ॥

7. Commanding thus, Shumbha the lord of the Asuras, the cruel despot set out surrounded by thousands of huge armies.

आयान्तं चण्डिका दृष्ट्वा तत्सैन्यमतिभीषणम् ।
ज्याखनैः पूरयामास धरणीगगनान्तरम् ॥ ८ ॥

8. Seeing that ferocious army advancing, Chandika filled the space between the earth and the sky with twangs of the bow-string.

ततः सिंहो महानादमतीव कृतवान् नृप ।
घण्टास्खनेन तान्नादानम्बिका चोपवृंहयत् ॥ ९ ॥

9. O King! Then the lion made a very big roar. The Mother amplified those sounds by the ring of the bell.

धनुर्ज्यासिंहघण्टानां नादापूरितदिङ्मुखा ।
निनादैर्भीषणैः काली जिग्ये विस्तारितानना ॥ १० ॥

10. Kali who filled the quarters with the noise coming out of her gaping mouth, submerged with her terrific roars the twangs of the bow-string, the roar of the lion and the ring of the bell.

तं निनादमुपश्रुत्य दैत्यसैन्यैश्चतुर्दिशम् ।
देवी सिंहस्तथा काली सरोषैः परिवारिताः ॥ ११ ॥

11. Hearing this noise, the infuriated armies of the Asuras surrounded the Devi, lion and Kali on all the four directions.

एतस्मिन्नन्तरे भूप विनाशाय सुरद्विषाम् ।
भवायामरसिंहानामतिवीर्यबलान्विताः ॥ १२ ॥

ब्रह्मेशगुहविष्णूनां तथेन्द्रस्य च शक्तयः ।
शरीरेभ्यो विनिष्क्रम्य तद्रूपैश्चण्डिकां ययुः ॥ १३ ॥

12-13. O King! Meanwhile for ensuring the destruction of the enemies of gods and the existence of the great gods, the force of Brahma, Siva, Guha, Vishnu and Indra, possessed of great valour and strength, emerged out of their respective forms.

यस्य देवस्य यद्रूपं यथा भूषणवाहनम् ।
तद्वदेव हि तच्छक्तिरसुरान् योद्धुमाययौ ॥ १४ ॥

14. Whatever was the form of the Godhead, whatever his ornaments and vehicle, in that very guise his force came to fight the Asuras.

हंसयुक्तविमानाग्रे साक्षसूत्रकमण्डलुः ।
आयाता ब्रह्मणः शक्तिर्ब्रह्माणीत्यभिधीयते ॥ १५ ॥

15. Seating on the aerial chariot yoked with swans, having the rosary of beads and water-pot came the force of Brahma. She is called *brahmānī*.

माहेश्वरी वृषारूढा त्रिशूलवरधारिणी ।
महाहिवलया प्राप्ता चन्द्ररेखाविभूषणा ॥ १६ ॥

16. Maheswari came mounted on the bull, holding the great trident, with huge serpents for bangles and with the digit of the moon for ornament.

कौमारी शक्तिहस्ता च मयूरवरवाहना ।
योद्धुमभ्याययौ दैत्यानग्निका गुहरूपिणी ॥ १७ ॥

17. The mother *kaumāri* came to fight the Asuras
in the form of Guha, mounted on the pretty peacock and
wielding the lance in her hand.

तथैव वैष्णवी शक्तिर्गरुडोपरि संस्थिता ।
शङ्खचक्रगदाशाङ्खखड्गहस्ताऽभ्युपाययौ ॥ १८ ॥

18. Likewise, Vaishnavi, the force of Vishnu, came
on the scene, seated on Garuda, with the conch, discus,
mace the bow *śārnga* and the sword in her hands.

यज्ञवाराहमतुलं रूपं या बिभ्रतो हरेः ।
शक्तिः साप्याययौ तत्र वाराहीं बिभ्रती तनुम् ॥ १९ ॥

19. The One who took the incomparable form of
Vishnu, the sacrificial boar, she also came as the Shakti
vārahi, in a boar-like form.

नारसिंही नृसिंहस्य बिभ्रती सदृशं वपुः ।
प्राप्ता तत्र सटाक्षेपक्षिप्तनक्षत्रसंहतिः ॥ २० ॥

20. *nārasimhi* came there as well, bearing a similar
form to that of Narasimha; and the constellations of stars
were scattered hither and thither whenever she shook her
mane.

वज्रहस्ता तथैवैन्द्री गजराजोपरि स्थिता ।
प्राप्ता सहस्रनयना यथा शक्रस्तथैव सा ॥ २१ ॥

21. Seated on the King of elephants, with a thunderbolt in hand and possessed of thousand eyes Aindri
joined the fray. She was just like Indra.

ततः परिवृतस्तामिरीशानो देवशक्तिभिः ।
हन्यन्तामसुराः शीघ्रं मम प्रीत्याह चण्डिकाम् ॥ २२ ॥

22. Thereupon, Shiva surrounded by those forces of the gods told Chandika: "Let the Asuras be killed without delay, out of love for me."

ततो देवीशरीरात्तु विनिष्क्रान्तातिभीषणा ।
चण्डिका शक्तिरत्युग्रा शिवाशतनिनादिनी ॥ २३ ॥

23. Then, from the body of the Goddess emerged a terrific force of Chandika, roaring frightfully like hundred jackals yelling together.

सा चाह धूम्रजटिलमीशानमपराजिता ।
दूतत्वं गच्छ भगवन् पार्श्वं शुम्भनिशुम्भयोः ॥ २४ ॥

24. She, the unvanquished, told Shiva of the matted smoke-hued hair : "Lord, please go as a messenger to the presence of Shumbha and Nishumbha."

ब्रूहि शुम्भं निशुम्भं च दानवावतिगर्वितौ ।
ये चान्ये दानवास्तत्र युद्धाय समुपस्थिताः ॥ २५ ॥

25. Tell those two arrogant Asuras Shumbha and Nishumbha, and the other Asuras that might be present there ready for the battle.

त्रैलोक्यमिन्द्रो लभतां देवाः सन्तु हविर्भुजः ।
यूयं प्रयात पातालं यदि जीवितुमिच्छथ ॥ २६ ॥

26. Let Indra get the sovereignty of the triple world. Let the gods partake the oblations. You go to the nether regions if you want to live.

बलावलेपादथ चेद्भवन्तो युद्धकाङ्क्षिणः ।
तदागच्छत तृप्यन्तु मच्छिवाः पिशितेन वः ॥ २७ ॥

27. Or else, proud of your strength if you desire battle, then come by all means. Let my jackals feed contentedly on your flesh.

यतो नियुक्तो दौत्येन तया देव्या शिवः खयम् ।
शिवदूतीति लोकेऽस्मिंस्ततः सा ख्यातिमागता ॥ २८ ॥

28. As that Devi employed Shiva himself as a messenger, she became renowned in this world as Shivaduti.

तेऽपि श्रुत्वा वचो देव्याः शर्वाख्यातं महासुराः ।
अमर्षापूरिता जग्मुर्यत्र कात्यायनी स्थिता ॥ २९ ॥

29. Those great Asuras, hearing the words of the Goddess communicated by Shiva were filled with indignation and repaired to the place where Katyayani stood.

ततः प्रथममेवाग्रे शरशक्त्यृष्टिवृष्टिभिः ।
ववर्षुरुद्धतामर्षास्तां देवीममरारयः ॥ ३० ॥

30. Then, in the beginning itself their fury roused, the enemies of the immortals showered on the Goddess volleys of arrows, lances and double-edged swords.

सा च तान् प्रहितान् बाणाञ्छूलशक्तिपरश्वधान् ।
चिच्छेद लीलयाध्मातधनुर्मुक्तैर्महेषुभिः ॥ ३१ ॥

31. And she cut asunder playfully with her powerful arrows released from her full-drawn bow the arrows, the spears, the lances and the hatchets aimed at her.

तस्याग्रतस्तथा काली शूलपातविदारितान् ।
खट्वाङ्गपोथितांश्चारीन्कुर्वती व्यचरत् तदा ॥ ३२ ॥

32. Then in front of him, Kali roamed about tearing the foes with the fall of her spear and mashing them with her skull-topped staff.

कमण्डलुजलाक्षेपहतवीर्यान् हतौजसः ।
ब्रह्माणी चाकरोच्छत्रून् येन येन स धावति ॥ ३३ ॥

33. Brahmani, at whomsoever she rushed, she made those enemies lose their strength and spirit by sprinkling on them the water from her water-pot.

माहेश्वरी त्रिशूलेन तथा चक्रेण वैष्णवी ।
दैत्याञ्जघान कौमारी तथा शक्त्याऽतिकोपना ॥ ३४ ॥

34. Maheshwari with her trident, Vaishnavi with her discus and the infuriated Kaumari with her lance slew the Asuras.

ऐन्द्रीकुलिशपातेन शतशो दैत्यदानवाः ।
पेतुर्विदारिताः पृथ्व्यां रुधिरौघप्रवर्षिणः ॥ ३५ ॥

35. The offsprings of Diti and Danu fell on the ground in hundreds split by the stroke of Aindri's thunderbolt, emitting streams of blood.

तुण्डप्रहारविध्वस्ता दष्ट्राग्रक्षतवक्षसः ।
वाराहमूर्त्या न्यपतंश्चक्रेण च विदारिताः ॥ ३६ ॥

36. Pounded by the assailing snout of the boarformed Goddess, wounded in the chest by the edge of her tusk and rent by her discus, they fell.

नखैर्विदारितांश्चान्यान् भक्षयन्ती महासुरान् ।
नारसिंही चचाराजौ नादापूर्णदिगम्बरा ॥ ३७ ॥

37. Filling the sky and the quarters with her roar,

Narasimhi roamed about in the battlefield devouring the other great Asuras torn by her claws.

चण्डाट्टहासैरसुराः शिवदूत्यमिदूषिताः ।
पेतुः पृथिव्यां पतितास्तांश्चखादाथ सा तदा ॥ ३८ ॥

38. Frustrated by the terrific loud laughter of Shivaduti, the Asuras fell on the ground and she promptly ate them up, as they fell.

इति मातृगणं क्रुद्धं मर्दयन्तं महासुरान् ।
दृष्ट्वाऽभ्युपायैर्विविधैनेशुदेवारिसैनिकाः ॥ ३९ ॥

39. Seeing the angry host of mothers smashing the great Asuras thus by various means, the troops of the foes of the gods took to their heels.

पलायनपरान् दृष्ट्वा दैत्यान् मातृगणार्दितान् ।
योद्धुमभ्याययौ क्रुद्धो रक्तबीजो महासुरः ॥ ४० ॥

40. Noticing that the Asuras assailed by the host of mothers were intent on running away, the great Asura Raktabija enraged came forward to fight.

रक्तबिन्दुर्यदा भूमौ पतत्यस्य शरीरतः ।
समुत्पतति मेदिन्यां तत्प्रमाणो महासुरः ॥ ४१ ॥

41. No sooner a drop of blood falls from his body on the ground than a great Asura of his size springs forth on the earth.

युयुधे स गदापाणिरिन्द्रशक्त्या महासुरः ।
ततश्चेन्द्री खवज्रेण रक्तबीजमताडयत् ॥ ४२ ॥

42. With mace in hand the great Asura combatted with Indra's force. Then Aindri struck Raktabija with her thunderbolt.

कुलिशेनाहतस्याशु बहु सुस्राव शोणितम् ।
समुत्तस्थुस्ततो योधास्तद्रूपास्तत्पराक्रमाः ॥ ४३ ॥

43. Struck by the thunderbolt, blood from him soon flowed out in abundance. From that sprang up warriors of his stature and of his might.

यावन्तः पतितास्तस्य शरीराद्रक्तबिन्दवः ।
तावन्तः पुरुषा जातास्तद्वीर्यबलविक्रमाः ॥ ४४ ॥

44. As many drops of blood fell from his body so many men were born of his valour, strength and prowess.

ते चापि युयुधुस्तत्र पुरुषा रक्तसम्भवाः ।
समं मातृभिरत्युग्रशस्त्रपातातिभीषणम् ॥ ४५ ॥

45. And those men born out of blood fought with the mothers more terribly hurling fierce weapons.

पुनश्च वज्रपातेन क्षतमस्य शिरो यदा ।
ववाह रक्तं पुरुषास्ततो जाताः सहस्रशः ॥ ४६ ॥

46. Again, when his head, was hurt with the fall of the thunderbolt the blood flowed; and from that men were born in thousands.

वैष्णवी समरे चैनं चक्रेणाभिजघान ह ।
गदया ताडयामास ऐन्द्री तमसुरेश्वरम् ॥ ४७ ॥

47. In the battle Vaishnavi struck him with the discus. Aindri hit that lord of the Asuras with a mace.

वैष्णवीचक्रभिन्नस्य रुधिरस्रावसम्भवैः ।
सहस्रशो जगद्व्याप्तं तत्प्रमाणैर्महासुरैः ॥ ४८ ॥

48. The world was pervaded by thousands of great Asuras of his size when they were born from the stream

of blood flowing out of the cut inflicted by Vaishnavi's discus.

शक्त्या जघान कौमारी वाराही च तथाऽसिना ।
माहेश्वरी त्रिशूलेन रक्तबीजं महासुरम् ॥ ४९ ॥

49. Kaumari struck him with her lance and Varahi with her sword. Maheswari assaulted the great Asura Raktabija with her trident.

स चापि गदया दैत्यः सर्वा एवाहनत् पृथक् ।
मातॄः कोपसमाविष्टो रक्तबीजो महासुरः ॥ ५० ॥

50. The great Asura Raktabija too, filled with anger struck the mothers with his mace individually and severally.

तस्याहतस्य बहुधा शक्तिशूलादिभिर्भुवि ।
पपात यो वै रक्तौघस्तेनासञ्छतशोऽसुराः ॥ ५१ ॥

51. Struck variously by lances, spears and other weapons, whenever the stream of blood fell on the ground, then from there sprung up Asuras in hundreds.

तैश्चासुरासृक्सम्भूतैरसुरैः सकलं जगत् ।
व्याप्तमासीत् ततो देवा भयमाजग्मुरुत्तमम् ॥ ५२ ॥

52. The entire world was pervaded by the Asuras born out of that Asura's blood. By that the gods became very much frightened.

तान् विषण्णान् सुरान् दृष्ट्वा चण्डिका प्राहसत्वरा ।
उवाच कालीं चामुण्डे विस्तीर्णं वदनं कुरु ॥ ५३ ॥

53. Seeing the gods dejected, Chandika laughed and soon said to Kali : O Chamunda, keep your mouth wide open.

मच्छस्त्रपातसम्भूतान् रक्तबिन्दून् महासुरान् ।
रक्तबिन्दोः प्रतीच्छ त्वं वक्त्रेणानेन वेगिना ॥ ५४ ॥

54. And with this mouth quickly take in the drops
of blood generated by the fall of my weapons and the great
Asuras generated out of the drops of blood.

भक्षयन्ती चर रणे तदुत्पन्नान् महासुरान् ।
एवमेष क्षयं दैत्यः क्षीणरक्तो गमिष्यति ॥ ५५ ॥

55. Roam about in the battlefield devouring the
great Asuras born out of him. Thus this Asura will perish
losing all his blood.

भक्ष्यमाणास्त्वया चोग्रा न चोत्पत्स्यन्ति चापरे ॥ ५६ ॥

56. As you will be devouring them, no more of the
fierce Asuras will come into being.

इत्युक्त्वा तां ततो देवी शूलेनाभिजघान तम् ।
मुखेन काली जगृहे रक्तबीजस्य शोणितम् ॥ ५७ ॥

57. Having directed her thus, the Goddess then
struck him with the spear. Kali caught in her mouth the
blood of Raktabija.

ततोऽसावाजघानाथ गदया तत्र चण्डिकाम् ।
न चास्या वेदनां चक्रे गदापातोऽल्विकामपि ॥ ५८ ॥

58. Then he struck Chandika with his mace. But the
stroke of the mace did not cause her pain in the least.

तस्याहतस्य देहात्तु बहु सुस्राव शोणितम् ।
यतस्ततस्तद्वक्त्रेण चामुण्डा सम्प्रतीच्छति ॥ ५९ ॥

59. On the other hand, blood flowed copiously from
the stricken parts of his body and wherever it flowed
Chamunda took it in with her mouth.

मुखे समुद्‌गता येऽस्या रक्तपातान्महासुराः ।
तांश्चखादाथ चामुण्डा पपौ तस्य च शोणितम् ॥ ६० ॥

60. And whoever were the Asuras born out of the blood taken in her mouth, Chamunda ate them up and went on drinking his blood.

देवी शूलेन वज्रेण बाणैरसिभिर्‌ऋष्टिभिः ।
जघान रक्तबीजं तं चामुण्डापीतशोणितम् ॥ ६१ ॥

61. The Goddess smote Raktabija whose blood was being drunk by Chamunda with spear, thunderbolt, shafts, swords and double-edged swords.

स पपात महीपृष्ठे शस्त्रसङ्घसमाहतः ।
नीरक्तश्च महीपाल रक्तबीजो महासुरः ॥ ६२ ॥

62. O the guardian of the earth, the great Asura Raktabija hit by a plethora of weapons and devoid of all blood fell on the lap of the earth.

ततस्ते हर्षमतुलमवापुस्त्रिदशा नृप ।
तेषां मातृगणो जातो ननर्तासृङ्मदोद्धतः ॥ ६३ ॥

63. O King! Then the gods attained happiness unparalleled. The host of mothers, born out of them danced intoxicated with the bouts of blood.

इति श्रीमार्कण्डेयपुराणे सावर्णिके मन्वन्तरे देवीमाहात्म्ये अष्टमः ॥ ८ ॥

Here ends the eighth of Devi Mahatmya in Markendeya Purana, during the period of Savarni, the Manu.

NINTH CHAPTER

राजोवाच ॥ १ ॥

1. The King said :

विचित्रमिदमाख्यातं भगवन् भवता मम ।
देव्याश्चरितमाहात्म्यं रक्तबीजवधाश्रितम् ॥ २ ॥

2. Sire, wonderful is this narration related by you, the glory of the Devi's deed pertaining to the slaying of Raktabija.

भूयश्चेच्छाम्यहं श्रोतुं रक्तबीजे निपातिते ।
चकार शुम्भो यत्कर्म निशुम्भश्चातिकोपनः ॥ ३ ॥

3. I want to hear further what act did Shumbha and the wrathful Nishumbha do when Raktabija was felled.

ऋषिरुवाच ॥ ४ ॥

4. The sage said :

चकार कोपमतुलं रक्तबीजे निपातिते ।
शुम्भासुरो निशुम्भश्च हतेष्वन्येषु चाहवे ॥ ५ ॥

5. When Raktabija was felled and the others killed in battle, the Asuras Shumbha and Nishumbha became exceedingly angry.

हन्यमानं महासैन्यं विलोक्यामर्षमुद्वहन् ।
अभ्यधावन्निशुम्भोऽथ मुख्ययाऽसुरसेनया ॥ ६ ॥

6. Flying into a passion on seeing his great army being slaughtered Nishumbha rushed forth with the chief forces of the Asuras.

तस्याग्रतस्तथा पृष्ठे पार्श्वयोश्च महासुराः ।
सन्दष्टौष्ठपुटाः क्रुद्धा हन्तुं देवीमुपाययुः ॥ ७ ॥

7. In front of him, at his back and on his sides great Asuras biting their lip in rage advanced for slaying the Goddess.

आजगाम महावीर्यः शुम्भोऽपि स्वबलैर्वृतः ।
निहन्तुं चण्डिकां कोपात् कृत्वा युद्धं तु मातृभिः ॥ ८ ॥

8. The great warrior Shumbha too accompanied by his forces arrived in fury to slay Chandika, after having fought with the mothers.

ततो युद्धमतीवासीद्देव्याः शुम्भनिशुम्भयोः ।
शरवर्षमतीघोग्रं मेघयोरिव वर्षतोः ॥ ९ ॥

9. Then there began an intense fight between the Goddess on one side and Shumbha, Nishumbha on the other, from whom the volley of arrows was intensely fierce like pourings from two clouds.

विच्छेदास्ताञ्छरांस्ताभ्यां चण्डिका स्वशरोत्करैः ।
ताडयामास चाङ्गेषु शस्त्रौघैरसुरेश्वरौ ॥ १० ॥

10. Chandika with her shower of arrows cut asunder their arrows and hit the lords of the Asuras on different parts of the body with a stream of weapons.

निशुम्भो निशितं खड्गं चर्म चादाय सुप्रभम् ।
अताडयन्मूर्ध्नि सिंहं देव्या वाहनमुत्तमम् ॥ ११ ॥

11. Nishumbha took a sharp sword and a shining shield and hit the lion, the superb vehicle of the Goddess, on the head.

ताडिते वाहने देवी क्षुरप्रेणासिमुत्तमम् ।
निशुम्भस्याशु चिच्छेद चर्म चाप्यष्टचन्द्रकम् ॥ १२ ॥

12. When her mount was hit, the goddess soon cut asunder with a sharp-edged arrow the superb sword and the shield figuring eight moons, of Nishumba.

छिन्ने चर्मणि खड्गे च शक्तिं चिक्षेप सोऽसुरः ।
तामप्यस्य द्विधा चक्रे चक्रेणासिमुखागताम् ॥ १३ ॥

13. When his sword and his shield were cut as under, that Asura threw the lance. She cut that also into two, as it came towards her, with a discus.

कोपाध्मातो निशुम्भोऽथ शूलं जग्राह दानवः ।
आयान्तं मुष्टिपातेन देवी तच्चाप्यचूर्णयत् ॥ १४ ॥

14. Then the Asura Nishumbha bloated with anger seized the spear. The Goddess powdered that also as it came towards her, with a blow of her fist.

आविध्याथ गदां सोऽपि चिक्षेप चण्डिकां प्रति ।
सापि देव्याः त्रिशूलेन भिन्ना भसत्वमागता ॥ १५ ॥

15. And he whirled his mace and threw it towards Chandika. That too was reduced to ashes split by her trident.

ततः परशुहस्तं तमायान्तं दैत्यपुङ्गवम् ।
आहत्य देवी बाणौघैरपातयत भूतले ॥ १६ ॥

16. Then the Goddess struck with a volley of arrows

that strong and eminent Asura advancing towards her with a battle-axe in his hand and laid him flat on the ground.

तस्मिन्निपतिते भूमौ निशुम्भे भीमविक्रमे ।
भ्रातर्यतीव संक्रुद्धः प्रययौ हन्तुमम्बिकाम् ॥ १७ ॥

17. When his brother, Nishumba, of terrible prowess was thus laid flat on the ground,(Shumbha) exceedingly angry set out to slay Ambika.

स रथस्थस्तथात्युच्चैर्गृहीतपरमायुधैः ।
भुजैरष्टामिरतुलैर्व्याप्याशेषं बभौ नभः ॥ १८ ॥

18. Standing in his chariot and pervading the entire sky with his incomparable lofty eight arms holding excellent weapons, he shone.

तमायान्तं समालोक्य देवी शङ्खमवादयत् ।
ज्याशब्दं चापि धनुषश्चकारातीव दुःसहम् ॥ १९ ॥

19. Seeing him advancing, the Goddess blew the conch and made a twang with her bow-string which was simply unbearable.

पूरयामास ककुभो निजघण्टास्वनेन च ।
समस्तदैत्यसैन्यानां तेजोवधविधायिना ॥ २० ॥

20. She filled the quarters with the sound of her bell, that rang the death knell to the splendour of all the hosts of Asuras.[1]

---

1 In external worship, the bell plays a significant part. Its ringing is a sign for invocation of the Deity, *devatāhvāna tāncanam* . For the coming in of the gods and for the driving away of demoniac forces one should ring the bell.

आगमार्थं तु देवानां गमनार्थं च रक्षसाम् ।
कुर्यात् घण्टारवं तत्र देवताह्वानलाञ्छनम् ॥

ततः सिंहो महानादैस्त्याजितेभमहामदैः ।
पूरयामास गगनं गां तथैव दिशो दश ॥ २१ ॥

21. Then the lion filled the sky, the earth and the ten-quarters with its loud roars, making the elephants there abandon their wild rut.

ततः काली समुत्पत्य गगनं क्ष्मामताडयत् ।
कराभ्यां तन्निनादेन प्राक्क्ष्वनास्ते तिरोहिताः ॥ २२ ॥

22. Thereupon, Kali jumped and slapped the sky and the earth with both her hands. In that sound all the previous sounds were submerged.

अट्टाट्टहासमशिवं शिवदूती चकार ह ।
तैः शब्दैरसुरास्त्रेसुः शुम्भः कोपं परं ययौ ॥ २३ ॥

23. Shivaduti began her thundering inauspicious laughter. By these sounds the Asuras were terrified. Shumbha became exceedingly angry.

दुरात्मंस्तिष्ठ तिष्ठेति व्याजहाराम्बिका यदा ।
तदा जयेत्यमिहितं देवैराकाशसंस्थितैः ॥ २४ ॥

24. No sooner the Mother exclaimed "Stand fast, O wicked one!" then the gods stationed in the sky proclaimed "Victory to thee"

शुम्भेनागत्य या शक्तिर्मुक्ता ज्वालातिभीषणा ।
आयान्ती वह्निकूटाभा सा निरस्ता महोल्कया ॥ २५ ॥

25. The lance, flaming fiercely, hurled by the advancing Shumbha was coming like a mount of fire. It was prevented by a big fire-brand.

सिंहनादेन शुम्भस्य व्याप्तं लोकत्रयान्तरम् ।
निर्घातनिःस्वनो घोरो जितवानवनीपते ॥ २६ ॥

26. The space between the three worlds was pervaded by Shumbha's war-cry. O Lord of earth, the dreadful thunder-stroke overpowered it.

शुम्भमुक्ताञ्छरान्देवी शुम्भस्तत्प्रहिताञ्छरान् ।
चिच्छेद स्वशरैरुग्रैः शतशोऽथ सहस्रशः ॥ २७ ॥

27. In hundreds and thousands, they cut with their
fierce arrows those of the opponent—the Goddess cutting
the arrows hurled by Shumbha and Shumbha cutting the
arrows released by her.

ततः सा चण्डिका क्रुद्धा शूलेनाभिजघान तम् ।
स तदाभिहतो भूमौ मूर्च्छितो निपपात ह ॥ २८ ॥

28. Then the enraged Chandika struck him with the
spear. Hit by that he fell swooning to the ground.

ततो निशुम्भः सम्प्राप्य चेतनामात्तकार्मुकः ।
आजघान शरैर्देवीं कालीं केसरिणं तथा ॥ २९ ॥

29. Then Nishumbha regaining consciousness, took
his bow and smote with his arrows, the Goddess, Kali and
the lion.

पुनश्च कृत्वा बाहूनामयुतं दनुजेश्वरः ।
चक्रायुतेन दितिजश्छादयामास चण्डिकाम् ॥ ३० ॥

30. Again the lord of the Asuras, son of Diti,
creating for himself ten thousand arms covered Chandika
with ten thousand discuses.

ततो भगवती क्रुद्धा दुर्गा दुर्गार्तिनाशिनी ।
चिच्छेद तानि चक्राणि स्वशरैः सायकांश्च तान् ॥ ३१ ॥

31. Then the Goddess Durga, the destroyer of pains

and perils, became angry and cut asunder those discuses and those arrows with her own arrows.

तती निशुम्भो वेगेन गदामादाय चण्डिकाम् ।
अभ्यधावत वै हन्तुं दैत्यसैन्यसमावृतः ॥ ३२ ॥

32. Then Nishumbha accompanied by the army of the Asuras swiftly taking his mace rushed forward to kill Chandika.

तस्यापतत पवाशु गदां चिच्छेद चण्डिका ।
खड्गेन शितधारेण स च शूलं समाददे ॥ ३३ ॥

33. As he was rushing, Chandika with a sharp-edged sword broke the mace to pieces. And he seized the spear.

शूलहस्तं समायान्तं निशुम्भममरार्दनम् ।
हृदि विव्याध शूलेन वेगाविद्धेन चण्डिका ॥ ३४ ॥

34. Chandika smote in the heart with a spear hurled with speed, Nishumbha, the afflicter of the gods, who was coming towards her with a spear in hand.

भिन्नस्य तस्य शूलेन हृदयान्निःसृतोऽपरः ।
महाबलो महावीर्यस्तिष्ठेति पुरुषो वदन् ॥ ३५ ॥

35. From his heart pierced by the spear emerged another person of great strength and of great valour exclaiming "Stop."

तस्य निष्क्रामतो देवी प्रहस्य खनवत्तमतः ।
शिरश्चिच्छेद खड्गेन ततोऽसावपतद् भुविः ॥ ३६ ॥

36. As he emerged, the Goddess laughed noisily and cut off his head with her sword. So he fell to the ground.

ततः सिंहश्चखादोग्रदंष्ट्राक्षुण्णशिरोधरान् ।
असुरांस्तांस्तथा काली शिवदूती तथापरान् ॥ ३७ ॥

37. Then the lion ground the necks of Asuras with its fierce teeth and ate them up. Likewise, Kali and Shivaduti, ate the others.

कौमारीशक्तिनिर्भिन्नाः केचिन्नेशुर्महासुराः ।
ब्रह्माणीमन्त्रपूतेन तोयेनान्ये निराकृताः ॥ ३८ ॥

38. Certain great Asuras perished pierced by the lance of *kaumari*. Others were repulsed by the water sanctified by the Mantra of *brahmani*.

माहेश्वरीत्रिशूलेन भिन्नाः पेतुस्तथापरे ।
वाराहीतुण्डघातेन केचिच्चूर्णीकृता भुवि ॥ ३९ ॥

39. Some others were cut asunder by the trident of Maheshwari and fell. Certain Asuras were smashed to powder on the ground by the assault of Varahi's snout.

खण्डं खण्डं च चक्रेण वैष्णव्या दानवाः कृताः ।
वज्रेण चैन्द्रीहस्ताग्रविमुक्तेन तथापरे ॥ ४० ॥

40. The Asuras were cut into bits and pieces by the discus of Vaishnavi. Similarly others were dealt with by the thunderbolt released from the forepart of Aindri's hand.

केचिद्विनेशुरसुराः केचिन्नष्टा महाहवात् ।
भक्षिताश्चापरे काली शिवदूतीमृगाधिपैः ॥ ४१ ॥

41. Some Asuras perished. Some fled from the great battle. Others were devoured by Kali, Shivaduti and the lord of animals.

इति श्रीमार्कण्डेयपुराणे सावर्णिके मन्वन्तरे देवीमाहात्म्ये
नवमः ॥ ९ ॥

Here ends the ninth of Devi Mahatmya in Markendeya Purana during the period of Savarni, the Manu.

TENTH CHAPTER

ऋषिरुवाच ॥ १ ॥

1. The Sage said :

निशुम्भं निहतं दृष्ट्वा भ्रातरं प्राणसम्मितम् ।
हन्यमानं बलं चैव शुम्भः क्रुद्धोऽब्रवीद्वचः ॥ २ ॥

2. Seeing his brother Nishumbha, who was to him as his own life, killed and his forces being slain Shumbha, furious, spoke these words:

बलावलेपदुष्टे त्वं मा दुर्गे गर्वमावह ।
अन्यासां बलमाश्रित्य युद्धसे यातिमानिनी ॥ ३ ॥

3. O Durga, wicked and proud of your strength, do not be haughty. You fight depending on the strength of others and yet you boast of your self-respect!

देव्युवाच ॥ ४ ॥

4. The Goddess said :

एकैवाहं जगत्यत्र द्वितीया का ममापरा ।
पश्यैता दुष्ट मय्येव विशन्त्यो मद्विभूतयः ॥ ५ ॥

5. In this world, I, the one, alone exist. Who is the second person other than myself ? Look, wicked one, these manifestations of mine enter into myself.

ततः समस्तास्ता देव्यो ब्रह्माणीप्रमुखा लयम् ।
तस्या देव्यास्तनौ जग्मुरेकैवासीत् तदाम्बिका ॥ ६ ॥

6. Then all those Devis headed by Brahmani got merged in the body of the Goddess. Then the Mother alone was there.

देव्युवाच ॥ ७ ॥

7. The Goddess said :

अहं विभूत्या बहुभिरिह रूपैर्यदास्थिता ।
तत्संहृतं मयैकैव तिष्ठाम्याजौ स्थिरो भव ॥ ८ ॥

8. I, by manifold manifestations, stood here in many forms. These are now withdrawn by me. Alone I stand. Be steadfast in the battle.

ऋषिरुवाच ॥ ९ ॥

9. The Sage said :

ततः प्रववृते युद्धं देव्याः शुम्भस्य चोभयोः ।
पश्यतां सर्वदेवानामसुराणां च दारुणम् ॥ १० ॥

10. Then started the battle between them both, the Goddess and Shumbha, striking terror in the witnessing Asuras and all the gods.

शरवर्षैः शितैः शस्त्रैस्तथा चास्त्रैः सुदारुणैः ।
तयोर्युद्धमभूद् भूयः सर्वलोकभयङ्करम् ॥ ११ ॥

11. With showers of arrows, the sharp weapons and with terrific missiles, there arose again a combat between them, fearful to the whole world.

दिव्यान्यस्त्राणि शतशो मुमुचे यान् यथाम्बिका ।
बभञ्ज तानि दैत्येन्द्रस्तत्प्रतीघातकर्तृभिः ॥ १२ ॥

12. What all divine missiles the Mother discharged in hundreds, the lord of the Asuras broke them all with nullifying weapons.

मुक्तानि तेन चास्त्राणि दिव्यानि परमेश्वरी ।
बभञ्ज लीलयैवोग्रहुङ्कारोच्चारणादिभिः ॥ १३ ॥

13. And what all divine missiles were hurled by him,
the great Goddess broke them all playfully with fierce
grunts and the like.

ततः शरशतैर्देवीमाच्छादयत सोऽसुरः ।
सापि तत्कुपिता देवी धनुश्चिच्छेद चेषुभिः ॥ १४ ॥

14. Then that Asura covered the Goddess with
hundreds of arrows. Angry at this, the Goddess too broke
his bow with her arrows.

छिन्ने धनुषि दैत्येन्द्रस्तथा शक्तिमथाददे ।
चिच्छेद देवी चक्रेण तामप्यस्य करे स्थिताम् ॥ १५ ॥

15. His bow broken, the lord of Asuras got hold of
the lance. The Goddess broke that also in his hand, with
a discus.

ततः खड्गमुपादाय शतचन्द्रं च भानुमत् ।
अभ्यधावत तां देवीं दैत्यानामधिपेश्वरः ॥ १६ ॥

16. Then the supreme sovereign of the Asuras
wielding a sword and shining shield figuring hundred
moons, rushed at the Goddess.

तस्यापतत एवाशु खड्गं चिच्छेद चण्डिका ।
धनुर्मुक्तैः शितैर्बाणैश्चार्कंकरामलम् ॥ १७ ॥

17. As he was rushing forward, Chandika with sharp
arrows released from her bow broke his sword as well as
his shield, spotless like the sun's rays.

अश्वांश्च पातयामास रथं सारथिना सह ।
हताश्वः स तदा दैत्यश्छिन्नधन्वा विसारथिः ॥ १८ ॥
जग्राह मुद्गरं घोरमम्बिकानिधनोद्यतः ।
चिच्छेदापततस्तस्य मुद्गरं निशितैः शरैः ॥ १९ ॥

18-19. She felled his horses and the chariot with the charioteer. Then, his horse killed, his bow broken and his charioteer missing, the Asura seized the terrible club, trying to kill the Goddess. She cut into pieces with her sharp arrows his club as he rushed towards her.

तथापि सोऽभ्यधावत्तां मुष्टिमुद्यम्य वेगवान् ।
स मुष्टिं पातयामास हृदये दैत्यपुङ्गवः ॥ २० ॥
देव्यास्तं चापि सा देवी तलेनोरस्यताडयत् ।
तलप्रहाराभिहतो निपपात महीतले ॥ २१ ॥

20. Even then, he leaped at her with speed, lifting his fist. The eminent Asura brought his fist down on the heart of the Goddess.

21. And the Goddess slapped him in the chest with her palm; smitten by the blow of her palm he fell on the ground.

स दैत्यराजः सहसा पुनरेव तथोत्थितः ।
उत्पत्य च प्रगृह्योच्चैर्देवीं गगनमास्थितः ॥ २२ ॥

22. The king of Asuras immediately rose again. He rose up and seizing the Goddess aloft jumped to the sky.

तत्रापि सा निराधारा युयुधे तेन चण्डिका ॥ २३ ॥

23. There also Chandika fought with him without any support.

नियुद्धं खे तदा दैत्यश्चण्डिका च परस्परम् ।
चक्रतुः प्रथमं सिद्धमुनिविस्मयकारकम् ॥ २४ ॥

24. Then causing wonder to the Siddhas and sages, for the first time, the Asura and Chandika began to wrestle with each other, in the sky.

ततो नियुद्धं सुचिरं कृत्वा तेनाम्बिका सह ।
उत्पाट्य भ्रामयामास चिक्षेप धरणीतले ॥ २५ ॥

25. Wrestling with him for a long time, the Mother uprooted and swung him round and flung him down on the earth.

स क्षिप्तो धरणीं प्राप्य मुष्टिमुद्यम्य वेगवान् ।
अभ्यधावत दुष्टात्मा चण्डिकानिधनेच्छया ॥ २६ ॥

26. Thus thrown, the wicked Asura reaching the ground jumped up with speed, raising his fist with the desire of slaying Chandika.

तमायान्तं ततो देवी सर्वदैत्यजनेश्वरम् ।
जगत्यां पातयामास भित्वा शूलेन वक्षसि ॥ २७ ॥

27. Then the Goddess seeing the lord of all the Asura folk advancing towards her, felled him on the earth, piercing him in the chest with her spear.

स गतासुः पपातोर्व्यां देवीशूलाग्रविक्षतः ।
चालयन् सकलां पृथ्वीं साब्धिद्वीपां सपर्वताम् ॥ २८ ॥

28. Pierced by the spear-point of the Goddess he fell to the ground lifeless, shaking the whole earth along with oceans, islands and mountains.

ततः प्रसन्नमखिलं हते तस्मिन् दुरात्मनि ।
जगत् स्वास्थ्यमतीवाप निर्मलं चाभवन्नभः ॥ २९ ॥

29. When that wicked one was slain, everything became clear and propitious. The world got its original state back again and the sky became spotless.

उत्पातमेघाः सोल्काः ये प्रागासंस्ते शमं ययुः ।
सरितो मार्गवाहिन्यस्तथासंस्तत्र पातिते ॥ ३० ॥

30. The portents of clouds with meteors which appeared previously, vanished and the rivers flowed in their courses, after his fall.

ततो देवगणाः सर्वं दर्षनिर्भरमानसाः ।
बभूवुर्निहते तस्मिन् गन्धर्वा ललितं जगुः ॥ ३१ ॥

31. As he was killed, all the hosts of gods were filled with delight in their minds and the Gandharvas sang sweetly.

अवादयंस्तथैवान्ये ननृतुश्चाप्सरोगणाः ।
ववुः पुण्यास्तथा वाताः सुप्रभोऽभूद्दिवाकरः ॥ ३२ ॥

32. Some played on musical instruments and the bevy of Apsara girls danced. The winds blew favourably and the sun became resplendent.

इति श्रीमार्कण्डेयपुराणे सावर्णिके मन्वन्तरे देवीमाहात्म्ये
दशमः ॥ १० ॥

Here ends the tenth of *Devi* Mahatmya   in Markendeya Purana, during the period of Savarni   the Manu.

ELEVENTH CHAPTER

ऋषिरुवाच ॥ १ ॥

1. The Sage said :

देव्या हते तत्र महासुरेन्द्रे सेन्द्राः सुरा वह्निपुरोगमास्ताम् ।
कात्यायनीं तुष्टुवुरिष्टलाभाद्विकाशिवक्त्राब्जविकासिताशाः ॥२॥

2. When the great lord of the Asuras was killed by the Goddess, the gods with Indra, headed by Agni, lauded Katyayani, illuminating the quarters with their moon-like faces, cheerful on account of the fulfilment of their desire:

देवी प्रपन्नार्तिहरे प्रसीद प्रसीद मातर्जगतोऽखिलस्य ।
प्रसीद विश्वेश्वरि पाहि विश्वं त्वमीश्वरी देवि चराचरस्य ॥ ३ ॥

3. O Devi, O Remover of the distress of those who take refuge in thee, Be pleased. May thou be gracious, O Mother of the entire world. Be pleased, O Sovereign of the Universe, protect the universe. O Devi, thou art the sovereign of the mobile and the immobile.

आधारभूता जगतस्त्वमेका महीस्वरूपेण यतः स्थितासि ।
अपां स्वरूपस्थितया त्वयैतदाप्यायते कृत्स्नमलङ्घ्यवीर्ये ॥ ४ ॥

4. Thou alone art the sole support and basis of the world ; because thou standest in the form of the vast earth. O, Thou whose valour cannot be challenged, the thirst of

238

all this is quenched by thee who standest in the form of water.[1]

त्वं वैष्णवीशक्तिरनन्तवीर्या विश्वस्य बीजं परमासि माया ।
सम्मोहितं देवि समस्तमेतत् त्वं वै प्रसन्ना भुवि मुक्तिहेतुः ॥५॥

5. Vishnu's shakti thou art, of infinite valour. The seed of the universe, thou art the supreme Maya : O Devi, all this is charmed and deluded by thee. If thou art gracious,[2] thou becomest the cause of liberation on the earth itself.

विद्याः समस्तास्तव देवि भेदाः स्त्रियः समस्ताः सकला जगत्सु ।
त्वयैकया पूरितमम्बयैतत् का ते स्तुतिः स्तव्यपरा परोक्तिः ॥६॥

6. O Devi, in the world, all ways of knowledge are thy different parts and all women are thee in entirety. This world is filled by thee, the Sole Mother. Thou art the supreme fit to be lauded. Thou art also the supreme laud. So, what laud can we make ?

सर्वभूता यदा देवी भुक्तिमुक्तिप्रदायिनी ।
त्वं स्तुता स्तुतये का वा भवन्तु परमोक्तयः ॥ ७ ॥

7. The Goddess has become all; she gives enjoyment and liberation - when thou art lauded thus, what more potent words can be for thy praise ?

सर्वस्य बुद्धिरूपेण जनस्य हृदि संस्थिते ।
स्वर्गापवर्गदे देवि नारायणि नमोऽस्तु ते ॥ ८ ॥

---

1 All this life is athirst for delight, the *rasa* , the divine waters *āpo devīh* that create and sustain existence.

2 The Sanskrit word is *prasanna* , clear. Devi is the supreme delusion. The delusion persists till the gracious Presence becomes clear *prasanna* , then one receives the grace, *prasāda* of the Devi. She that is delusion becomes the cause of liberation as well.

8. O thou who standest in the form of intelligence in the heart of every person, giver of heaven and liberation, Devi, Narayani, salutation be to thee.

कलाकाष्ठादिरूपेण परिणामप्रदायिनि ।
विश्वस्योपरतौ शक्ते नारायणि नमोऽस्तु ते ॥ ९ ॥

9. O thou who grantest the evolution in the form of *kala kastha* ,[1] the force left even after the cessation of the universe, Narayani, salutations be to thee.

सर्वमङ्गलमाङ्गल्ये शिवे सर्वार्थसाधिके ।
शरण्ये ऽयम्बके गौरि नारायणि नमोऽस्तु ते ॥ १० ॥

10. O the auspiciousness in all that is auspicious, O the good, the accomplisher of all objects, O adept in giving refuge, the mother of the triple world, lady immaculate (Gowri) Narayani, salutation be to thee.

सृष्टिस्थितिविनाशानां शक्तिभूते सनातनि ।
गुणाश्रये गुणमये नारायणि नमोऽस्तु ते ॥ ११ ॥

11. O thou who becomest the force behind creation, preservation and destruction, O Eternal one, O resort to the *gunas* (Purusha) O the make-up of *gunas* (Prakriti), Narayani, salutation be to thee.

शरणागतदीनार्तपरित्राणपरायणे ।
सर्वस्यार्तिहरे देवि नारायणि नमोऽस्तु ते ॥ १२ ॥

12. O thou, resolved to protect the weak and the distressed who take refuge in thee, O the remover of sufferings of every being, Devi Narayani, salutation be to thee.

---

1 Measurements of time. Eighteen minutes make one *kāṣṭha* and thirty *kāṣṭhās* make one *kalā*.

हंसयुक्तविमानस्थे ब्रह्माणीरूपधारिणि ।
कौशाम्भःक्षरिके देवि नारायणि नमोऽस्तु ते ॥ १३ ॥

13. O Narayani, seated in the areal chariot yoked to swans, bearing the form of Brahmani and sprinkling the waters with *kusa* grass, Devi, salutation be to thee.

त्रिशूलचन्द्राहिधरे महावृषभवाहिनि ।
माहेश्वरीखरूपेण नारायणि नमोऽस्तु ते ॥ १४ ॥

14. O Narayani, in the form of Maheswari, wearer of the trident, moon and the snake, mounted on the great bull, salutation be to thee.

मयूरकुक्कुटवृते महाशक्तिधरेऽनघे ।
कौमारीरूपसंस्थाने नारायणि नमोऽस्तु ते ॥ १५ ॥

15. O Narayani, appearing in the form of Kaumari, O wielder of the great lance, O Pure one, surrounded by the cock and the peacock, salutation be to thee.

शङ्खचक्रगदाशार्ङ्गगृहीतपरमायुधे ।
प्रसीद वैष्णवीरूपे नारायणि नमोऽस्तु ते ॥ १६ ॥

16. O Narayani, in the form of Vaishnavi, be gracious. O wielder of the superb weapons, conch, discus, mace and the bow Sarnga, salutation be to thee.

गृहीतोग्रमहाचक्रे दंष्ट्रोद्धृतवसुन्धरे ।
वराहरूपिणि शिवे नारायणि नमोऽस्तु ते ॥ १७ ॥

17. O Narayani, in the form of the great boar : O thou who lifted up the earth with thy tusk, wielder of the great fierce wheel, O Auspicious, salutations be to thee.

नृसिंहरूपेणोग्रेण हन्तुं दैत्यान् कृतोद्यमे ।
त्रैलोक्यत्राणसहिते नारायणि नमोऽस्तु ते ॥ १८ ॥

18. O Narayani, who in the terrible form of Narasimha is engaged in killing the Asuras and affording constant protection to the three worlds, salutations be to thee.

किरीटिनि महावज्रे सहस्रनयनोज्ज्वले ।
वृत्रप्राणहरे चैन्द्रि नारायणि नमोऽस्तु ते ॥ १९ ॥

19. O Narayani, Indra's force, O thou with the crown, the great thunderbolt and the thousand eyes resplendent, Vritra' life-taker, salutations be to thee.

शिवदूतीस्वरूपेण हतदैत्यमहाबले ।
घोररूपे महारावे नारायणि नमोऽस्तु ते ॥ २० ॥

20. O Narayani, in the form of Shivaduti, O the vanquisher of the great armies of the Asuras, O of terrible form and tremendous noise, salutation be to thee.

दंष्ट्राकरालवदने शिरोमालाविभूषणे ।
चामुण्डे मुण्डमथने नारायणि नमोऽस्तु ते ॥ २१ ॥

21. O Narayani, O Chamunda, the smasher of Munda, O thou with the garland of heads as ornament, O thou of terrific teeth and mouth, salutation be to thee.

लक्ष्मि लज्जे महाविद्ये श्रद्धे पुष्टि स्वधे ध्रुवे ।
महारात्रि महामाये नारायणि नमोऽस्तु ते ॥ २२ ॥

22. O Narayani, O prosperity, modesty, great knowledge, faith, nourishment, self-sustenance, constancy, O the great night, O the great delusion, salutation be to thee.

मेधे सरस्वति वरे भूति बाभ्रवि तामसि ।
नियते त्वं प्रसीदेशे नारायणि नमोऽस्तु ते ॥ २३ ॥

23. O Narayani, O the intellect united with God, all-flowing knowledge, O the best, O the white Satva, the

242

tawny Rajas, the dark Tamas, O the fixed principle beyond the triad of gunas, O Sovereign,[1] be pleased, salutation be to thee.

सर्वस्वरूपे सर्वेशे सर्वशक्तिसमन्विते ।
भयेभ्यस्त्राहि नो देवि दुर्गे देवि नमोऽस्तु ते ॥ २४ ॥

24. O the form of all, the master of all, O thou
accompanied by all the forces, Devi protect us from fear.
O Devi Durga, salutation be to thee.

पतत्ते वदनं सौम्यं लोचनत्रयभूषितम् ।
पातु नः सर्वभूतेभ्यः कात्यायनि नमोऽस्तु ते ॥ २५ ॥

25. May this thy lovely face adorned with eyes,
guard us from all beings. O Katyayani, salutation be to
thee.

ज्वालाकरालमत्युग्रमशेषासुरसूदनम् ।
त्रिशूलं पातु नो भीतेर्भद्रकालि नमोऽस्तु ते ॥ २६ ॥

26. May the trident sharp-edged, flaming terribly,
destroyer of the Asuras in entirety, protect us from terror
O Auspicious Kali, salutation be to thee.

हिनस्ति दैत्यतेजांसि स्वनेनापूर्य या जगत् ।
सा घण्टा पातु नो देवि पापेभ्योऽनः सुतानिव ॥ २७ ॥

27. O Devi, May that bell which filling the world
with its sound destroys the prowess of the Asuras protect
us from evil, as a living being protects its children.

असुरासृग्वसापङ्कचर्चितस्ते करोज्ज्वलः ।
शुभाय खड्गो भवतु चण्डिके त्वां नता वयन् ॥ २८ ॥

---

1. She is gunamayi also gunatita. She is in the form of three gunas,
the fixed principle niyali, beyond the three gunas and the master
sovereign Isa.

28. O Chandika, may thy sword smeared with the mire of blood and marrow of the Asuras, resplendent in thy hand be for our good. We bow down to thee.

रोगानशेषानपहंसि तुष्टा रुष्टा तु कामान् सकलानभीष्टान् ।
त्वामाश्रितानां न विपन्नराणां त्वामाश्रिता ह्याश्रयतां प्रयान्ति ॥

29. If pleased thou destroyest all diseases; if angry thou destroyest all the desires longed for. No calamity befalls the men who depend on thee. Those who depend on the thee and resort to thee become a haven of refuge.

एतत् कृतं यत् कदनं त्वयाद्य धर्मद्विषां देवि महासुराणाम् ।
रूपैरनेकैर्बहुधात्ममूर्तिं कृत्वाऽम्बिके तत् प्रकरोति काऽन्या ॥ ३०

30. Who else can do this, this slaughter that has been done by thee now, of the great Asuras, the haters of Dharma, by making thy form manifold, into very many forms.

विद्यासु शास्त्रेषु विवेककदीपेष्वाद्येषु वाक्येषु च का त्वदन्या ।
ममत्वगर्तेऽतिमहान्धकारे विभ्रामयस्येतदतीव विश्वम् ॥ ३१ ॥

31. Who else except thee is said in the paths of knowledge, in the sciences, in those original statements, the lamps of discrimination ? Yet, in the blindest darkest abyss of my-ness, thou throwest this universe and makest it whirl.

रक्षांसि यत्रोग्रविषाश्च नागा यत्रारयो दस्युबलानि यत्र ।
दावानलो यत्र तथाब्धिमध्ये तत्र स्थिता त्वं परिपासि विश्वम् ॥

32. Where there are demons, serpents with dreadful poison, where there are foes, troops of robbers, where there is wild fire, in the midst of the sea, there thou standest and savest the universe.

विश्वेश्वरि त्वं परिपासि विश्वं विश्वात्मिका धारयसीह विश्वम् ।
विश्वेशवन्द्या भवती भवन्ति विश्वाश्रया ये त्वयि भक्तिनम्राः ॥

33. Thou art the sovereign of the universe. Thou protectest the universe. The soul of the universe, thou upholdest and sustainest here the universe. Thou art worthy to be adored even by the lord of the universe. The whole universe takes refuge in those who bow to thee in devotion.

देवि प्रसीद परिपालय नोऽरिभीतेर्नित्यं यथाऽसुरवधादधुनैव सद्यः ।
पापानि सर्वजगतां प्रशमं नयाशु उत्पातपाकजनितांश्च महोपसर्गान् ॥

34. O Devi, be gracious Just as thou hast now immediately saved us by killing the Asuras, likewise, always save us from the fear of the foes. Please subdue the sins of all the worlds and the great calamities that are produced by the maturing of evil portents.

प्रणतानां प्रसीद त्वं देवि विश्वार्तिहारिणि ।
त्रैलोक्यवासिनामीड्ये लोकानां वरदा भव ॥ ३५ ॥

35. Be gracious to those who bow to thee. O Devi, Destroyer of the distress of the universe, O thou worthy of praise by the inhabitants of the three worlds, grant what is best to all the worlds.

देव्युवाच ॥ ३६ ॥

36. The Goddess said :

वरदाऽहं सुरगणा वरं यन्मनसेच्छथ ।
तं वृणुध्वं प्रयच्छामि जगतामुपकारकम् ॥ ३७ ॥

37. O host of gods, I shall grant the boon. Whatever boon you desire by the mind, choose that: I shall give for the benefit of the world.

देवा ऊचुः ॥ ३८ ॥

38. The gods said:

सर्वाबाधाप्रशमनं त्रैलोक्यस्याखिलेश्वरि ।
एवमेव त्वया कार्यमस्मद्वैरिविनाशनम् ॥ ३९ ॥

39. O Sovereign of all, just like this, thou shouldst accomplish the destruction of our foes, the appeasement of all the afflictions of the three worlds.

देव्युवाच ॥ ४० ॥

40. The Goddess said :

वैवस्वतेऽन्तरे प्राप्ते अष्टाविंशतिमे युगे ।
शुम्भो निशुम्भश्चैवान्यावुत्पत्स्येते महासुरौ ॥ ४१ ॥

41. In the time of Vaivasvata Manu, when the twenty eighth yuga comes, two other great Asuras Shumbha and Nishumbha will be born.

नन्दगोपगृहे जाता यशोदागर्भसम्भवा ।
ततस्तौ नाशयिष्यामि विन्ध्याचलनिवासिनी ॥ ४२ ॥

42. Born in the womb of Yasoda, growing in the house of Nandagopa I shall then destroy them, taking abode in the Vindhya mountain.

पुनरप्यतिरौद्रेण रूपेण पृथिवीतले ।
अवतीर्य हनिष्यामि वैप्रचित्तांश्च दानवान् ॥ ४३ ॥

43. Again, I shall descend on earth in the most terrible form and shall slay the Asuras Vaiprachittas.

भक्षयन्त्याश्च तानुग्रान् वैप्रचित्तान् महासुरान् ।
रक्ता दन्ता भविष्यन्ति दाडिमीकुसुमोपमाः ॥ ४४ ॥

44. When I eat up those great Asuras, Vaiprachittas, my teeth will become as red as the pomegranate flower.

ततो मां देवताः स्वर्गे मर्त्यलोके च मानवाः ।
स्तुवन्तो व्याहरिष्यन्ति सततं रक्तदन्तिकाम् ॥ ४५ ॥

45. Then the gods in heaven and the men in the mortal world when praising shall always speak of me as Raktadantika.

भूयश्च शतवार्षिक्यामनावृष्ट्यामनम्भसि ।
मुनिसिः संस्तुता भूमौ सम्भविष्याम्ययोनिजा ॥ ४६ ॥

46. Again, when for hundred years there will be no water on account of failure of rains, praised by the sages I shall come into being on earth, without being born in a womb.

ततः शतेन नेत्राणां निरीक्षिष्याम्यहं मुनीन् ।
कीर्तयिष्यन्ति मनुजाः शताक्षीमिति मां ततः ॥ ४७ ॥

47. Then I shall look at the sages with a hundred eyes. Then the offsprings of Manu shall extol me as *sataksi*.

ततोऽहमखिलं लोकमात्मदेहसमुद्भवैः ।
भरिष्यामि सुराः शाकैरावृष्टेः प्राणधारकैः ॥ ४८ ॥

48. O gods, then till the rains come, I shall fill and nourish the entire world with life-sustaining vegetables produced out of my own body.

शाकम्भरीति विख्यातिं तदा यास्याम्यहं भुबि ॥ ४९ ॥

49. Then I shall get renown in the world as *sākambhari*.

तत्रैव च वधिष्यामि दुर्गमाख्यं महासुरम् ।
दुर्गादेवीति विख्यातं तन्मे नाम भविष्यति ॥ ५० ॥

50. There itself I shall slay a great Asura named Durgama. Then I shall get the famous name of Goddess Durga.

पुनश्चाहं यदा भीमं रूपं कृत्वा हिमाचले ।
रक्षांसि भक्षयिष्यामि मुनीनां त्राणकारणात् ॥ ५१ ॥

तदा मां मुनयः सर्वे स्तोष्यन्त्यानम्रमूर्तयः ।
भीमादेवीति विख्यातं तन्मे नाम भविष्यति ॥ ५२ ॥

51-52. Again, when for the sake of protecting the sages, I shall take a terrific form in the mountain Himalayas and devour the demons, then all the sages with their bodies bent in salutation will be extolling me. Then my name will become famous as Goddess *bhīmā*.

यदाऽरुणाख्यस्त्रैलोक्ये महाबाधां करिष्यति ।
तदाऽहं भ्रामरं रूपं कृत्वाऽसङ्ख्येयषट्पदम् ॥ ५३ ॥

त्रैलोक्यस्य हिताथार्य वधिष्यामि महासुरम् ।
भ्रामरीति च मां लोकास्तदा स्तोष्यन्ति सर्वतः ॥ ५४ ॥

53-54. When in the three worlds one Aruna will be creating great havoc, I shall take the form of a cluster consisting of innumerable bees and shall slay the great Asura for the benefit of the three worlds. Then everywhere people will laud me as Bhramari.

इत्थं यदा यदा बाधा दानवोत्था भविष्यति ।
तदा तदाऽवतीर्याहं करिष्याम्यरिसंक्षयम् ॥ ५५ ॥

55. Thus, whenever there shall be oppression arising out of the Asuras. I shall descend and accomplish the destruction of the foes.

इति श्रीमार्कण्डेयपुराणे सावर्णिके मन्वन्तरे देवीमाहात्म्ये
एकादशः ॥ ११ ॥

Here ends the eleventh of Devi Mahatmya in Markendeya Purana during the period of Savarni, the Manu

TWELFTH CHAPTER

देव्युवाच ॥ १ ॥

1. The Goddess said :

एभिः स्तवैश्च मां नित्यं स्तोष्यते यः समाहितः ।
तस्याहं सकलां बाधां शमयिष्याम्यसंशयम् ॥ २ ॥

2. Whoever with concentration praises me constantly with these lauds, I shall without doubt put an end to all his troubles.

मधुकैटभनाशं च महिषासुरघातनम् ।
कीर्तयिष्यन्ति ये तद्वद्धं शुम्भनिशुम्भयोः ॥ ३ ॥

3. Whoever extols my deeds relating to the destruction of Madhu and Kaitabha, the killing of Mahishasura and likewise the slaughter of Shumbha and Nishumbha,

अष्टम्यां च चतुर्दश्यां नवम्यां चैकचेतसः ।
श्रोष्यन्ति चैव ये भक्त्या मम माहात्म्यमुत्तमम् ॥ ४ ॥

4. Whoever with one-pointed mind listens with devotion to my glories sung in this Mahatmyam on the eighth, fourteenth and ninth days of the lunar fortnight,

न तेषां दुष्कृतं किञ्चिद् दुष्कृतोत्था न चापदः ।
भविष्यति न दारिद्र्यं न चैवेष्टवियोजनम् ॥ ५ ॥

5. To them nothing bad happens, neither misfortunes arising out of bad happenings. No poverty is faced by them nor separation from the near and dear ones.

शत्रुभ्यो न भयं नस्य दस्युतो वा न राजतः ।
न शस्त्रानलतोयौघात् कदाचित् सम्भविष्यति ॥ ६ ॥

6. No fear comes to them from foes, robbers or even from kings—neither from weapons, fire and floods.

तस्मान्ममैतन्माहात्म्यं पठितव्यं समाहितैः ।
श्रोतव्यं च सदा भक्त्या परं स्वस्त्ययनं महत् ॥ ७ ॥

7. Therefore this, my Mahatmyam, should be recited by those of concentrated mind and listened to constantly with devotion. It is the sublime and supreme way to welfare.

उपसर्गानशेषांस्तु महामारीसमुद्भवान् ।
तथा त्रिविधमुत्पातं माहात्म्यं शमयेन्मम ॥ ८ ॥

8. This Mahatmyam will alleviate all sufferings due to epidemic like small-pox as well as the threefold portents.[1]

यत्रैतत् पठ्यते सम्यङ्नित्यमायतने मम ।
सदा न तद्विमोक्ष्यामि सान्निध्यं तत्र मे स्थितम् ॥ ९ ॥

9. I shall never leave the abode where this Mahatmyam is well recited constantly. My standing presence is there.

बलिप्रदाने पूजायामग्निकार्ये महोत्सवे ।
सर्वं ममैतन्माहात्म्यमुच्चार्यं श्राव्यमेव च ॥ १० ॥

---

1 Portents indicate the calamities that are going to befall on a person. They are threefold, affecting the physical, vital and mental beings of men: the portents that appear before illness invades the body, the portents that indicate the advent of anger, lust etc. to vitiate the vital and the portents of confused or perverse thinking which foretell the onslaught on the right thinking of the mind. Some classify the threefold portents as pertaining to oneself *ādhyātmika*, pertaining to other beings *ādhibhautika* and pertaining to acts of God *adi-daivika*-calamities arising from anger, jealousy, malice etc; fear from ghosts, goblins, fire, water etc; sufferings caused by earthquake, fall of thunder etc.

10. When offerings are made, in worship, in rituals with fire and on great festive occasions, this my *Mahatmyam* should be completely recited and listened to.

जानताजानता वापि बलिपूजां यथाकृताम् ।
प्रतीक्षिष्याम्यहं प्रीत्या वह्निहोमं तथाकृतम् ॥ ११ ॥

11. I shall accept with satisfaction the offering, the worship and the fire-ritual thus done, whether so done knowingly or unknowingly.

शरत्काले महापूजा क्रियते या च वार्षिकी ।
तस्यां ममैतन्माहात्म्यं श्रुत्वा भक्तिसमन्वितः ॥ १२ ॥

सर्वबाधाविनिर्मुक्तो धनधान्यसमन्वितः ।
मनुष्यो मत्प्रसादेन भविष्यति न संशयः ॥ १३ ॥

12-13. During the time of the Great Worship done in the autumnal season as well as in the beginning of the year,[1] by hearing this my Mahatmyam with devotion, man by my grace is released from all sufferings and acquires wealth and corn. There is no doubt.

श्रुत्वा ममैतन्माहात्म्यं तथा चोत्पत्तयः शुभाः ।
पराक्रमं च युद्धेषु जायते निर्भयः पुमान् ॥ १४ ॥

14. Listening to this my Mahatmyam, to the auspicious manifestations and to my prowess in battles, man becomes fearless.

रिपवः संक्षयं यान्ति कल्याणं चोपपद्यते ।
नन्दते च कुलं पुंसां माहात्म्यं मम श्रृण्वताम् ॥ १५ ॥

---

1 The Great Worship is during the *navarātri*, the sacred nine days which occur twice in a year, one at the beginning of the year, in Spring, *vasantā navarātri* and the other in the month of Ashwin' during *śarat*, autumn, the *śarada navarātri*.

15. To the men who listen to my Mahatmyam, the enemies are destroyed and welfare is produced. Their families rejoice.

शान्तिकर्मणि सर्वत्र तथा दुःस्वप्रदर्शने ।
ग्रहपीडासु चोग्रासु माहात्म्यं श्रृणुयान्मम ॥ १६ ॥

16. My Mahatmyam should be listened to in all alleviation-rites, on seeing a bad dream and when great afflictions arise due to planetary positions.

उपसर्गाः शमं यान्ति ग्रहपीडाश्च दारुणाः ।
दुःस्वप्नं च नृभिर्दृष्टं सुस्वप्नमुपजायते ॥ १७ ॥

17. Troubles subside and also the terrible affliction of planets. The bad dream seen by men turns out to be a good dream.

बालग्रहाभिभूतानां बालानां शान्तिकारकम् ।
सङ्घातभेदे च नृणां मैत्रीकरणमुत्तमम् ॥ १८ ॥

18. It tranquillises the effects of maladies in children caused by certain obsessions: it is the best means of re-establishing the links of friendship amongst men where there occurs a break in relationships.

दुर्वृत्तानामशेषाणां बलहानिकरं परम् ।
रक्षोभूतपिशाचानां पठनादेव नाशनम् ॥ १९ ॥

19. It destroys most effectively the strength of evil-doers, without exception. Demons, goblins and ghosts perish at the mere reading of this.

सर्वं ममैतन्माहात्म्यं मम सन्निधिकारकम् ॥ २० ॥

20. This Mahatmyam of mine in its entirety evokes my presence.

पशुपुष्पार्घधूपैश्च गन्धदीपैस्तथोत्तमैः ।
विप्राणां भोजनैर्हेमैः प्रोक्षणीयैरहर्निशम् ॥ २१ ॥

अन्यैश्च विविधैर्भोगैः प्रदानैर्वत्सरेण या ।
प्रीतिमें क्रियते सास्विन्सकृदुच्चरिते श्रुते ॥ २२ ॥

21-22. What satisfaction I shall derive by worship day and night for full year with these aids viz. animal for the offering, flowers, costly incense, best scents, lamps, feeding the Brahmans, fire rituals, sacramental sprinkling of water, various other objects of enjoyment and gifts, the same satisfaction I shall get by reciting or listening to this once.

श्रुतं हरति पापानि तथारोग्यं प्रयच्छति ।
रक्षां करोति भूतेभ्यो जन्मनां कीर्तनं मम ॥ २३ ॥

23. Hearing removes the sins and grants freedom from illness. The recital of my manifestations affords protection from evil spirits.

युद्धेषु चरितं यन्मे दुष्टदैत्यनिबर्हणम् ।
तस्मिङ्छ्रुते वैरिकृतं भयं पुंसां न जायते ॥ २४ ॥

24. If my deeds of demolishing the wicked Asuras in battles are heard, people will have no fear of the doings of their enemies.

युष्माभिः स्तुतयो याश्च याश्च ब्रह्मर्षिभिः कृताः ।
ब्रह्मणा च कृतास्तास्तु प्रयच्छन्तु शुभां मतिम् ॥ २५ ॥

25. Let the lauds made by you, those made by the divine seers and those others made by Brahma give auspiciousness in thought.

अरण्ये प्रान्तरे वापि दावाग्निपरिवारितः ।
दस्युभिर्वा वृतः शून्ये गृहीतो वापि शत्रुभिः ॥ २६ ॥

26. In a forest, on a lone path or surrounded by a forest fire or encircled by robbers or else seized by enemies in a desolate place,

सिंहव्याघ्रानुयातो वा वने वा वनहस्तिभिः ।
राज्ञा क्रुद्धेन चाज्ञप्तो वध्यो बन्धगतोऽपि वा ॥ २७ ॥

27. Or in a jungle pursued by lion, tiger or wild elephants, or else on the command of an irate king thrown into prison or sentenced to death,

आघूर्णितो वा वातेन स्थितः पोते महार्णवे ।
पतत्सु चापि शस्त्रेषु सङ्ग्रामे भृशदारुणे ॥ २८ ॥

28. Or caught in a boat tossed by winds on the high seas, or else facing the volley of arrows in an intense terrific battle,

सर्वाबाधासु घोरासु वेदनाभ्यर्दितोऽपि वा ।
स्मरन् ममैतच्चरितं नरो मुच्येत सङ्कटात् ॥ २९ ॥

29. Or in the midst of all kinds of terrible troubles or afflicted with pain, remembering this my *carita*, a man gets out of straits.

मम प्रभावात् सिंहाद्याः दस्यवो वैरिणस्तथा ।
दूरादेव पलायन्ते स्मरतश्चरितं मम ॥ ३० ॥

30. By my power, animals like lions, robbers and enemies, flee at a distance from one who remembers my charita.

ऋषिरुवाच ॥ ३१ ॥

31. The Sage said :

इत्युक्त्वा सा भगवती चण्डिका चण्डविक्रमा ।
पश्यतां सर्वदेवानां तत्रैवान्तरधीयत ॥ ३२ ॥

32. Having said this, the great Chandika, of fierce prowess, vanished there itself, even as all the gods were gazing at her.

तेऽपि देवा निरातङ्काः स्वाधिकारान् यथा पुरा ।
यज्ञभागभुजः सर्वं चक्रिर्विनिहतारयः ॥ ३३ ॥

33. Their enemies having been destroyed, the gods, relieved of uncertainty in their minds, began to enjoy their shares in sacrifices and wield their authority as before.

दैत्याश्च देव्या निहते शुम्भे देवरिपौ युधि ।
जगद्विध्वंसके तस्मिन् महोग्रेऽतुलविक्रमे ॥ ३४ ॥

निशुम्भे च महावीर्ये शेषाः पातालमाययुः ॥ ३५ ॥

34-35. When in battle, Shumbha the enemy of the gods and the afflicter of the world as well as the great fierce Nishumbha of unparalleled prowess and high valour were slain by the Goddess, the remaining Asuras entered the nether worlds.

एवं भगवती देवी सा नित्याऽपि पुनः पुनः ।
सम्भूय कुरुते भूप जगतः परिपालनम् ॥ ३६ ॥

36. O King, thus the Goddess, Bhagavati, though eternal manifesting herself again and again carries out the protection of the world.

तयैतन्मोह्यते विश्वं सैव विश्वं प्रसूयते ।
सा याचिता च विज्ञानं तुष्टा ऋद्धिं प्रयच्छति ॥ ३७ ॥

37. This universe is deluded by her and it is she who gives birth to the universe. Entreated, she grants supreme knowledge and gratified, she confers prosperity.

व्याप्तं तयैतत् सकलं ब्रह्माण्डं मनुजेश्वर ।
महादेव्या महाकालीमहामारीस्वरूपया ॥ ३८ ॥

256

38. Master of men, all this cosmos (lit. Brahma's egg) is pervaded by the great Goddess in the form of *mahākāli* and *mahāmāri*.[1]

सैब काले महामारी सैव सृष्टिर्भवत्यजा ।
स्थिर्ति करोति भूतानां सैव काले सनातनी ॥ ३९ ॥

39. At one time she is *Mahamari* [1]. She the unborn becomes the creation (at another time) And also she the eternal attends to the preservation of beings at the appropriate time.

भवकाले नृणां सैव लक्ष्मीर्वृद्धिप्रदा गृहे ।
सैवाभावे तथाऽलक्ष्मीर्विनाशायोपजायते ॥ ४० ॥

40. During the time of having, she is verily *lakṣmi* for men, granting growth and prosperity in the house. At the time of not having, she herself is *alakṣmi* and brings about ruin.

स्तुता सम्पूजिता पुष्पैर्गन्धधूपादिभिस्तथा ।
ददाति वित्तं पुत्रांश्च मतिं धर्मे तथा शुभाम् ॥ ४१ ॥

41. Lauded and worshipped with flowers, fragrance, incense etc. she confers wealth, offsprings and an auspicious mind bent on Dharma.

इति श्रीमार्कण्डेयपुराणे सावर्णिके मन्वन्तरे देवीमाहात्म्ये
द्वादशः ॥ १२ ॥

Here ends the twelfth of Devi Mahatmya in the Markendeya Purana, during the period of Savarni, the Manu.

---

1 Kala is time and *mahākāli* denotes the great time factor while *mahāmāri* denotes Death (*mar*, to die). The Goddess pervades the cosmos in the form of Time and Death, *mahākāli* and *mahāmāri*.
1 doing the destruction, *samhara*.

THIRTEENTH CHAPTER

ऋषिरुवाच ॥ १ ॥

1. The Sage said :

एतत्ते कथितं भूप देवीमाहात्म्यमुत्तमम् ॥ २ ॥

2. O king, this sublime Devi Mahatmyam has been narrated to you.

एवम्प्रभावा सा देवी ययेदं धार्यते जगत् ।
विद्या तथैव क्रियते भगवद्विष्णुमायया ॥ ३ ॥

3. Of such glory is the Goddess by whom this world is upheld and sustained. Likewise knowledge is produced by the Yoga Maya of Lord Vishnu.

तया त्वयेष वैश्यश्च तथैवान्ये विवेकिनः ।
मोहान्ते मोहिताश्चैव मोहमेष्यन्ति चापरे ॥ ४ ॥

4. By her, you, this Vaishya and others of discriminating intellect are deluded. Others have been deluded before and many others will be deluded in the future.

तामुपैहि महाराज शरणं परमेश्वरीम् ।
आराधिता सैव नृणां भोगस्वर्गापवर्गदा ॥ ५ ॥

5. O great king, take refuge in her the supreme Goddess. She indeed when worshipped confers enjoyment, heaven and liberation.

मार्कण्डेय उवाच ॥ ६ ॥

6. Markendeya said :

इति तस्य वचः श्रुत्वा सुरथः स नराधिपः ।
प्रणिपत्य महाभागं तमृर्षि संशितव्रतम् ॥ ७ ॥
निर्विण्णोऽतिममत्वेन राज्यापहरणेन च ।
जगाम सद्यस्तपसे स च वैश्यो महामुने ॥ ८ ॥

7-8. Hearing his words, O great sage, Suratha, the lord of men, despondent at the loss of his kingdom and his excessive sense of my-ness, bowed down to that sage of great parts and of severe penances and started immediately for performing *tapas*. The Vaishya too went with him.

सन्दर्शनार्थमम्बाया नदीपुलिनमास्थितः ।
स च वैश्यस्तपस्तेपे देवीसूक्तं परं जपन् ॥ ९ ॥

9. They repaired to the sandy banks of a river for getting the vision of the Mother. He and Vaishya performed the *tapas*, using for japa, the great *devī sūkta*.

तौ तस्मिन् पुलिने देव्याः कृत्वा मूर्तिं महीमयीम् ।
अर्हणां चक्रतुस्तस्याः पुष्पधूपाग्नितर्पणैः ॥ १० ॥

10. They both made on the bank an image of the Devi out of earth and worshipped her in the image with flowers, incense, fire-ritual and offerings of water.

निराहारौ यताःत्मानौ तन्मनस्कौ समाहितौ ।
ददतुस्तौ बलिं चैव निजगात्रासृगुक्षितम् ॥ ११ ॥

11. Without partaking food, exercising sel-fcontrol, with the thought of that and nothing else, and concentrated, they gave the offering dipped in the blood drawn out of their own bodies.

एवं समाराधयतोस्त्रिभिर्वर्षैर्यतात्मनोः ।
परितुष्टा जगद्धात्री प्रत्यक्षं प्राह चण्डिका ॥ १२ ॥

12. As they were worshipping like this, exercising
self-control, in three years' time, the upholder and sustainer
of the worlds, Chandika became pleased, appeared before
them and spoke :

देव्युवाच ॥ १३ ॥

13. The Goddess said :

यत् प्रार्थ्यते त्वया भूप त्वया च कुलनन्दन ।
मत्तस्तत्प्राप्यतां सर्वं परितुष्टा ददामि ते ॥ १४ ॥

14. O King, whatever is prayed for by you and O
(Vaishya) delight of your family, whatever by you too,
get those all from me. I am pleased. I shall give to you.

मार्कण्डेय उवाच ॥ १५ ॥

15. Markendeya said :

ततो वव्रे नृपो राज्यमविभ्रंश्यन्यजन्मनि ।
अत्रैव च निजं राज्यं हतशत्रुबलं बलात् ॥ १६ ॥

16. Then the king chose the kingdom which will not
get out of his hands even in a future life, while in this life
his own kingdom captured back by strength by killing the
armies of his enemies.

सोऽपि वैश्यस्ततो ज्ञानं वव्रे निर्विण्णमानसः ।
ममेत्यहमिति प्राज्ञः सङ्गविच्युतिकारकम् ॥ १७ ॥

17. But then the wise Vaishya despondent in the
mind chose the knowledge which gives release from the
attachment of I-ness and my-ness.

260

देव्युवाच ॥ १८ ॥

18. The Goddess said :

खल्पैरहोभिर्नृपते स्वं राज्यं प्राप्स्यते भवान् ॥ १९ ॥

19. O King, in a few days you are going to get back
your kingdom.

हत्वा रिपूनस्खलितं तव तत्र भविष्यति ॥ २० ॥

20. After killing the enemies, it will not slip from
you any more.

मृतश्च भूयः सम्प्राप्य जन्म देवाद्विवस्वतः ॥ २१ ॥
सावर्णिको मनुर्नाम भवान् भुवि भविष्यति ॥ २२ ॥

21-22. After death, again you will get birth from the
Sun-God and become on earth the famous Manu, *savarni*.

वैश्यवर्य त्वया यश्च वरोऽस्मत्तोऽभिवाञ्छितः ॥ २३ ॥
तं प्रयच्छामि संसिद्ध्यै तव ज्ञानं भविष्यति ॥ २४ ॥

23-24. O the best amongst Vaishyas, what you
desired out of me, that boon I shall confer. The knowledge
will bring you fulfilment.

मार्कण्डेय उवाच ॥ २५ ॥

25. Markendeya said :

इति दत्वा तयोर्देवी यथाभिलषितं वरम् ।
बभूवान्तर्हिता सद्यो भक्त्या ताभ्यामभिष्टुता ॥ २६-२८ ॥

26-28. Thus after giving both of them boons as they
desired, the Goddess immediately vanished, lauded by
them with devotion.[1]

---

1 The verses 26 and 27 have to be repeated again as verses
28 and 29 to end the Mahatmyam.

एवं देव्या वरं लब्ध्वा सुरथः क्षत्रियर्षभः ।
सूर्याज्जन्म समासाद्य सावर्णिर्भविता मनुः ॥ २७-२९ ॥

27-29. Thus, Suratha, the best of the Kshatryas, having got the boon from the Goddess will become the Manu Savarni by taking birth from the Sun-god.[1]

ह्रीं ओम् श्री मार्कण्डेयपुराणे सावर्णिके मन्वन्तरे देवीमाहात्म्ये
त्रयोदशः ॥ १३ ॥

KLIM OM.

Here ends the thirteenth of Devi Mahatmya in Markendeya Purana during the period of Savarni, the Manu.

DEVI SUKTA

In the thirteenth chapter it is said that the King and the Vaishya in order to see the Mother face to face did *tapas*, reciting the great Devi Sukta, *devi suktam param japan*. Which is the Devi Sukta referred to ?

Some would hold that the laud in the fifth chapter commencing *namo devyai maha devyai* is the Devi Sukta. But it is the considered opinion of many that the famous Devi Sukta in the Rig Veda is the one referred to here.

The Vedas are held as the authority and always an attempt is made to trace all the spiritual practices and religious rituals prevalent to the primary source of the Vedas. The Tantra pursues the Vedic teaching perhaps from a different angle altogether but it always holds the Veda in great respect. Considering the unique place occupied by this text Saptasati in Tantric literature and its occult practices, it is quite natural to seek for something explicit or implicit in the Vedic wisdom setting its seal of approval on this Sadhana. It is true that the story, ritual or mode of worship mentioned in Saptasati does not find a place in Rig Veda. But if we study carefully the Devi Sukta, the 125th hymn in the tenth Mandala of the Rig Veda and delve into its thought, we find that for the first time the glory of the Goddess, *devi mahatmya* is delineated here. Thought, spirit and Mantra-force vie with one another squandering the wealth of the Divine Afflatus through the words of Ambhrni Vak. The seer of the hymn is a Rishika, the daughter of Ambhrna and her name itself is Vak. She expresses the Divine Glory revealed to her through the inspired word in the form of this hymn. There are many hymns in the tenth Mandala where the name of the seer and the name of the deity he sees are one and the same. The reason is that the seer is one with the godhead he sees in himself completely identified and as a result the name of the godhead becomes also his name. Likewise in this hymn' the name of the *Rishika* and the name of the deity are one and the same, viz, *vāk*, because the daughter of Ambhrna realises in her the creative Word, the primary *nāda*, the *parā śakti* of the Tantra, becomes that and expresses herself through this hymn. "It will be more correct to say that the Female Energy of the Supreme Godhead *para-devata* realising herself in or choosing the embodiment of Vak Ambhrni utters the Word, the Mantra."[1]

Even a cursory reading of the hymn will bring home to the reader the glory of the Goddess. In the Devi Mahatmya, Mahalakshmi is mentioned as the primordeal Prakriti made up of the three qualities, *sattva, rajas* and *tamas* and from her manifest Mahakali and Mahasaraswati. This will be clear when one reads the *rahasya-traya*. The middle episode describes how this Mahalakshmi came into being. Though she is the Prime Mover, the *śaktis* of all the gods joined together to make her as the *parā śakti*. This important concept of the Devi Mahatmya is portrayed in the phrase *tām mā devā vyadadhuḥ*, in the third

---

1 Further Lights : The Veda and the Tantra by Sri Kapali Sastriar.

Rik of the Devi Sukta. The immanent form of the Goddess described in a series of verses beginning with *yā devī sarvabhūtesu* is explained in the fourth Rik *mayā so annam atti.* In the declaration of Vak in the fifth Rik it is said that whomsoever she loves, she makes him mighty, him a Brahman, him a Rishi, him a man of pure understanding, *tam rsim tam sumedhām.* Can it be an accidental coincidence that it is Rishi Sumedha who narrates the glory of the Goddess to the monarch and the merchant ? The cardinal doctrine of the Sapasati that the Goddess takes birth to protect the worlds and slay the wicked, we find already proclaimed in the sixth Rik of Devi Sukta. *āham rudrāya dhanur atanomi brahmadviṣe śarave hantavā u.* The universal and trancendental form of the Divine Mother is expressed in the last line *paro divā para enā pṛthivyai tāvatī mahinā sambabhūva* What is thus expressed directly in the Veda is portrayed with epic grandeur in the striking verses of Saptasati.

"The tread of her feet bent the earth low, the top of her crown scraped the welkin high. With the twang of her bow string, she shook the entire nether-world and with a thousand arms, she stood covering all the quarters."

(II.38,39)

Thus, we find a close correlation between the sum and substance of Devi Mahatmya and the Devi Sukta in the Rig Veda. And on the strength of the phrase *dēvī suktam param japan*, found in the thirteenth chapter, we can conclude that the recital of the Devi Sukta in the Rig Veda has been a part of Chandi worship and the Vedic basis of Devi Mahatmyam has to be found in this Devi Sukta of Vak Ambhrni.

DEVI SUKTAM *

ॐ अहं रुद्रेभिर्वसुभिश्चराम्यहमादित्यैरुत विश्वदेवैः ।
अहं मित्रावरुणोभा विभर्म्यहमिन्द्राग्नी अहमश्विनोभा ॥ १ ॥

1. I walk with the Vasus and Rudras, with the
Adityas, as also with the All-Gods, Vishva Devah.

Mitra and Varuna, both I hold aloft, even so Indra
and Agni I do and the Ashwin-twins too.

अहं सोममाहनसं विभर्म्यहं त्वष्टारमुत पूषणं भगम् ।
अहं दधामि द्रविणं हविष्मते सुप्राव्ये यजमानाय सुन्वते ॥ २ ॥

2. I uphold and cherish the Soma that is to be pressed
out (for the delight of the Gods) and am the supporter of
the Divine sculptor Twashtri, and of Bhaga and Pushan
I hold the wealth for the sacrificer who reaches to the Gods
the pleasing offerings of Soma and Havis.

अहं राष्ट्री सङ्गमनी वसूनां चिकितुषी प्रथमा यज्ञियानाम् ।
तां मा देवा व्यदधुः पुरुत्रा भूरिस्थात्रां भूर्यावेशयन्तीम् ॥ ३ ॥

3. The Queen, I am the dispenser of wealth ; conscious, I am the first among the Gods (for whom the
sacrifice is meant).

Such am I (the One) and the Gods have found me
established in the Many, permeating and taking possession of the Manifold (existence)

---

*The translation provided here is that of Sri Kapali Sastriar—
Vide *Further Lights : The Veda and the Tantra*.

मया सो अन्नमत्ति यो विपश्यति यः प्राणिति य ईं श्रृणोत्युक्तम् ।
अमन्तवो मां त उप क्षियन्ति श्रुधि श्रुत श्रद्धिवं ते वदामि ॥ ४ ॥

4. It is by Me (by the sole Power) that one eats his food, sees, breathes and hears what is said.

They that ignore me (with their thought not turned to me) run to ruin. Hear, I declare to thee, the truth of faith, hearken!

अहमेव स्वयमिदं वदामि जुष्टं देवेभिरुत मानुषेभिः ।
यं कामये तं तमुग्रं कृणोमि तं ब्रह्माणं तमृषिं तं सुमेधाम् ॥ ५ ॥

5. Of my own accord, I announce this (truth) which the Gods as well as men strive to reach.

Whomsoever I love, I make them mighty, him a Brahman, him a Rishi, him a man of pure understanding.

अहं रुद्राय धनुरा तनोमि ब्रह्मद्विषे शरवे हन्तवा उ ।
अहं जनाय समदं कृणोम्यहं द्यावापृथिवी आ विवेश ॥ ६ ॥

6. For Rudra I stretch the bow-for the destruction of the tyrant, of the Veda—hater (Brahma-dvit) On the people I bestow equal joy in battle and I have permeated Heaven and Earth.

अहं सुवे पितरमस्य मूर्धन् मम योनिरप्स्वन्तः समुद्रे ।
ततो वि तिष्ठे भुवनानु विश्वोतामूं द्यां वर्ष्मणोप स्पृशामि ॥ ७ ॥

7. I gave birth to the Father (Heaven) at the summit of This (creation, Earth). My origin is in the Waters in the Inner Ocean.[1] Thence I extend pervading all the

---

1 Ocean is the image of the Infinite Conciousness and Being, in the conception of the ancients ; the word 'inner' before the 'ocean' (antas-samudra) here removes the veil over the Truth indicated by Ocean and Waters, *samudra* and *apah*.

worlds; and yonder Heaven I closely touch and penetrate with the showering and flowing body of mine, *varṣmaṇā*.

अहमेव वात इव प्र वाम्यारभमाणा भुवनानि विश्वा ।
परो दिवा पर एना पृथिव्यैतावती महिना सं बभूव ॥ ८ ॥

8. Like the winds, I blow vehemently, myself commencing all the worlds; far beyond the heavens, far (beneath) the Earth—so vast by my largeness I have become.

THE TRIPLE SECRET

The Sage Medhas imparts the secret of worship of the Goddess to the king and the merchant. This is described in the three secrets, *rahasya traya*.

The first secret deals with the process of creation. It is the secret about the *mula prakrti* who is the cause of creation. In the language of the Sankhyas, the *mula prakrti* is the important one, *pradhana*; hence the name *pradhanika rahasya* for the first secret. Creation takes place because of the existence of the qualities of *sattva, rajas* and *tamas*. Mahalakshmi is the first one existing, pervading everything and containing in her these three *gunas*. When the desire for creation appears, the quality *rajas* necessary for doing action predominates in her. There is a movement, a throb amongst the three qualities which were hitherto in equilibrium. From the quality *tamas* manifested Mahakali and from the quality *sattva* manifested Mahasaraswati. In the picturesque language of the Tantra it is said that Mahalakshmi bears on her head the serpent, *linga* and *yoni—nagam lingam ca yonim ca bibhrati*. The serpent is the symbol for Time and *linga* and *yoni* denote the male and female principles. The supreme beyond Time and beyond sex limited itself by Time and took upon it the male and female principles for the purpose of creation. These three Maha Shaktis, independently created each a pair of male and female.

Mahalakshmi created Lakshmi and Brahma, Mahakali brought forth Siva and Saraswati and Mahasaraswati Vishnu and Gauri. It will now be abundantly clear that the Mahakali, Mahalakshmi and Mahasaraswati of the Saptasati are not the popular Gauri, Lakshmi and Saraswati but Powers infinitely superior to them. So, in popular parlance Lakshmi became Brahma's sister and shared the common characteristic of a lotus-seat. Saraswati became Siva's sister, both the repositories and givers of true knowledge. Parvati became Vishnu's sister, which fact has become famous through the Puranas which are known as *bhāgavata* in both the cases. For the purpose of creation, these three pairs became a different set of couples. Brahma took Saraswati as his consort, Vishnu Lakshmi and Siva Parvati and respectively presided over the creation, preservation and destruction of the universe. This is the first secret.

In the second secret is described how the Godhead beyond change subjected itself to change, how the *mūla prakṛti*, became *vikṛti*; hence the name *vaikṛtika rahasya* to the second secret. The primordeal Shakti Mahalakshmi manifested from the bodies of all the gods and became a mass Para Sakti, for carrying out the destruction of Mahishasura. From her who has eighteen hands manifest Mahakali of the ten hands and Mahasaraswati of the eight hands. Mahakali manifested to kill Madhu and Kaitabha, while Mahasaraswati was the godhead that appeared to vanquish Shumbha, Nishumbha and others. The second secret describes in detail the mode of worshipping these three deities.

In the third secret, *murti rahasya*, the incarnations, the *avatāra mūrtis* of the Goddess are mentioned. In the eleventh chapter of the text the Goddess herself proclaims her future incarnations on earth for the purpose of destroying the wicked and re-establishing the Divine Law on earth. *mūrti rahasya* deals in brief with the mode of worship of these great incarnations, Nandaja, Raktadantika, Shakambhari, Satakshi, Durga, Bhima and Bhramari.

PRADHANIKA RAHASYA

अस्य श्रीसप्तशतीरहस्यत्रयस्य ब्रह्मविष्णुरुद्रा ऋषयः । महा
काली महालक्ष्मी महासरस्वत्यो देवताः । अनुष्टुप् छन्दः ।
नवदुर्गा महालक्ष्मी बीजम् श्रीं शक्तिः । ममाभीष्टफलसिद्धये
सप्तशती पाठान्ते जपे विनियोगः ॥

For the three secrets, the seers are Brahma, Vishnu
and Rudra. The deities are Mahakali, Mahalakshmi and
Mahasaraswati. Mahalakshmi, Navadurga is the seed and
Srim is the force. The application is in Japa at the end of
the Saptasati recital, for the fruition of my desires.

राजोवाच ।

The King said :

भगवन्नवतारा मे चण्डिकाया स्त्वयोदिताः ।
एतेषां प्रकृतिं ब्रह्मन् प्रधानं वक्तुमर्हसि ॥ १ ॥

1. Sire, you have mentioned to me about the manifestations of Chandika. Knower of Brahman, please oblige
by telling me about their nature and importance.

आराध्यं यन्मया देव्याः स्वरूपं येन वै द्विज ।
विधिना ब्रूहि सकलं यथावत् प्रणतस्य मे ॥ २ ॥

2. Which of the deities have I to worship, in what
form, with what ritual? O, twice-born, I have bowed to
you. Tell me all the facts.

ऋषिरुवाच

The Sage said :

इदं रहस्यं परमं अनाख्येयं प्रचक्षते ।
भक्तोऽसीति न मे किंचित् तवावाच्यं नराधिप ॥ ३ ॥

3. This is a great secret. It is said that it should not be mentioned. But you are devoted to me, O lord of men and there is nothing that I cannot mention to you.

सर्वस्याद्या महालक्ष्मीस्त्रिगुणा परमेश्वरी ।
लक्ष्यालक्ष्यस्वरूपा सा व्याप्य कृत्स्नं व्यवस्थिता ॥ ४ ॥

4. Mahalakshmi is the first and foremost of all. Supreme sovereign, she is of the three qualities. All the manifested and unmanifested are her form. Pervading in entirety, she stands.

मातुलिंगं गदां खेटं पानपात्रं च बिभ्रती ।
नागं लिंगं च योनिं च बिभ्रती नृप मूर्द्धनि ॥ ५ ॥

5. She holds the citron,[1] mace, shield and the drinking vessel. O king, she bears on her head the serpent, the male and the female principles.

तप्तकाञ्चनवर्णाभा तप्तकाञ्चनभूषणा ।
शून्यं तदखिलं स्वेन पूरयामास तेजसा ॥ ६ ॥

6. Her complexion is that of melted gold and her ornaments too made of melted gold. She filled all the void with her light.

शून्यं तदखिलं लोकं विलोक्य परमेश्वरी ।
बभार रूपमपरं तमसा केवलेन हि ॥ ७ ॥

7. The Supreme sovereign seeing the entire world a void bore another form by mere *tamas*.

सा मिश्राञ्जनसंकाशा दंष्ट्राञ्चितवरानना ।
विशाललोचना नारी बभूव तनुमध्यमा ॥ ८ ॥

---

1 The fruit containing many seeds, symbolising the manifold creation.

8. The form became a woman of slender waist and expansive eyes. Her shapely mouth was marked by fangs and she shone like cut collyrium.

खड्गपात्रशिरःखेटै रलंकृतचतुर्भुजा ।
कबन्धधारं शिरसा बिभ्राणा हि शिरःस्रजम् ॥ ९ ॥

9. Her four hands were adorned with the sword, the drinking vessel, the head and the shield. In her breast she wore a garland of headless trunks and in her head, a string of heads.

तां प्रोवाच महालक्ष्मी स्तामसीं प्रमदोत्तमाम् ।
ददामि तव नामानि यानि कर्माणि तानि ते ॥ १० ॥

10. Mahalakshmi said to that superb woman, predominant in *tamas*. I shall give you your names and your field of action.

महामाया महाकाली महामारी क्षुधा तृषा ।
निद्रा तृष्णा चैकवीरा कालरात्रिर्दुरत्यया ॥ ११ ॥

11. Mahamaya, Mahakali, Great Death, hunger, thirst, sleep, hankering, the sole warrior, dark night, the impassable.

इमानि तव नामानि प्रतिपाद्यानि कर्मभिः ।
एभिः कर्माणि ते ज्ञात्वा योऽधीते सोऽश्नुते सुखम् ॥ १२ ॥

12. These are your names indicated by your actions. One who studies your actions knowing them from these names attains happiness.

तामित्युक्त्वा महालक्ष्मीः स्वरूपमपरं नृप ।
सत्त्वाख्येनातिशुद्धेन गुणेनेन्दुप्रभं दधौ ॥ १३ ॥

13. O king, having said this to her, Mahalakshmi

took another form of moon-like lustre through the very pure quality, known as *sattwa*.

अक्षमालांकुशधरा वीणापुस्तकधारिणी ।
सा बभूव वरा नारी नामान्यस्यै च सा ददौ ॥ १४ ॥

14. The form became a nice lady holding the garland of beads and goad and carrying in her hands the book and the Vina. To her as well she gave the names.

महाविद्या महावाणी भारती वाक् सरस्वती ।
आर्या ब्राह्मी कामधेनुवेंदगर्भा सुरेश्वरी ॥ १५ ॥

15. Great knowledge, Great Word, Bharati, Vak, Saraswati, Arya, Brahma's consort, the cow yielding all desires, one who carries in her womb the Veda and the Sovereign lady of the gods.

अथोवाच महालक्ष्मीर्महाकालीं सरस्वतीम् ।
युवां जनयतां देव्यौ मिथुने खानुरूपतः ॥ १६ ॥

16. The Mahalakshmi said to Mahakali and Mahasaraswati. You two goddesses, please produce twins according to your own nature.

इत्युक्त्वा ते महालक्ष्मीः ससर्ज मिथुनं खयम् ।
हिरण्यगर्भौ रुचिरौ स्त्रीपुंसौ कमलासनौ ॥ १७ ॥

17. Telling them thus, Mahalakshmi herself produced twins, a male and a female seated on the lotus, both beautiful as they were delivered out of the golden womb.

ब्रह्मन् विधे विरिंचेति धातरित्याह तं नरम् ।
श्रीःपद्मे कमले लक्ष्मीत्याह माता स्त्रियं च ताम् ॥ १८ ॥

18. The Mother accosted the male ' O Brahma, Fate,

Virinchi, Ordainer' and she addressed the female 'O Sri, Padma, Kamala, Lakshmi.'

महाकाली भारती च मिथुने सृजतः सह ।
पत्योरपि रूपाणि नामानि च वदामि ते ॥ १९ ॥

19. Mahakali and Mahasaraswati produced together twins. I shall tell you their names and forms.

नीलकण्ठं रक्तबाहुं श्वेतांगं चन्द्रशेखरम् ।
जनयामास पुरुषं महाकाली सितां स्त्रियम् ॥ २० ॥

20. Mahakali produced a male of blue neck, red arm, white limb, having the moon in the crest and she also produced a white female.

स रुद्रः शंकरः स्थाणुः कपर्दी च त्रिलोचनः ।
त्रयी विद्या कामधेनुः सा स्त्री भाषा स्वराक्षरा ॥ २१ ॥

21. He is Rudra, the doer of good, the unchanging fixed one, the three-eyed with the matted hair *kaparda*. That female is knowledge, the three Vedas, the cow fulfilling all wants, language, Swara and the immutable letter.

सरस्वती स्त्रियं गौरीं कृष्णं च पुरुषं नृप ।
जनयामास नामानि तयोरपि वदामि ते ॥ २२ ॥

22. Mahasaraswati produced a female of golden yellow colour and a male of dark complexion. I shall tell you their names as well, O, King!

विष्णुः कृष्णो हृषीकेशो वासुदेवो जनार्दनः ।
उमा गौरी सती चण्डी सुन्दरी सुभगा शिवा ॥ २३ ॥

23. Vishnu, Krshna the dark one, the lord of the senses, Vasudeva, Janardana, Uma, Gauri, Sati, Chandi, Sundari, Subhaga, Siva.

एवं युवतयः सद्यः पुरुषत्वं प्रपेदिरे ।
चक्षुष्मन्तो नु पश्यन्ति नेतरे तद्विदो जनाः ॥ २४ ॥

24. Thus the ladies instantaneously attained manhood. Those who have eyes will see. The rest of the people will not know about it.

ब्रह्मणे प्रददौ पत्नीं महालक्ष्मीर्नृप त्रयीम् ।
रुद्राय गौरीं वरदां वासुदेवाय च श्रियम् ॥ २५ ॥

25. O King, Mahalakshmi gave Saraswati in the form of three Vedas as wife to Brahma, Gauri the giver of the best of Rudra and Lakshmi to Vasudeva.

स्वरया सह संभूय विरिंचोऽण्डमजीजनत् ।
बिभेद भगवान् रुद्रस्तद् गौर्या सह वीर्यवान् ॥ २६ ॥

26. Brahma united with Saraswati in the form of Sound and created the cosmos, The valorous Lord Rudra joined with Gauri and broke it.

अण्डमध्ये प्रधानादि कार्यं जातमभून्नृप ।
महाभूतात्मकं सर्वं जगत् स्थावरजंगमम् ॥ २६ ॥

27. O King, in the middle of the cosmos sprang up resultant actions like Mula Prakrti and all this universe of mobile and immobile objects, composed of the great elements.

पुपोष पालयामास तल्लक्ष्म्या सह केशवः ।
महालक्ष्मीरेवमज्ञा राजन् सर्वेश्वरेश्वरी ॥ २८ ॥

निराकारा च साकारा सैव नानाभिधानभृत् ।
नामान्तरैर्निरूप्यैषा नाम्ना नान्येन केनचित् ॥ २९ ॥

28-29. Vishnu nourished and protected that along with Lakshmi. O King, thus the Goddess of all the gods

Mahalakshmi had no birth and no form. She is also with form and bears varied names. She has to be proved by other names and yet by no other name can she be proved.

इति प्राधानिकरहस्यं संपूर्णम्

Thus Pradhanika Rahasya is complete.

VAIKRTIKA RAHASYA

ऋषिरुवाच

The Sage said :

त्रिगुणा तामसी देवी सात्त्विकी या त्वयोदिता ।
सा शर्वा चण्डिका दुर्गा भद्रा भगवतीर्यते ॥ १ ॥

1. The Goddess who is triply classified as the one composed of the three gunas, the one predominant in *tamas* and the one predominant in *satva* is mentioned as Sarva, Chandika, Durga, Bhadra and Bhagavati.

योगनिद्रा हरेरुक्ता महाकाली तमोगुणा ।
मधुकैटभनाशार्थं यां तुष्टावाम्बुजासनः ॥ २ ॥

2. The one whom Brahma of the lotus-seat praised for the purpose of destroying Madhu and Kaitabha, she is said to be Vishnu's superconscient sleep, Mahakali in whom *tamas* predominates.

दशवक्त्रा दशभुजा दशपादाञ्जनप्रभा ।
विशालया राजमाना त्रिंशल्लोचनमालया ॥ ३ ॥

3. She has ten faces, ten arms, ten feet and has the lustre of collyrium. She shines with her thirty large eyes knit like a garland.

स्फुरद्दशनदंष्ट्रा सा भीमरूपाऽपि भूमिप ।
रूपसौभाग्यकान्तीनां सा प्रतिष्ठा महाश्रियाम् ॥ ४ ॥

4. Protector of the world, though she is terrible in appearance with her glittering teeth and fangs, she is the mainstay of the great opulence of beauty, auspiciousness and lustre.

खड्गवाणगदाशूलशङ्खचक्रभुशुण्डिभृत् ।
परिघं कार्मुकं शीर्षं निश्च्योतद्रुधिरं दधौ ॥ ५ ॥

5. She wields the sword, the shaft, the mace, the trident, the conch, the discus and the sling. She bears also the iron club, the bow and the head dripping with blood.

एषा सा वैष्णवी माया महाकाली दुरत्यया ।
आराधिता वशीकुर्यात् पूजाकर्तुश्चराचरम् ॥ ६ ॥

6. She is the delusion of Vishnu, the impassable, Mahakali. If worshipped she will bring under the control of the worshipper all the mobile and the immobile in the universe.

सर्वदेवशरीरेभ्यो याऽऽविभूताऽमितप्रभा ।
त्रिगुणा सा महालक्ष्मीः साक्षान्महिषमर्दिनी ॥ ७ ॥

7. The one who manifested out of the bodies of all the gods with immeasurable light, she is Mahalakshmi containing the three gunas, verily the destroyer of Mahisha.

श्वेतानना नीलभुजा सुश्वेतस्तनमण्डला ।
रक्तमध्या रक्तपादा रक्तजङ्घोरुरुन्मदा ॥ ८ ॥

8. Her face white, arms black and the breasts extremely white, she has her hip red, her feet red, her shanks and thighs red. She is the form of supreme delight.

सुचित्रजघना चित्रमाल्यांबरविभूषणा ।
चित्रानुलेपना कान्तिरूपसौभाग्यशालिनी ॥ ९ ॥

9. Her lap is of varied hues. Her garland, garment, ornament, smearing on the body all are of various hues. She is full of lustre, beauty and auspiciousness.

अष्टादशभुजा पूज्या सा सहस्रभुजा सती ।
आयुधान्यत्र वक्ष्यन्ते दक्षिणाधःकरक्रमात् ॥ १० ॥

10. Though she is possessed of thousand arms, she should be worshipped as one with eighteen arms. The weapons are now enumerated from the bottom - most right hand.

अक्षमाला च कमलं बाणोऽसिः कुलिशं गदा ।
चक्रं त्रिशूलं परशुः शंखो घण्टा च पाशकः ॥ ११ ॥

11. The garland of beads, lotus, shaft, sword, thunderbolt, mace, discus, trident, battle axe, conch, bell, noose,

शक्तिर्दण्डश्चर्म चापं पानपात्रं कमण्डलुः ।
अलंकृतभुजामेमिरायुधैः कमलासनाम् ॥ १२ ॥

12. The lance, staff, shield, bow, drinking vessel, water-pot with these weapons her arms are adorned and her seat is on the lotus.

सर्वदेवमयीमीशां महालक्ष्मीमिमां नृप ।
पूजयेत् सर्वलोकानां स देवानां प्रभुर्भवेत् ॥ १३ ॥

13. O King, one who worships this Mahalakshmi, the Goddess come out of all the gods, he will become the master of all the worlds and the gods.

गौरीदेहात् समुद्भूता या सर्वैकगुणाश्रया ।
साक्षात् सरस्वती प्रोक्ता शुभासुरनिबर्हिणी ॥ १४ ॥

284

14. The one who was born out of the body of Gauri having as her base only the *sattva* guna, she is verily Mahasaraswati, the slayer of Shumbhasura.

दधौ चाष्टभुजा बाणान्मुसलं शूलचक्रभृत् ।
शंखं घण्टां लांगलं च कार्मुकं वसुधाधिप ॥ १५ ॥

15. O, the lord of the earth, she wields in her eight arms, arrows, pestle, trident, discus, conch, bell, ploughshare and the bow.

एषा संपूजिता भक्त्या सर्वज्ञत्वं प्रयच्छति ।
निशुम्भमथिनी देवी शुम्भासुरनिबर्हिणी ॥ १६ ॥

16. This is the goddess who crushed Nishumbha and killed the Asura Shumbha. If she is worshipped with devotion, she grants omniscience to the worshipper.

इत्युक्तानि स्वरूपाणि मूर्तीनां तव पार्थिव ।
उपासनं जगन्मातुः पृथगासां निशामय ॥ १७ ॥

17. O King, the forms of these embodiments have thus been told. Hear and know the worship of the World-mother as well as of these embodiments distinctly.

महालक्ष्मीर्यदा पूज्या महाकाली सरस्वती ।
दक्षिणोत्तरयोः पूज्ये पृष्ठतो मिथुनत्रयम् ॥ १८ ॥

18. When Mahalakshmi is worshipped, you have to worship on her right and left Mahakali and Mahasaraswati, at the back of these three the three couples.

विरिञ्चिः स्वरया मध्ये रुद्रो गौर्या च दक्षिणे ।
वामे लक्ष्म्या हृषीकेशः पुरतो देवतात्रयम् ॥ १९ ॥

19. At the back, in the middle, Brahma with Saraswati, on the right, Rudra with Gauri and on the left Vishnu with Lakshmi. In the front the three goddesses.

अष्टादशभुजा मध्ये वामे चास्या दशानना ।
दक्षिणेऽष्टभुजा लक्ष्मीर्मेढतीति समर्चयेत् ॥ २० ॥

20. (In the front), in the middle, the eighteen armed. To her left the ten-faced and on the right the eight-armed. Mahalakshmi has to be worshipped as the important deity.

अष्टादशभुजा चैषा यदा पूज्या नराधिप ।
दशानना चाष्टभुजा दक्षिणोत्तरयोस्तदा ॥ २१ ॥

21. O master of men, when this eighteen-armed one and on right and left the ten-faced and the eight-armed are worshipped,

कालमृत्यू च संपूज्यौ सर्वारिष्टप्रशान्तये ।
यदा चाष्टभुजा पूज्या शुम्भासुरनिबर्हिणी ॥ २२ ॥

22. *Kala*, time and *Mrtyu*, death have to be worshipped for mitigating all calamities. When the eight armed, the slayer of Asura Sumbha is worshipped,

नवास्याः शक्तयः पूज्यास्तथा रुद्रविनायकौ ।
नमो देव्या इति स्तोत्रैर्महालक्ष्मीं समर्चयेत् ॥ २३ ॥

23. Her nine Saktis have to be worshipped as well as Rudra and Vinayaka. Mahalakshmi should be worshipped with the laud commencing *namo devyai*.

अवतारत्रयार्चायां स्तोत्रमन्त्रा स्तदाश्रयाः ।
अष्टादशभुजा चैषा पूज्या महिषमर्दिनी ॥ २४ ॥

24. In the worship of the three manifestations, the

lauds mentioned in the three episodes should relate to the respective manifestations. This destroyer of Mahisha, of eighteen arms has to be specially worshipped.

महालक्ष्मीर्महाकाली सैव प्रोक्ता सरस्वती ।
ईश्वरी पुण्यपापानां सर्वलोकमहेश्वरी ॥ २५ ॥

25. She herself is called as Mahakali, Mahalakshmi and Mahasaraswati. She is the Great Goddess of all the worlds, the dispenser of merit and sin.

महिषान्तकरी येन पूजिता स जगत्प्रभुः ।
पूजयेउज्जगतां धात्रीं चण्डिकां भक्तवत्सलाम् ॥ २६ ॥

26. One who worships the destroyer of Mahisha becomes the lord of the world. One should worship Chandika, endearing to the devotees, the sustainer and upholder of the worlds-

अर्घ्यादिभिरलंकारैर्गन्धपुष्पैस्तथोत्तमैः ।
धूपैर्दीपैश्च नैवेद्यैर्नानाभक्ष्यसमन्वितैः ॥ २७ ॥

27. By Arghya etc., by decking with ornaments, by sandal paste, flowers, by the best incense, lamps, by offerings of food containing various eatables,

रुधिराक्तेन बलिना मांसेन सुरया नृप ।
प्रणामाचमनीयेन चन्दनेन सुगन्धिना ॥ २८ ॥

28. By offering of sacrifice steeped in blood, by flesh, by wine, by salutations, sipping of water, fragrant sandal,

सकर्पूरैश्च तांबूलैर्भक्तिभावसमन्वितैः ।
वामभागेऽग्रतो देव्यादिच्छन्नशीर्षं महासुरम् ॥ २९ ॥

पूजयेन्महिषं येन प्राप्तं सायुज्यमीशया ।
दक्षिणे पुरतः सिद्धं समग्रं धर्ममीश्वरम् ॥ ३० ॥

वाहनं पूजयेद्देव्या धृतं येन चराचरम् ।
ततः कृताञ्जलि भूत्वा स्तुवीत चरितैरिमैः ॥ ३१ ॥

29-31. By offering *tāmbūla* with camphor with an
attitude of devotion in all these acts. In front of the
Goddess, on the left side, one should worship the great
Asura Mahisha whose head had been severed by the
Goddess and who had attained union with her. In front
on the right, one should worship the vehicle of the Goddess, the lion which is no other than the whole mighty
Dharma upholding and sustaining the mobile and the
immobile. Then with folded hands one should offer prayers
with these episodes.

एकेन वा मध्यमेन नैकेनेतरयोरिह ।
चरितार्धं तु न जपेज्जपन् छिद्रमवाप्नुयात् ॥ ३२ ॥

32. Or by the middle episode alone ; but not by any
one of the other episodes. One should not stop recital in
the middle of an episode. If he does so, it will be a chink
in his armour.

स्तोत्रमन्त्रैः स्तुवीतेमां यदि वा जगदम्बिकाम् ।
प्रदक्षिणानमस्कारान् कृत्वा मूर्ध्नि कृतांजलिः ॥ ३३ ॥

33. Or else, he should go round the deity with
reverence, offer salutations and with hands folded on the
head pray to the World-mother by means of the lauds.

क्षमापयेज्जगद्धात्रीं मुहुर्मुहुरतन्द्रितः ।
प्रतिश्लोकं च जुहुयात् पायसं तिलसर्पिषा ॥ ३४ ॥

34. Again and again, without any lassitude one
should seek the pardon of the sustainer of the worlds. With
each verse he should offer in the fire oblations of rice
cooked in milk, sesamum and ghee.

जुहुयात् स्तोत्रमन्त्रैर्वा चण्डिकायै शुभं हविः ।
नमो नमः पदैर्देवीं पूजयेत् सुसमाहितः ॥ ३५ ॥

35. Or with the verses of the lauds he can offer the
auspicious oblations to Chandika. He should withdraw
into himself, concentrate, utter the words *namo namah*
"salutations, salutations" and worship the Devi.

प्रयतः प्रांजलिः प्रह्वः प्राणानारोप्य चात्मनि ।
सुचिरं भावयेद्देवीं चण्डिकां तन्मयो भवेत् ॥ ३६ ॥

36. Controlled, with folded hands, highly plastic
with a surrendered attitude, he should impose his Prana
on his Self and meditate on the Goddess Chandika for
quite a long time. He will become full of her.

एवं यः पूजयेद्भक्त्या प्रत्यहं परमेश्वरीम् ।
भुक्त्वा भोगान् यथाकामं देवीसायुज्यमाप्नुयात् ॥ ३७ ॥

37. One who worships thus daily, the supreme
Goddess experiences all enjoyments to his heart's content
and attains union with the Goddess.

यो न पूजयते नित्यं चण्डिकां भक्तवत्सलाम् ।
भस्मीकृत्यास्य पुण्यानि निर्दहेत् परमेश्वरी ॥ ३८ ॥

38. If one does not worship daily Chandika, endearing to the devotees, the supreme Goddess reduces to ashes his merits and consumes him.

तस्मात् पूजय भूपाल सर्वलोकमहेश्वरीम् ।
यथोक्तेन विधानेन चण्डिकां सुखमाप्स्यसि ॥ ३९ ॥

39. Therefore, O king, worship as per the prescribed method Chandika, the great Goddess in all the worlds. You will get happiness.

इति वैकृतिकरहस्यं संपूर्णम्

This Vaikrtika Rahasya is complete.

MŪRTI RAHASYA

ऋषिरुवाच

The Sage said :

नन्दा भगवती नाम या भविष्यति नन्दजा ।
सा स्तुता पूजिता ध्याता वशीकुर्याज्जगत्त्रयम् ॥ १ ॥

1. The goddess who is going to be born of Nanda
with the name Nanda Bhagavati, if she is lauded, worshipped, contemplated upon, she will bring under the
control of the worshipper the triple world.

कनकोत्तमकान्तिः सा सुकान्तिकनकांबरा ।
देवी कनकवर्णाभा कनकोत्तमभूषणा ॥ २ ॥

2. She whose complexion will be that of pure gold
will be wearing garments of shining gold. She with the
golden lustre will be wearing ornaments of pure gold.

कमलांकुशपाशाब्जैरलंकृतचतुर्भुजा ।
इन्दिरा कमला लक्ष्मीः सा श्रीः रुक्मांबुजासना ॥ ३ ॥

3. Her four arms will be adorned by lotus, goad,
noose and conch. She is Lakshmi, Kamala, Indira, Sri,
seated on the golden lotus.

या रक्तदन्तिका नाम देवी प्रोक्ता मयानघ ।
तस्याः स्वरूपं वक्ष्यामि श्रृणु सर्वभयापहम् ॥ ४ ॥

4. O Spotless one, I mentioned a goddess named Raktadantika; hear about her form, it will allay all fears.

रक्तांबरा रक्तवर्णा रक्तसर्वांगभूषणा ।
रक्तायुधा रक्तनेत्रा रक्तकेशातिभीषणा ॥ ५ ॥

5. Her garment is red, her colour is red, all the ornaments in her body are red, her weapons are red, Her eyes are red and her hair is red. She is terrible.

रक्ततीक्ष्णनखा रक्तदशना रक्तदंष्ट्रिका ।
पतिं नारीवानुरक्ता देवी भक्तं भजेज्जनम् ॥ ६ ॥

6. She has sharp red nails, red teeth and red fangs. But she will look after her devotee as a loving wife her husband.

वसुधेव विशाला सा सुमेरुयुगलस्तनी ।
दीर्घौ लंबावतिस्थूलौ तावतीव मनोहरौ ॥ ७ ॥

7. Vast is her form like the earth. Her pair of breasts is like the mountain Meru, long, protruding and very huge, exquisitely beautiful.

कर्कशावतिकान्तौ तौ सर्वानन्दपयोनिधी ।
भक्तान् संपाययेद्देवी सर्वकामदुघौ स्तनौ ॥ ८ ॥

8. Those hard captivating breasts are oceans of the perfect bliss. With those yielding all wishes, she feeds her devotees.

खड्गपात्रं च मुसलं लांगलं च बिभर्ति सा ।
आख्याता रक्तचामुण्डा देवी योगेश्वरीति च ॥ ९ ॥

9. She bears the sword, the drinking vessel, the pestle and the ploughshare. She is known as the goddess Rakta Chamunda, the sovereign of Yoga.

अनया व्याप्तमखिलं जगत् स्थावरजङ्गमम् ।
इमां यः पूजयेद्रुक्त्या स व्याप्नोति चराचरम् ॥ १० ॥

10. By her is pervaded the entire world, the mobile and the immobile. One who worships her with devotion extends himself in the mobile and in the immobile.

अधीते य इमं नित्यं रक्तदन्त्या वपुःस्तवम् ।
तं सा परिचरेद्देवी पतिं प्रियमिवांगना ॥ ११ ॥

11. As a woman would on her dear husband, the goddess waits on the one who constantly studies this laud describing the form of Raktadantika.

शाकंभरी नीलवर्णा नीलोत्पलविलोचना ।
गंभीरनाभि स्त्रिवलीविभूषिततनूदरी ॥ १२ ॥

12. Sakambhari is blue in complexion and her eyes are like the blue lotus. Deep is her navel and her slender abdomen is adorned by the three folds.

सुकर्कशसमोत्तुंगवृत्तपीनघनस्तनी ।
मुष्टिं शिलीमुखैः पूर्णं कमलं कमलालया ॥ १३ ॥

13. Her breasts are pretty hard, even, lofty, round, fat and dense. Her abode is in the lotus. Lotus, a handful of arrows,

पुष्पपल्लवमूलादिफलाढ्यं शाकसंचयम् ।
काम्यानन्तरसैयुक्तं क्षुत्तृण्मृत्युजरापहम् ॥ १४ ॥

14. a heap of victuals rich in flowers, tendrils, roots, fruits etc. having in it all the desired infinite variety of tastes and removing hunger, thirst, death and old age,

कार्मुकं च स्फुरत्कान्ति बिभर्ति परमेश्वरी ।
शाकंभरी शताक्षी स्यात् सैव दुर्गा प्रकीर्तिता ॥ १५ ॥

15. and a bow of glittering lustre—all these the great goddess Sakambhari bears. She herself is Satakshi, also known as Durga.

शाकंभरीं स्तुवन् ध्यायन् जपन् संपूजयन् नमन् ।
अक्षय्यमश्नुते शीघ्रमन्नपानादि सर्वशः ॥ १६ ॥

16. If one lauds, contemplates upon, recites about, worships or salutes Sakambhari one gets speedily in all possible ways food and drink of undiminishing quantity.

भीमापि नीलवर्णा सा दंष्ट्रादशनभासुरा ।
विशाललोचना नारी वृत्तपीनघनस्तनी ॥ १७ ॥

17. Bhima also is of blue complexion. A woman of large eyes and shining teeth and fangs, her breasts are round, fat and massive.

चन्द्रहासं च डमरुं शिरःपात्रं च बिभ्रती ।
एकवीरा कालरात्रिः सैवोक्ता कामदा स्तुता ॥ १८ ॥

18. She holds the sabre, the little drum, and the bowl made of human skull. She is mentioned as Ekavira, the sole warrior, Kalaratri the dark night. She is praised as the giver of desires.

तेजोमण्डलदुर्धर्षा भ्रामरी चित्रकान्तिभृत् ।
चित्रभ्रमरसंकाशा महामारीति गीयते ॥ १९ ॥

19. Bhramari is unassailable, encircled by light. Her splendour is of wonderful variety. She appears like a multi-coloured bee and is praised as Mahamari.

इत्येता मूर्तयो देव्या व्याख्याता वसुधाधिप ।
जगन्मातुश्चण्डिकायाः कीर्तिताः कामधेनवः ॥ २० ॥

20. O lord of earth, thus are explained the embodiments of the World-Mother, of the Goddess Chandika.

These are said to be verily Kamadhenus, the milch-cows yielding all desires.

इदं रहस्यं परमं न वाच्यं यस्य कस्यचित् ।
व्याख्यानं दिव्यमूर्तीनामधीष्वावहितः स्वयम् ॥ २१ ॥

21. This is the supreme secret, not to be told to anybody. Make by yourself a concentrated study of the explanations about these divine embodiments.

दैव्या ध्यानं तवाख्यातं गुह्याद् गुह्यतरं महत् ।
तस्मात् सर्वप्रयत्नेन सर्वकामफलप्रदम् ॥ २२ ॥

22. The great secret of secrets, meditation on the goddess has been imparted to you. So if an all-out effort is made, an all-fulfilling result will be achieved.

इति मूर्तिरहस्यं संपूर्णम्

Thus Murti Rahasya is complete.

A PRAYER CRAVING PARDON

अपराधसहस्राणि क्रियन्तेऽहर्निशं मया ।
दासोऽयमिति मां मत्वा क्षमस्व परमेश्वरि ॥ १ ॥

1. Day and night, I commit a thousand mistakes, O Supreme Goddess, pardon them considering that I am thy slave.

आवाहनं न जानामि न जानामि विसर्जनम् ।
पूजां चैव न जानामि क्षम्यतां परमेश्वरि ॥ २ ॥

2. I do not know how to invoke thy presence and how to revoke it. I do not know how to worship thee. Pardon, O Supreme Goddess.

मन्त्रहीनं क्रियाहीनं भक्तिहीनं सुरेश्वरि ।
यत् पूजितं मया देवि परिपूर्णं तदस्तु ते ॥ ३ ॥

3. O the queen of gods, let no shortcoming in Mantra, ritual or devotion vitiate the fullness of my worship to thee.

अपराधशतं कृत्वा जगदम्बेति चोच्चरेत् ।
यां गतिं समवाप्नोति न तां ब्रह्मादयः सुराः ॥ ४ ॥

4. If a man commits a hundred faults but utters the invocation, 'O World-Mother', the status he attains, even Brahma and other gods do not attain.

सापराधोऽस्मि शरणं प्राप्तस्त्वां जगदम्बिके ।
इदानीमनुकम्प्योऽहं यथेच्छसि तथा कुरु ॥ ५ ॥

5. I am full of faults. O World-Mother, I seek refuge in thee. Now I have to be pitied. Do as thou likest.

अज्ञानाद्विस्मृते भ्रान्त्या यन्न्यूनमधिकं कृतम् ।
तत् सर्वं क्षम्यतां देवि प्रसीद परमेश्वरि ॥ ६ ॥

6. Devi, pray, pardon my acts of omission and commission through ignorance, forgetfulness or error; O Supreme Goddess may thou be pleased.

कामेश्वरि जगन्मातः सच्चिदानन्दविग्रहे ।
गृहाणार्चामिमां प्रीत्या प्रसीद परमेश्वरि ॥ ७ ॥

7. O the lady of love, mother of the world, embodiment of Truth- Consciousness - Bliss, pray accept with satisfaction this worship. O Supreme Goddess, may thou be pleased.

गुह्यातिगुह्यगोप्त्री त्वं गृहाणास्मत्कृतं जपम् ।
सिद्धिर्भवतु मे देवि त्वत्प्रसादान्महेश्वरि ॥ ८ ॥

8. Devi, thou art the protector of the most occult secrets. Please accept the japa done by me. Great Goddess, let fulfilment come to me by thy grace.

PRAYOGA

The *saptaśati* has been acclaimed as a great *sādhana sastra*, a practical manual, an *artha śāstra* a purposive science. The Tantric seers have laid down certain methods by practising which the text becomes an unfailing companion in the journey of life. As many have followed these methods and achieved results, they are sure and safe. We shall discuss such methods, *prayogas*, here.

First and foremost we have to appreciate a fact which is fundamental to Mantra Sadhana. "Prayer to an indefinite something, to an Impersonal divinity can only evoke an impersonal or indefinite response. If a response, is sought to be evoked for a particular need, the prayer could be fruitful when it is addressed to a canalised centre of the Divinity, the Personal form which is active for the purpose in question, and that is precisely what the Devata in its higher sense is in the Tantra."[1] It is true that there is one Supreme Deity presiding over everything. It is also true that there exists a number of gods and goddesses. The one does not negate the many. The one god does not overrule the other gods in their respective fields of operation. He is the soul, they are his limbs *sa ātmā angāni anyā devatāḥ*. And each limb of his has a specific function to perform in creation. There is a gradation and a heirarchy

---

1 *Further Lights : The Veda and the Tantra* by Sri Kapali Sastriar.

of delegated functions and the gods deriving their authority from the supreme Godhead are posited in various planes on the rising tier of consciousness. It is very easy for the human being to get in touch with the gods in the lower levels of this pyramidal structure of consciousness. They are posited in levels very near to him and so the results are spectacular in the beginning. But these lower classes of deities, *kṣudra devatās*, do not lead a person very far. Soon, the progress comes to a standstill. But if a person chooses a deity in the higher cadre and is guided properly by a Guru in his quest, slowly but surely he progresses and gets indications of the grace of the deity he worships. Marvelling at the abounding grace, he grows in devotion towards the Godhead. Slowly a relationship is established and a living concourse takes place between the sadhaka and his chosen deity. *iṣṭa devatā*. He gets into the habit of referring every one of his acts to the deity within him and learns to wait on the Divine Grace for the success of his undertakings. Most men take to the worship of a deity to achieve some objective in life. But the worship results in strengthening the bonds between the sadhaka and the deity and in course of time that has a greater pull and attraction than the objective with which he orginally started the worship. Finally, these objectives pale into insignificance or vanish altogether because they either become fulfilled or replaced by higher objectives and all these objectives finally converge towards the supreme objective in life which is the ultimate goal of all spiritual paths.

As we have explained, a specific deity will help in the achievement of a specific objective. For example,

Vighneswara will help in the removal of all obstacles, Saraswati in the acquisition of knowledge, Lakshmi in the acquisition of wealth etc. But if one has the supreme aim in view, and takes to a benevolent deity, by its grace the Sadhana proceeds on safe and sound lines. Gradually, the burden of the whole Sadhana is taken up by the deity and the sadhaka is brought nearer and nearer to his great aim. To give an example, if a person's aim is supreme knowledge, *brahma vidyā* and he approaches Vighneswara for it, the elephant-headed god not only breaks the obstacles on the way of knowledge, but also does whatever is necessary for the progress of the sadhaka at appropriate time. The sadhaka need not approach Saraswati. If Saraswati's grace becomes necessary for the achievement of the sadhaka's aim, Vighneswara himself arranges for that.

Closer the relationship between two persons the more intimate is the contact. If one is able to build up a relationship with the Divine, he gets the Divine's care and protection. And what more does a person want in this world?

The means of establishing this relationship between God and man is known in the Tantra as Prayoga. Prayoga is *prakarsa yoga* , union par excellence with the Divine. In each act one should unite with the Divine. That is why the Tantrics say that *prayoga* is necessary for any *kārya siddhi*, accomplishment of purpose.

There are specific *prayogas* for specific acts to be accomplished. In the hands of real aspirants, *prayoga* is a powerful tool for progress. It creates a stumbling block to progress in the hands of the ignorant who turn it into a barter deal between themselves and their god. If it is said that the recital of *Saptasati* five times ensures removal of the evil effects of planetary combinations, it is not equivalent to pressing the button of a machine five times for achieving the result. Prayoga is a thing much more than mere cause and effect. A *prayoga* is fruitful only if it is done with absolute faith and devotion, which lead ultimately to an identification with the Divine. The same *prayoga* in the hands of the wicked and mischievous is a dangerous tool and like all divine tools used perversely ultimately destroys the user.[1]

It is said that an act done without any expectation or desire for result, *niṣkāmya karma* is the best. For this purpose the sadhaka should develop an attitude that the Divine knows what is best for him and the Divine's Will is his will. But this is not easy. Until this attitude is developed, it is not at all wrong to invoke the Godhead and seek His help for the fulfilment of one's desires. It

---

1 The prayoga in such cases is known as *ābhlchāra*, perverse, usually called black magic. There is a picturesque description in Sri Aurobindo's epic Savitri :(11.8)

"Thought sat, a Priestess of Perversity,
On her black tripod of the triune snake,
Reading by opposite signs the eternal script,
A sorceress reversing Life's God-frame.
In darkling aisles with evil eyes for lamps
And fate voices chanting from the apse,
In strange infernal dim basilicas
Intoning the magic of the unholy Word,
The ominous profound Initiate
Performed the ritual of her Mysteries."

is far better that way than relying on fellow human beings who are subject to the same disabilities as the aspirant. If for the fulfilment of anything, big or small, significant or insignificant, one begins to invoke the Divine and wait on His grace, that itself is a great *tapas* . Every minute, every action becomes related to the Divine. The sadhaka progresses fast in his Sadhana and even his daily routine becomes a sort of worship to the Divine, *soparya paryāyastava bhavatu yan me vilasitam.* A state comes, as described in Vasishta Ganapati Muni's *umāsahasram* , when the sadhaka exclaims : "O Mother of the worlds, for the fulfilment of paltry desires, this person is depending on thee. O Lady of the breaker of cities, for the fulfilment of intermediate desires, he is depending on thee. O one of vast compassion, for the fulfilment of ultimate desires, he is depending on thee. O Bhagavati supreme, even when devoid of desires he is depending on thee."[1] This is the secret of Prayoga. Then the whole life on earth becomes a *prayoga* done by the embodied soul for the ultimate identification with the Divine.

It is said that the prescribed *niyama* , principle, has to be observed in the case of *kāmya prayogas, prayoga* for the fulfilment of an objective while it is not necessary in the case of *niṣkāmya prayogas* , *prayogas* done without any desire. If *prayoga* has to confer Siddhi, one should learn these disciplines and act accordingly. Even for the

---

[1] जननि जगतां स्वल्पे कामेऽप्ययं त्वयि लम्बते
पुरभिदबले मध्ये कामेऽप्ययं त्वयि लम्बते ।
बहुलकरुणे श्रेष्ठे कामेऽप्ययं त्वयि लम्बते
भगवति परे वीते कामेऽप्ययं त्वयि लम्बते ॥

worship to be fruitful there are certain secret disciplines *niyamas* to be observed. For example, a man who worships Hanuman should observe brahmacharya, celibacy, in thought, word, and deed. Then only the worship will be effective. Those who worship Saraswati, should always be reading or writing—devoted to studies. Then only Her grace is obtained.[1]

When a *prayoga* is performed for Siddhi, propitious surroundings have to be chosen as they hasten the fulfilment. The Tantra prescribes certain places of natural grandeur and scenery where the Divine presence is more palpable, like the summit of a mountain, or the bank of a river, *parvatāgre nadī tire*. In the Devi Mahatmya also it is said that Suratha and Samadhi repaired to the vicinity of a river, *nadī pulinam āsthitah* for perceiving the Mother. Similarly certain days are said to be propitious for the Sadhana. Recital of *Saptasati* on the eighth, ninth and fourteenth day of the lunar fortnight hastens the siddhi. The Goddess herself has proclaimed *astamyām ca caturdaśyām navamyām caikacetasah*

The *nitya candi vidhāna* describes the method or reciting *candi* daily while *nava candi* describes the procedure to be followed during worship on the nine sacred nights Navaratri. *sata candi* is to recite the text a hundred times. This is usually done by employing ten Brahmins to recite in chorus the text once on the first day, twice on the second day, thrice on the third day and four times on the fourth day, thus completing the count. To

---

1 I came to know of these for the first time through my Acharya Sri Kapali Sastriar. He favoured me with these secrets saying that these were not to be found in books.

complete the *prayoga, homa* is done on the fifth day. Similarly *sahasra candi* is to arrange for the recital of the text a thousand times by competent persons. Both *śata candi* and *sahasra candi* are forms of congregational worship and are done to invoke a Powerful Presence for promoting general welfare of people, warding off calamities due to floods, famine, pestilence, invasion from a foreign power etc. There is besides a *prayoga* known as *rūpacandi* for individual worship. Each verse of the text has to be bracketed before and after with the *navākṣari mantra* and the line *rupam dehi jayam dehi yaso dehi dviso jahi* and then recited. This is said to fulfil all desires.[1]

In all these prayogas, *homa* offering of oblations in the sacred fire is done by reciting each verse of the text; *pratiślokam ca juhuyāt pāyasam tilasarpiṣā*. It is said that the Mantras of the *kavaca* should not be used in Homa. Kumari Puja is a special rite of Chandi worship. This should not be confused with the Suvasini puja of the *śrividya* worship. The latter is the worship of married women whose husbands are alive, while the former is the worship of little girls who are far below the age of puberty. In Kumari puja nine little girls ranging from the ages of 2 to 10 are worshipped as the forms of the nine Durgas.

In order that the *prayogas* may yield results quickly, it is customary to do the prayogas of *śāpoddhāra* and *utkīlana* first. But many hold that *saptaśati* is a *siddha*

---

[1] रूपं देहीति संयोज्य नवार्णमनुना सह ।
संपुटत्वेन संयोज्य प्रतिश्लोकं जपेत्तथा ।
रूपचण्डीति सा प्रोक्ता सर्वाभीष्टफलप्रदा ॥

mantra and there is no curse about it. But as the Tantras refer to these, we make a passing mention here. The *śapoddhāra* is effected by reciting the chapters of *Saptaśati* in this order : 13,1; 12, 2; 11,3; 10,4; 9, 5; 8, 6; and 7,7. The *utkīlana* is done by reciting first the middle episode, then the first episode and finally the last episode *madhyādyāntam*.

We said that *navākṣari japa* is rarely done by itself and in the worship of Chandi, *navaksari japa* forms a limb of the *pārāyana* (reading) of the text. Even then, Damara Tantra prescribes certain *prayogas* for the nine-lettered mantra. If one stands up to the navel in water and recites the Mantra a thousand times, he gets poetic faculty.[1] If the Mantra is done ten thousand times, one gets release even if imprisoned by the king.[2]

There are numerous prayogas for the *pārāyana* of *saptaśati*. The result depends upon the number of times the *parayana* is done. If done thrice, all miseries of a minor nature will vanish. If done five times, ill-effects due to planetary combinations will be removed. If done seven times, it results in the allaying of great fear. Thus, Varahi Tantra goes on enumerating the results and finally says that all siddhis are accomplished by reading the Chandi text a hundred times. *candyāh satāvṛttipāthat sarvāh siddhyanti siddhayah.*

The *prayoga* of reciting the *saptaśati* verses along with special verses of the text or other great Mantras is

---

सहस्रमस्य मन्त्रस्य नवबीजस्य यो जले ।
नाभिमात्रे जपेत् संयक् कविद्वं लभते ध्रुवम् ॥
अयुतं नवतत्वस्य राजबन्धनसङ्कटैः ।

explained in detail in the *kātyāyani tantra*. This is three-fold. Reciting the mantra as a suffix of each sloka of the text is known as *pallava* ; if it is joined as a prefix of each sloka of the text, it is known as *yojana* and if the same Mantra is repeated both as a prefix and suffix of each sloka it is known as *samputa*. All the important *prayogas* enumerated below can be done in the above threefold manner:

Mantra siddhi is got if each sloka is joined with the *pranava*, Aum or Navaksari.

Speedy siddhi is assured if one recites *aum bhūh bhuwah suvah* as a prefix of the sloka and *suvah bhuwah bhuw aum* as the suffix.

All desires will be fulfilled if the famous *jātavedase* Rik is used with each sloka.

Death can be postponed and prevented if the recital is done with the Rik, *'tryambakam yajāmahe'*

The sloka *'sulena pahi no devi'* can be used with the verses or alone. Untimely or accidental deaths are warded off.

When the sloka *'saraṇāgata dīnārta'* is used, all acts are accomplished.

'sarva mangala māngalye' - this sloka confers allround auspiciousness.

The sloka *'durge smṛtā'* removes all distress and prevents all dangers.

The sloka *'ittham yadā yadā bādhā'* will cure small pox and allied diseases.

The sloka *'hinasti daitya tejāmsi'* will restore to normalcy children possessed by evil spirits.

The famous sloka *'rogan asesan'* will cure all diseases.

The japa of the sloka '*jnáninámapi cetámsi*' acts as a charm in captivating others.

The sloka '*ityuktvá sá tada devi*' will give knowledge, will cure stammering in speech.

The Rik '*kámsosmitám*' read with the slokas, brings into play the gracious glance of Lakshmi.

The Rik '*Anrna asmin*' when read with the slokas, frees one from indebtedness.

The japa of '*devi prapannartihare*' removes all distress and bestows all desires.

We shall conclude the list by mentioning a very important and fruitful *prayoga*. This is to use the *sataksári Vidyá* with each sloka. This Vidya of 100 letters[1] consists of three great Riks—the Durga Mantra in the *Tristub* metre of 44 letters, the Mrtyunjaya Mantra in the *Anustub* metre of 32 letters, and the famous *Gayatri* mantra in the *Gayatri* metre of 24 letters and is mentioned in the *Prapancasara* Tantra whose authorship is ascribed to Sri Acharya Sankara.

játavedese sunaváma somam arátiyato nidaháti vedah

sa nah parsadati durgáni visvá náveva sindhum duritátyagnih

"To the knower of all Birth (Agni) we press Soma, to him who consumes the knowledge (or wealth) of the enemy. Let Agni carry us across all the obstructions like a boat over the river."

This is the first Mantra. In the Veda it is the Mantra of Agni and in the Tantra, the Mantra of Durga.

---

1 For a fuller explanation, vide *Further Lights* : *The Veda and the Tantra* .

tryambakam yajāmahe sugandhim pusti vardhanam
urvārukamiva bandanāt mṛtyor muksiya māmrtāt.

"We adore the Father of the three worlds, Tryambaka of auspicious Fame, increaser of fullness and strength. May I be detached from Death like cucumber from the shell (or the stem) not from the Immortal."

This is the second Mantra and the Mantra of Shiva who conquers death.

tat savitur varenyam bhargo devasya dhimahi dhiyo
yo nah pracodayāt.

"We meditate upon that excellent splendour of the Lord Savitr. My he activate our thoughts."

This is the third Mantra, the Mantra of Surya Narayana, the visible godhead in the universe.

Thus, the *sātakṣari vidyā* places on the same supreme level of adoration Durga, Shiva and Vishnu in its three Mantras and so it is said to be a very fruitful *prayoga* in the recital of *saptaśati*.

Those who cannot do these *prayogas* meticulously need not despair. Knowingly, or unknowingly, *jānatājānatā vāpi* the Mother has to be invoked. Devotion and surrender to the *Sakti* are the important things. She always responds with Her Grace which does the whole sadhana.

"This Light comes not by struggle or by thought ;
In the mind's silence the Transcendent acts
And the hushed heart hears the unuttered Word'
                                    (Sri Aurobindo: *Savitri*)

SOME QUESTIONS ANSWERED

Q. *If one recites Devi Mahatmyam, should one also perform Sandhyavandanam? Can Sandhyavandanam be stopped if Devi Mahatmyam is read regularly?*

A. Your question arised from a comparison between Devi Mahatmayam and Sandhyavandanam. Sandhyavandanam is taken as a method of worship of the Divine Mother. Is it really so? Of course, in the popular conception, Sandhyavandanam is taken to be the worship of Sandhya and Sandhya being in the feminine gender, of the goddess Sandhya and hence, of the goddess Gayatri, etc. Really, Sandhyavandanam is the worship of the sun during the Sandhyas and the Mantra used for Japa is that of Savitr, the Sun God. As this Mantra is in the Chandas Gayatri, the Mantra is popularly known as Gayatri Mantra and is mistaken to be addressed to goddess Gayatri.

I do not deny that the Tantrics have developed the concept of Gayatri Devi and have ascribed this Vedic Mantra of Surya Savitr, seen by the Sage Viswamitra, to Gayatri Devi. There are similar traditions. The Vedi Rik 'Jatavedase' to the Deity Agni is ascribed to Durga in the Tanta. So Sandhyavandanam is originally a worship offered to the Sun God Surya Savitr, in the form of 'Mitra' at dawn, 'Savitr' at noon and 'Varuna' in the evening.

As the Puranas have later on identified Surya with Vishnu, the names of Vishnu like Kesava, Narayana, etc. are used in the Achamana, Nyasa, etc. Sandhyavandanam is really a worship at the Sandhyas and not a worship of the Sandhya and so the term can be used for any worship at the Sandhyas. But Sandhyavandanam, as come down to us, is a happy amalgam of invocations of Vedic Riks, Yogic practices like Pranayama and Tantric rituals like Arghya, Achaman, etc. and Japa of Gayatri. The details of the rituals and the mantras to be used vary according to the three Vedas and the follower of each Veda has his own way of Sandhyavandanam. Similarly the Tantriks have prescribed their own Sandhyavandanam, especiallly the worshippers of the Goddess as Sri Vidya.

Sandhyavandanam is ordained as a daily act, nitya karma - and so, any other act like Parayana of Devi Mahatmyam is normally done by orthodox in its place. Sandhyavandanam, if done properly with the proper understanding, of its significance is efficacious. It has lost much of its efficacy because it is done as a dull daily routine.

It is not quite correct to compare Sandhya-vandanam, Devi Mahatmyam or any other mode of worship because each has its own place and caters to the different need of the aspirant.

You have asked whether a person can leave Sandhyavandanam ane do Saptasati instead. The answer is simple. Whenever an aspirant does

Sandhyavandanam—we are not talking here of a person who does it as a daily ritual because he is afraid of society or he has been asked to do by others—we take it he feels a need for it and as long as there is a need, the outward rituals will continue. It is always the rule in the Sadhana that one should not leave the ritual one is accustomed to; rather the ritual should leave him. The meaning is that the rituals are there for the development of the Sadhana in the being of the individual and they will exist as long as there is a need. When there is no need for ritual, the ritual will automatically drop away from the person. However, the importance of outward ritual cannot be under-rated because even in an advanced stage of spiritual Sadhana, for keeping a happy balance between the physical and inner progress, it is necessary to have some outward act like recitation, prayer, puja or sitting for meditation, etc.

Q. *There is an assurance in the Bhagavat Gita that a person who resorts to God will not come to grief. Is there any such assurance in Devi mahatmyam?*

A. Just as there is an assurance in the Bhagavat Gita that there is no bad reaction (prathyayava) and the man who does auspicious things never reaches a sorry state, in the Devi Mahatmyam also, there are definte assurances. The whole of the 12th Chapter is an assurance by Devi Herself that the very recital of the Mahatmyam will evoke Her full presence and the Sadhana has to be done knowingly or unknowingly—*jānatā janata vāpi.*

Q. *In the Keelaka stotra, there is a prayer "Patneem Manoramam Dehi". If a woman does the parayanam, should she change it to "patim manoramam dehi"?*

A. When 'Patni' is mentioned in the text, an ordinary wife is not meant. It is the 'Shakti' who does the Sadhana, who is prayed for. Whether a person is a man or a woman, the witness 'Purusha' and the active 'Prakriti' are there in each and to perform the Sadhana, both for man and woman, the help of 'Shakti' is necessary. This will be clear when you study the phrase 'Kulotbavam' which not only means 'born of a good family' but born of 'Kula' meaning the 'Kundalini Shakti'.

Q. *After the japan, one is asked to do the nyasa. Has one to do all the 11 nyasa? When they should be done?*

A. It is not necessary to do all the 11 Nyasas. They can be done when there is inclination and time. The 11th Nyasa is said to give the benefits of all the other Nyasas and so it is usually done along with Moola Shadanga Nyasa. Anyway, Moola Shadanga Nyasa is always done. Whatever Nyasa or Nyasas are done in the beginning, the same Nyasa or Nyasas should be done at the end also. The order will be like this : Kavacha, Argals, Keelaka, Nyasa, Japa, Ratri Sukta, Three Charitas, Devi Suktha, Japa and then Nyasa and then the Rahasya Traya.

Q. In the kavacha stotra, 'Gowri' occuring in the 4th sloka is translated as the 'White one' while the same work occuring in the 22ndd sloka of pradhanika rahasya has beem translated as 'Golden yellow'. Which is right?

A. 'Gowra' means 'white' as well as 'yellow' (vide Amara kosha). In the Kavacha 'Gowri' is translated as 'white' in contrast to 'Kala Ratri' while in Rahasya Traya, the same word is translated as 'Golden yellow' as She is 'Hiranya Varna'.

Q. *In the murthi rahasya, in the 6th and 9th slokas, it is mentioned that the goddess protects her devotees as a loving wife devotes herself to her husband. Generally we understand that the mother's loved to the child is the most perfect love because the mother does not expect any return from the child. Please enlighten why this comparison of wife and husband is used instead of mother and child, which is the most appropriate.*

A. The relation between the Deity and the devotee need not be restricted to the relationship of the mother and the child. There may also be the Master and servant relationship as well as the Lover and the Beloved relationship. In Vaishnava traditio, God is considered as the Lover and the individual soul the Beloved, yearning after Him. In fact, this kind of relationship gives Sayujya 'oneness' with the Divine, while the others may give only 'Sameepya'— 'proximity'—or 'Salokya'—being in the same world'. In Shakti cult also, the worshipper is considered as Shiva and Deity as his Shakti. That is why, the comparison of the wife and husband is given.